NOTES

NOTES

Living **BIG**
on a SMALL Income

The *Classy* Cheapskate Way!

NOTES

Living **BIG**
on a SMALL Income

The *Classy* Cheapskate Way!

PATH TO A
- **FINANCIALLY SECURE,**
- **COMFORTABLE,**
- **DEBT FREE,**
- **FLEXIBLE,**
- **JOYFUL**
  LIFE!

JAMIE JAY

JAMIE JAY
STUDIOS
SUNBURY, PENNSYLVANIA

Printed by CreateSpace

Contact information located at jamiejayart.com.

Book design, photographs, and illustrations by Jamie Jay

This publication provides a wide range of information pertaining to the subject matter covered. It is sold with the understanding that the publisher/author is not to be held responsible for any results of personal actions taken by a reader or listener – good, bad, or indifferent. Any decisions and/or actions made are solely the choice of the person carrying them out. Following any tip is the personal choice of each individual and they are to be held accountable for their own actions.

Publisher's Cataloging-in-Publication Data

Jay, Jamie.
    Living big on a small income the classy cheapskate way! : path to a financially secure, comfortable, debt free, flexible, joyful life! / Jamie Jay.
        p. cm.
        ISBN-13: 978-1502471345
        ISBN-10: 1502471345

1. Finance, personal. 2. Thriftiness 3. Consumer education. 4. Home economics. 5. Sustainable living. 6. Self-reliant living. I. Title.

HG179.J39 2014
332.024–dc22
Library of Congress Control Number: 2014918136

ACKNOWLEDGMENTS

THANKS TO GOD for giving me wisdom, creativity, and a variety of talents that I enjoy using and sharing. A special thank you goes out to my family and friends for embracing my cheapskate – resourceful, frugal ways. May everyone who reads this book find great treasure within and learn to use everything to its greatest potential.

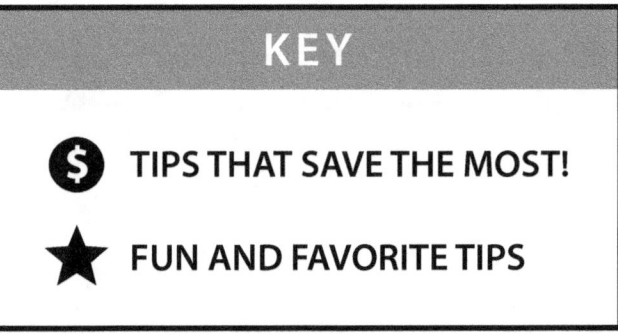

KEY

$ TIPS THAT SAVE THE MOST!

★ FUN AND FAVORITE TIPS

NOTES

CONTENTS

NOTES

PLAIN AND SIMPLY, this book is here to show you how to live big on a small income. By using resources wisely and thinking outside of the box, you can make your money stretch farther than ever expected. I'm really excited to share my techniques with you. I've included lots of savings calculations that should blow you away. You'll be able to see exactly how I am able to hoard away so much money on a less than average income. Nobody wants to worry how they will pay their next bill. My goal is to show you how you can obtain financial security, washing away financial burdens right along with any associated stress. If you already have a big salary, this book is for you too! You can simply live larger! You'll find well organized chapters filled with money and time saving tips that will help you to live debt free and obtain financial security if you apply them to your life as I have. If you are in deep debt, you really should free yourself of it. Start here with this book. Any money you save should be applied to paying off your loans and debt.

When you complete a tip in this book, you can even check off that you have completed it using special pages in the back of this book. By doing this, it will help you to get in the habit of living a frugal and resourceful lifestyle (the classy cheapskate way). Each tip will show information such as an *estimated amount of money that you should save or earn each year* by following the tip, the typical *amount of time required to complete the task* each year, a short list of applicable steps, and even the amount of *time that can be saved*. Please see an example tip shown on the next page; and keep in mind that the savings shown and time involved are for one entire year. The amounts are averages and are to give you an idea of what your savings could be. Each tip shows the savings as it would apply to one person. Some tips will show a *FINAL SAVINGS* which takes extra variables into consideration - the money saved, time invested, and time saved. Time is really important to factor into the equation since *time is money*. If you are saving time, you can use the extra time to make even more money. If you choose not to use the time to make additional money, you can use it in other valuable ways. I'm sure you'll see how everything works as you read further along. Finally, calculations are based on average prices and income in the United States at the time of writing this book.

1. **THIS IS YOUR EXAMPLE TIP.** This is the awesome explanation of the example tip that is supposed to change your life for the better. Yippee!

SAVINGS – $250; TIME INVOLVED – 1 HOUR (step 1, step 2, step 3)
TIME SAVED – 5 HOURS (time is money!)
FINAL SAVINGS – $350

NOTE: some tips will even show the final savings for the *first year* followed by the savings for *each additional year*. This is because it requires time and/or money to put the tip into action, whereas the following years do not because the tip has already been put into motion. Here is how this type of tip summary will look:

1ST YEAR'S FINAL SAVINGS – $500; **FUTURE YEARS** – $750

Really take advantage of the complete list of tips in the back of this book. When you first begin trying new tips, you can concentrate your efforts on the tips that have the most yearly savings to get the biggest bang for your buck and time.

In addition, most books have blank pages that are useless. Since I strive to be resourceful (attempting to waste nothing), I have taken those blank pages and added lines to them so that you may make note of your own money saving ideas when they arise. If you are reading the digital version of this book, then simply enjoy staring at the horizontal lines or print a page or two out for note taking.

All right, so now you get the gist of this book, how it is put together, and how to utilize it. Now let me give you a little background on myself. I am an artist, designer, writer, demonstrator, entrepreneur, and more. At age 35 I had raised two children to the ages of 9 and 10 without spending a penny on child care; owned 4 houses, 6 vehicles, and several successful businesses, all without a penny of debt while still stockpiling plenty of money for retirement; schooled myself, worked for myself, and did taxes myself. I was not born into wealth, I was born without a penny to my name. I am no genius. *Or, am I?* Every business I started cost less than $100 to start up. Where I saw a demand, it was supplied. I have a life that I feel in control of, though I let God lead the way. I enjoy flexibility to a very good degree. I work when I want and play when I want. I am never bored and my dreams are being fulfilled. Allow me to share with you how it all came to be!

For starters, I do almost everything myself (to a certain extent). I am the author, illustrator, photographer, layout artist, proofreader, and editor of this book. You may try some of the tactics in this book, but I am not to be held liable for your actions or the result of your actions. Use your own judgment. I am also my own lawyer. Do you know how much money I just saved?! Excuse me if you see any misspellings or typos in this book. I am not embarrassed by it. I think I am doing a pretty good job so far at communicating efficiently with the skills that I have. Punctuation is not my *best* friend, but we are fairly good friends.

Back on subject, money is pretty important to have. It gets you what you want and need. So you'll need to learn how to control your money and how to get money. In order to have control over your money, it is good to start by being organized. This book is organized into chapters that are clearly labelled so that you can read what you want to read when you want to read it. For example, maybe you will never read Chapter 5 which deals with children if you don't have children or grandchildren. But, if you do plan to have children, read the chapter as soon as you can (especially take notice of tip #5)! Read what pertains to you. Time is money. Don't ever forget that. TIME IS MONEY. Money is a tool that can offer stability, flexibility, comfort, security, and joy. In this book, I will show you how to get a big bang for your buck!

It's not how much money you make, but how you handle it that really counts. I want you to know that this book is written by an ordinary person that just happens to be blessed with the knowledge on how to make an income stretch way farther than expected. If I have anyone to thank for my knowledge of money management, it is God. All of the glory goes to him. You might say that an income of about $28,000 per year is low. But if I am able to save 50% or more on all of my purchases, I am living at a higher standard; way above my income level. Keep in mind that I am a stay at home mom who runs businesses from my home, living with a husband who has a normal job. We do not make loads of money, but we have way more money, property, and items than the average person. We dress nicely. We also have great experiences and adventures. At the time of writing this book, our combined gross income was just under $56,000 for the past year. This is normal for us. There is not a year of work that we made much more or less. We do not make a lot of money (our yearly income is simply average), but we consider ourselves wealthy because we save a very large portion of the money that we make.

According to a nationwide U.S. survey, the average amount saved (stored away) by people ages 33-44 (my range) is $61,000 (Shin). Both my husband and I greatly surpass that figure. In fact we are doing a much better job at saving than the group that is older than us who should be retiring. My husband and I save much of the money we earn each year due to our consistently frugal ways and we invest our savings properly. Because of that, we are actually on our way to becoming millionaires and I'd like to share with you how we do it. You don't even have to cook at home the rest of your life to achieve this (unless you enjoy it). We eat out at restaurants like Applebee's, Hoss's, Red Robin, and Texas Roadhouse. Just to let you know, we don't skimp on all of life's pleasures and you shouldn't have to either. Below I have listed the average amount of money that people have saved (put away, set aside) in different age groups. You can reference this and compare it to your own savings. If you follow some of the examples in the chapters that follow and find ways to save in many aspects of your life, you should be able to attain what my family has attained in a fairly short amount of time. Remember, it is not how much you make that is important. It is how much you save and how you handle your money. There are rich athletes and entertainers out there who end up going bankrupt.

Ages 25-32 – Median Savings $12,000
Ages 33-44 – Median Savings $61,000
Ages 45-54 – Median Savings $101,000 (Shin)

Before we get started with the juicy, money-saving chapters of this book, I would like to share one more point. I consider myself a *classy* cheapskate for three reasons. The first reason being, I don't do anything illegal, sleazy, or dangerous to save a buck (that I know of). Some people copy music, games, and movies (not me). Others sneak into movie theaters, drive-in theaters, or don't report winnings on their tax returns. I'm not one of those people who sleep in their vehicle in a hotel parking lot and then go inside in the morning to partake of the free meal that is supposed to be for paying guests. Some people take money out of wishing wells and fountains. Other people melt down older pennies because the copper is worth more than the penny itself. And still others throw their garbage in their employers dumpster. I save so much money the right way that I don't even need to consider doing those things. Besides that, I like to do good works. I believe that what goes around comes around. I also do not cause a big stink in a restaurant if a meal is late or undercooked trying to get a free meal out of it. If a chicken patty is pink and frozen solid, what do I do? I stop eating it and say, "This is pink and frozen solid" and I send it back to be nuked (not a biggie). I don't take leftover food from strangers. If it isn't obvious why, it's because I don't want to get sick and I assume that everyone wants their leftovers. Who wouldn't? Waste not, want not. I don't cut tumors out of my big toe with an X-Acto knife or remove my own moles (like some people I know). I don't pull my own adult teeth (I assume that could cause an infection). Besides, I've never had a cavity and know how to care for my teeth (check out Chapter 15). I've talked a lot about what I won't do. You'll get to see some of the creative ideas that I will do to save a buck in the meaty, straight to the point chapters that follow. For instance, what I will do is make fine art sculptures out of used cat litter. But I am *classy* because I wear gloves and remove the clumps first (well most of them). I also bake the art to over 1000 degrees Fahrenheit. You can read more about this in Chapter 7.

The second reason I consider myself a *classy* cheapskate is that I act classy when I am being cheap. I have a bit of cheapskate etiquette in me. For instance, if I am going to use a *free item* coupon, or accept a free hot dog at an event, I do it with a friendly smile, and with a bit of charm. I am sure to say, "Thank you." If I wish to rummage through a fancy business's dumpster, I ask politely first and then explain what I am looking for. At the last dumpster I had the pleasure of visiting, the owner thanked me and actually helped to load the items into my vehicle. He was happy that he didn't have to pay to have the items hauled away. A smile, friendly conversation, and a thank you go a long way.

Finally, the third reason I consider myself a *classy* cheapskate is that I don't skimp on all of life's pleasures just for the sake of being cheap. If skimping or saving is going to make me unhappy in a particular situation, then I'll opt not to save at all. I believe that the whole point of saving money is for present and future security; and to help provide more funds for entertainment. But if the process of saving money causes unhappiness, then there is not much reason to do it. According to TLC's online cheapskate quiz, I am only *mildly cheap*. They stated, "You know that there's a fine line between being too cheap and just thrifty. You border the too-cheap line, but in general have a good grasp of when to skimp and when to spend" (TLC). For instance, I use my air conditioning with not much fear of the cost. I am not going to sweat all day long and suffer just to save a few dollars. I take long, hot showers with no regrets. I even let my kids play with the hose, even though we are charged for each unit of water used (I don't water my lawn so this makes up for it). I save in as many ways as I can without diminishing my quality of life (or my family's quality of life). My definition of a classy cheapskate is a highly resourceful, clever, friendly, and courteously cheap person. Through your cheapskate journeys, remember to have FUN! Don't take yourself too seriously and keep a smile on your face. Being cheap (resourceful) is a good thing. Cherish it. My childhood quote was "Life is an Adventure" and I still feel that way. Get ready to set aside some of your pride – the bad kind of pride where you are too proud to do something because you think you are above others. Are you too proud to walk into a thrift store? I hope not because you are missing out on some spectacular savings if you are. I'm not too proud to wear pre-worn clothing. Even if I was a billionaire, I wouldn't think twice about shopping secondhand. Okay, I'm done preparing you to board the *Extreme Roller Coaster of Savings*. Now let's get started with the money saving tips!

Oh, by the way, you'll find me mentioning companies and products throughout this book. No companies have paid me to mention them or their products. I simply speak from experience and a desire to share my awesome, money saving tips with you.

NOTES

1.   **FREQUENT LOCAL AUCTIONS.** By attending local estate auctions, you can stock up on lots of supplies saving a bundle of cash. I have literally filled my van from top to bottom for under $5. I make it my goal to spend as little as possible at auction. Don't let cool items at the auction tempt you. Go for the dollar boxes. You might not know it, but there are treasures hidden inside of those junk boxes. I usually wait until the dollar box section is picked through pretty good and then buy up the entire lot of boxes that are left for only a buck.

Don't spend all day at the auction unless you have the time to spare. I find out when the dollar boxes are coming up for sale and just stay for that hour, pay for my goods, and then get out of there. After attending a few auctions, you should catch on to when the dollar boxes are usually brought up for sale. It should save you time if you call the auctioneer in advance to find out exactly when the box lots will be sold.

It is so much fun to pick through the treasures with my family when I get home from an auction. In the dollar boxes, you can find things like batteries, gift wrap, gift boxes, bows, cleaning supplies, rugs, and useful gadgets. Anything you don't need can be donated or sold. The savings calculation on the following page assumes that you go to 3 auctions per year.

SAVINGS – $750; TIME INVOLVED – 9 HOURS (attend auction, sort, clean, donate)
EARNINGS – $250; TIME INVOLVED – 3 HOURS (sell unwanted goods)
TIME SAVED – 9 HOURS (no need to shop for items at retail stores)
FINAL SAVINGS – $925

2. **USE ARTIFICIAL FLOWERS IN YOUR LANDSCAPING.** It saves both time and money since you don't have to purchase real flowers every year. You don't have to plant them, water them, or prune them. You will always have bright beautiful flowers and you will never have to dig a hole. Rearranging them is a snap as well. You just pull the flower bundle out of the ground and poke it in somewhere else. It's so easy!

You can find artificial flowers cheap at auctions, yard sales, secondhand stores, and online. I have received many compliments on my artificial flowers (many people think they are real, until I reveal otherwise). I have even noticed neighbors copying my idea. I spray the flowers with UV protective, matte, clear coat so that the color stays true over time. This protects them from the elements. I can even get the can of clear coat for free by using credit card rewards and making the purchase online at *amazon.com*. I can get many years of use out of artificial flowers. They are so easy to maintain and they don't die like regular flowers. I let wildflowers and greenery pop up naturally in my flower beds which makes things look even more believable when I place the artificial flowers in the ground at the start of each season. By using artificial flowers, I maintain a bright, colorful yard, and save hundreds of dollars each year. I also save loads of time and as I've stated before – time is money.

You don't have to make a special trip to purchase artificial flowers. You can simply gather them throughout the year as you come across them (in free boxes, at auction, or at secondhand stores). Maybe you already own some (check your attic). If worse comes to worse, you can shop for outdoor faux flowers online through discount websites.

SAVINGS – $250; TIME INVOLVED – 20 MINUTES (gather, place, apply clear coat)
TIME SAVED – 8 HOURS (no need to plant, water, fertilize, spray, or weed)
FINAL SAVINGS – $440

3. **LAY FAKE GRASS.** If you don't have grass, you don't have to mow, water, weed, weed whack, edge, seed, or fertilize your lawn. There are actually companies out there that make fake grass. I like the real looking faux grass. It costs a bit more, but it is worth it. I saw skids of it for sale this year at Ollie's Bargain Outlet. I was so excited!

Having an artificial lawn can save water if you require watering to keep your grass healthy, and of course you will save plenty of time by not having to care for real grass. Keep in mind that it is much less expensive to lay faux turf yourself than if you hire someone to do it for you.

Some people might argue that artificial grass is bad for the environment because natural grass helps to create oxygen. I would argue back that about half of the world's oxygen comes from phytoplankton which lives in the ocean (Roach). If anyone is worried about oxygen, then plant a small tree on your property. It will keep your faux grass cool, but you'll have to rake up the leaves. I am not against real plants, grass, and trees altogether. I just know that they are a lot of maintenance when having them near a built structure such as my home. Have no worries – my family has plenty of forest land where we donate way more than our fair share of the world's oxygen by allowing hundreds, if not thousands of trees to grow naturally. I just want my home property to look taken care of without a lot of extra work.

Did you know that there are Earth-friendly benefits to laying artificial grass? It saves water because there is no need to water a lawn, there is no need to use chemical fertilizers or herbicides, and it keeps 20 million rubber tires from reaching landfills each year according to The Synthetic Turf Council (Gordon).

If you have a pet, I would suggest that you keep a small corner of your yard planted with real grass so that your animal can poop and pee there. That way you do not have to worry about your beautiful fake grass needing hosed off.

Before you lay faux grass, make sure it is allowed in your municipality. Some water companies actually offer rebates for customers who lay faux turf if it is a drought-prone area. So definitely check into that. In the end, you can expect a faux lawn to last about 20 years. I got my faux grass for $1.34 per square foot. The average spent on faux grass including installation is usually $12.50 per square foot, but I always shoot for a bargain. So to cover a 400 square foot space it would cost about $536 if you are a thrifty shopper like me. On the other hand, the costs of maintaining a regular lawn of the same size including watering and fertilizing comes to $190 per year. This does not include the cost of hired lawn care and mowing (Gordon). The final savings calculation is shown below.

TIME INVOLVED – 12 HOURS (lay artificial grass in the first year)
TIME SAVED – 16 HOURS (no need to care for your lawn)
1ST YEAR'S FINAL SAVINGS – $0; **2ND YEAR** – $344; **FUTURE YEARS** – $590

4. **FORM A MOW-FREE LANDSCAPE.** If you create a landscape that requires no mowing, you will save by not having to keep a lawnmower in operation – which could include costly repairs and gas. You will also save valuable time by not having to mow.

So, how do you create a yard that has no grass? Well, you can begin by planting another type of ground cover. There are so many different types to choose from and they come in a variety of colors. Many of these plants flower during the year. So as an added bonus, you can have fresh flower arrangements in your home. Check out some of my favorites. I like the fast spreading varieties because you can get a bigger bang for your buck. I also prefer perennials because they are known to come back season after season and many keep their leaves year round. Finally, I like easy care. All of the following perennial ground covers are easy to care for:

Creeping Thyme* – takes foot traffic, flowers, evergreen, full sun, well-drained soil, 3" (zones 4-8)

Creeping Speedwell* – light foot traffic, fast growing, flowers, evergreen, sun, 2" (zones 4-8)

Ajuga* – light foot traffic, evergreen, flowers, shade; moist, well-drained soil, 6" (zones 4-9)

Irish Moss* – creeping, walkway cracks, moist, part shade, well-drained soil, 1" (zones 4-10)

Ice Plant* – showy flowers, evergreen, rock gardens, sun, well drained soil, 3" (zones 5-10)

Sedum* – between pavers, rock gardens, evergreen, drought tolerant, sun, 3" (zones 4-11)

Hens-and-Chicks* – stone path crevices, evergreen, full sun, well-drained soil, 4" (zones 3-9)

Armeria* – low, grassy appearance, flowers, full sun, well drained soil, 6" (zones 3-9)

Dwarf Mondo Grass* – evergreen, grassy clumps, part shade, slow-spreading, 3" (zones 6-10)

Green Brass Buttons – can take foot traffic, evergreen, full sun, well-drained soil, 2" (zones 5-9)

Lamium – fast growth, light foot traffic, flowers, shade; moist, well-drained soil, 8" (zones 4-8)

Western Wild Ginger – fast-spreading, light foot traffic, shade, well-drained soil, 4" (zones 7-9)

Lily-of-the-Valley – very fast-spreading, shade, well-drained soil, 8" (zones 3-8)

Bishop's Weed – fast-spreading, shade, well-drained soil, 12" (zones 4-9)

Golden Moneywort – fast-spreading vine, shade, moist soil, 2" (zones 4-10)

I prefer to grow my plants from seed to save money. I marked plants in the list with an *asterisk* if I am able to easily find seed packs for sale online. You can buy seeds from many online stores such as **burpee.com** or **outsidepride.com**. I favor **outsidepride.com** because more of the seeds I love are available and in stock. They also advertise that the seeds are non-GMO and have several varieties of my favorite ground cover – *Creeping Thyme*. Buying the plants when they are already grown is too costly. Even better than purchasing seeds, I like to collect the plants or seeds from family, friends, or neighbors. Exchanging is always fun. Visit **plantswap.net** if you want to swap plants with others online.

I'm not a big fan of chemicals, so I opt to do weeding myself if necessary. If you are going to use a pre-emergent herbicide to deal with weeds, expect to spend about $35. The product also has a short shelf life. So you'll need to use your supply in full each spring and fall to prevent weeds from coming up. Established plants will not be affected by the chemicals.

I would suggest breaking up some of your ground cover by adding walking paths. You can create these paths using found stones, bricks from auctions, or free mulch from your city. You can also create decorative borders using large stones. Some locations allow you to take away a very large amount of rocks for a small fee. For example, many national and state forests allow you to obtain a permit for about $10 as long as you collect and haul the rocks away yourself.

Another way to fill up space in your yard so that you do not have to mow is to plant bushes or other plants that don't require pruning. No pruning means saved time. Ferns do well for me. My ferns come back every year, multiply, and require no care. I suppose if there is a dead leaf, you could pull it off if it is unsightly. That doesn't take much time at all.

TIME INVOLVED – 10 HOURS FIRST YEAR (plant new ground cover)
TIME SAVED – 15 HOURS (no need to mow)
1ST YEAR'S FINAL SAVINGS – $105; **FUTURE YEARS** – $375

Check out the yard plan I created which I feel is ideal:

YARD PLAN
(GOOD FOR ZONES 4 - 8)

AJUGA
LIGHT FOOT TRAFFIC
LIKES SHADE

STONE BORDER

CREEPING THYME
TAKES
FOOT TRAFFIC

STEPPING STONE PATH

CREEPING SPEEDWELL
LIGHT FOOT TRAFFIC
VERY SHORT GROUND COVER

5. **USE A REEL LAWN MOWER.** A *reel* lawn mower does not require gas or electricity. You just push it around and blades cut your grass. So if you are set on having a grass lawn, this might be the mowing option for you if you wish to save money. You can get a reel mower for a hundred dollars or less. If you shop at an estate auction, it will be a lot less. On the other hand, if you go with a regular, *gas powered* lawn mower you will easily shell out two to three hundred dollars. Plus, you have to pay for gas to run the thing and pay for any necessary repairs as they arise.

TIME INVOLVED – NO EXTRA (when you need a new mower, get a reel mower)
1ST YEAR'S FINAL SAVINGS – $185; **FUTURE YEARS** – $35

6. **ACCEPT HAND-ME-DOWNS.** You can literally save thousands of dollars if you make a home for these used items which I often call family heirlooms. My house is loaded with free items that found a home here including a dining room table, buffet, bed, vanity, dresser, and cedar chest – just to name a few. If you don't like the item, take it anyway. You can always alter it with paint or come up with some other creative idea.

Even my silverware is handed down to me. Though at this point, my husband has lost so many pieces of silverware at work that it is a hodgepodge of different patterns in order to make one complete set (at least my dishes match). Well, the color of my dishes doesn't match, but the pattern does. I have **Fiesta** dinnerware which makes a great mix and match set. It is so festive to have a variety of fun-colored dishes all on one table when we are dining! Anyway, you can collect hand-me-down items over a period of several years or all at once. Sometimes a person who is moving might give you more than one item at a time. I still have several pairs of my grandmother's socks which I inherited when she passed away. Nobody else wanted them. They are quite comfortable and stylish, though some are starting to form holes now.

The following savings assumes you are taking in one furniture item rather than making a new purchase.

SAVINGS – $750; TIME INVOLVED – 1 HOUR (accept the offer, pick item up)
TIME SAVED – 2 HOURS (no need to shop for the item)
FINAL SAVINGS – $775

7.   **ASSIGN COLORS TO EACH PERSON** in your household. I do this for towels, cups, and dishes as well. This way we don't get things mixed up causing more laundry and cups to wash. There is no wondering if someone else accidentally drank out of your cup if they are color coded. We only drink water, so we use the same drinking cup all day long. Over the course of a year (for a household), using color coded items does help to save money by reducing the amount of washing that needs done due to mix-ups. It's the little things that add up. In this scenario, I based the calculations on 2 extra cups per person needing washed per day and 1 extra towel per person needing washed 4 times per week. It is also assuming that a load of dishes costs 50 cents to wash and a load of laundry costs 75 cents to wash and dry.

SAVINGS – $25/PERSON; TIME INVOLVED – 1 HOUR (shop for color coded items)
TIME SAVED – 16 HOURS (less washing to do)
1ST YEAR'S FINAL SAVINGS – $400; **FUTURE YEARS** – $425

8.   **KEEP YOUR FRIDGE FULL.** It is more efficient to keep a refrigerator full because it will not have to run as often. You can fill jugs, bottles, or containers with tap water and place them into the fridge to help keep it full if you don't have enough food. The same thing can be done with your freezer. It can be filled with ice packs, partly filled water bottles, or water-filled freezer bags. Another smart thing to do would be to pull your refrigerator away from the wall. "Your refrigerator/freezer combo is the biggest energy consumer among all of your appliances – seriously. It gobbles down around $100 in energy each year. . . . pulling it forward one inch

can reduce the energy usage of the refrigerator by as much as 40% ..." (Trent).

SAVINGS – $50; TIME INVOLVED – 5 MINUTES (pull fridge away from wall, fill bottles with water, place in fridge)
FINAL SAVINGS – $48

9. **SAVE NAPKINS.** I never buy napkins. Always save your extra napkins when dining out. This includes drive through restaurant orders and table dining (if you do not use all that were provided by the wait staff). If you take extra napkins (such as inside a fast food restaurant), that would be stealing. Only take what you were given. Use these napkins for at home. We have a stack on our dining room table. Also, if you are a woman who has a shiny face, you can use napkins to blot your face instead of purchasing fancy paper blotters from the store. Brown Taco Bell napkins are my personal favorite. One thing I can't stand is when you go through a drive through with 4 people and they only give you 1 or 2 napkins. Bummer! Then I actually have to rip napkins in half to share them with everyone and have none leftover for at home.

If you don't dine out, you could opt to use cloth napkins at home instead of paper. I rarely need to use a napkin though because I eat carefully. I don't smear food all over my face by shoving too much in my mouth all at once. So if you eat carefully, you can just forget about napkins altogether and you'll look more refined.

SAVINGS – $20/PERSON; TIME INVOLVED – 1 MINUTE (save napkins)

10. **SKIP THE PAPER TOWELS.** If it were up to me, I would never buy paper towels. I use a rag to clean up messes. A rag can be rinsed out over and over again. My husband loves paper towels. In our house, paper towels are for guests and my husband only.

"The average family uses two rolls of paper towels per week, and at $14 for an 8-pack you could be spending up to $182 a year for that convenience" (Cheung).

SAVINGS – $182 (ditch the paper towels, use a rag)

11. **USE TOILET PAPER INSTEAD OF TISSUES.** You could use a hanky, but I think that is disgusting. I don't want to wad up a bunch of germs in my pocket. I have never purchased tissues – ever. Guests in our house need to use toilet paper if they have a nose problem. I can get a roll of good quality, soft toilet paper on sale for about 50 cents a roll (I just did actually). A box of tissues costs about $2.50. I'm sure a box of tissues would last someone about a month. So would a roll of toilet paper used as a substitute. By staying in good health, you could make a roll last a year – I'm sure. I know I can. Just blow your nose daily in the shower. That's high class right there. Take it from the master. LOL.

SAVINGS – $24/PERSON (use toilet paper to blow your nose)

12. **SAVE MAIL ENVELOPES.** Never buy note paper or mailing envelopes again. When you get mail, slice the letter open with a letter opener. Then place the envelopes in a special basket, holder, or pile so that whenever you need scratch paper you can just grab a sheet. I never feel guilty about writing too many notes because I'm writing on garbage anyway so there is no waste involved.

What I really treasure are the envelopes within envelopes. These are the envelopes that are unused and are meant for replying back to junk mail offers. I just used one to send my child's lunch money to school. It didn't have any writing on it – just a clear window and lines for writing. It was perfect. Sometimes I use a white address label to cover up pre-printed addresses on the envelopes so that I can use them for other purposes. These *rare* types of envelopes are stored right beside my *scratch paper* envelopes.

SAVINGS – $35 (do not buy note paper or envelopes)
TIME SAVED – 1 HOUR (no need to shop for paper or envelopes)
FINAL SAVINGS – $60

13. **FORGET THE SCENTS.** You should not have to mask the real smell of your home by using scented candles and sprays. I do not purchase these items. Though I do sometimes win these items in junk boxes at auctions or in raffle drawings. Then I usually give the items away as gifts. I also do not wear perfume. I have no odor to hide. Besides, I happen to be highly allergic to many scents. You'll know you have a clean home if you don't have to cover up a smell using yet another smell.

"U.S. consumers are buying up household fragrances like room deodorizers, scented oils and candles to the tune of more than $5 billion each year. That's money spent on items designed to evaporate or burn" (Forbes). Perfume is right up there at $4.2 billion per year (Reilly).

SAVINGS – $300 (don't buy scents)
TIME SAVED – 3 HOURS (no more shopping for fragrant items)
FINAL SAVINGS – $375

14. **REMOLD JUNK CANDLES.** If you are interested in making fresh, new looking candles out of old junky candles, this is how I do it. I save ugly candles from estate auctions and yard sales that nobody wants. They are unwanted either because they are dirty, an undesirable color, unscented, mostly used, or melted and bent from being stored in an attic. I use a butter knife to scrape off any dirt. Then I use the double boiler method to melt the candle. To do this, simply place about an inch of water in a large metal pot or pan. Bring it to a boil. Reduce heat, and then place a smaller glass or metal bowl in the center of the first pot. Add the old candles into the smaller pot. Once melted, I remove the wick(s) from the liquid using pliers and save them for later. A bunch of crayons are added to create the

color desired. The mixture is stirred together with a metal spoon. I may add a little essential oil from my medicine cabinet to make the candle aromatic. After this, it is time to pour the wax into a new container or form.

If I want a fancy shaped candle, I tape the saved wick into the center of a JELL-O mold leaving an inch of wick under the tape which will be the exposed portion of the wick when the candle is removed from the mold (the candle is being made upside down). I hold the other end of the wick upward and then pour the warm liquid wax into the mold. It will start to set up at which point I let go of the wick. Once the candle completely sets up and is removed from the mold, it is ready for use. On the other hand, if I don't want to get fancy with my candle and wish to play things simple; I just use an old canning jar and pour the wax into it dangling the wick from above right down into the center of the wax. Voilà, that's it.

INGREDIENT AND SUPPLY LIST:
old candles
crayon(s) with wrappers removed
water
large pot or pan
smaller metal or glass bowl
JELLO-O mold or canning jar
spoon
butter knife
pliers

SAVINGS – $30; TIME INVOLVED – 30 MINUTES (gather supplies, remold candles)
FINAL SAVINGS – $17

15. **DO NOT WASH YOUR TOWELS OFTEN.** Some people I know wash their towels every day. I wash our household towels once every two weeks (or when needed). If they don't smell and they don't look dirty, then I don't see why they should need washed. As long as you hang the towels properly to dry, use a fan to draw moisture

out of your bathroom, and wash your body in the shower before you dry off, you should have no problem with being sanitary. I save over 93% by not washing our towels every day.

SAVINGS – $25/PERSON (only wash towels once every two weeks)
TIME SAVED – 28 HOURS (less washing, drying, and folding to do)
FINAL SAVINGS – $725

16. **DO NOT WASH YOUR BEDDING OFTEN.** Yes, I also know people who wash these items every single day! For one, I do not have time to do this. If you plan your showers before bed and/or wear pajamas, don't eat in your bed, don't let pets sleep in your bed, don't pee the bed, poop the bed, or puke in the bed, then I see no need to wash your sheets. This might sound disgusting, but I only wash my bedding once or twice per year. Don't dis me yet! The bedding doesn't smell or look dirty at all. My family is almost never sick. I know families who do more laundry than we do and are sick often. In fact, feel free to check into my children's school records (our medical records too). My kids only go to the doctor's office once a year for their yearly physicals. They have collected many perfect attendance awards over the years. I must be doing something right. Come on! I'm sure cave people slept on dirt and bugs (I'm still civilized since I'm not to that point and I hope I never am). By the way, if we have a guest, you'll receive freshly washed linens. So friends and relatives, feel free to keep visiting! In summary, I save 99% or more by following this strategy. For the savings summary, let's assume normal people wash their bedding once per week. But, if you currently wash your bedding every day (by following this tip, the savings would be much greater than shown – over a thousand dollars). Just a note, if you have pets that sleep on your bed, you might have pet hair accumulating; or even flea larvae and eggs living in your bed linens. By all means, wash your bedding often. It will be worth it and probably necessary to stay clean and sanitary.

SAVINGS – $37.50/PERSON (only wash bedding twice per year)
TIME SAVED – 7 HOURS (less stripping, washing, and drying linens; less time spent making the bed)
FINAL SAVINGS – $213

17. **OPEN YOUR BLINDS.** I am constantly catching my husband in a room during the day with the blinds closed and the lights on. The sun is free! Hello? Free light is the best light. Another thing I don't do is leave the TV on when nobody is in the room. A television sucks more energy than a light bulb (of course). If you simply turn items off when not in use, you could cut your energy use reducing your electric bill.

"According to the U.S. Energy Information Service, lights represented roughly 14 percent of the average household electric bill in 2010" (Brunot).

For this savings calculation, I'll assume that the household electric bill is usually $100 and that natural light is let in during the daylight hours as opposed to using electricity.

SAVINGS – $112 (let natural light come in through a window instead of flicking on a light switch)

18. **CLOSE YOUR BLINDS.** Ha! You're like, "What are ya talkin' about?" You just told us to open the blinds. Yes, but did you know that your house will stay cooler if you close those blinds or curtains on warmer days? So, when it is hot out, this is a great thing to remember to do (especially on the side of the house receiving sun at the time). For example, yearly savings in the Chicago area average "$15-35" (Energy Impact Illinois).

Some people have shade trees to help with this sort of thing, but I won't grow large trees (in a residential area) because of the cost of cutting them down when they get too old or too large (plus, it's a danger). My mother just got a quote on getting a large tree cut down and it was nearly a thousand dollars. I'll keep my small trees and shrubs.

By the way (thinking in reverse), on cooler days, let that light shine through the windows to help warm your home or office.

SAVINGS – $25 (close your blinds to keep the sun's heat out, you have to close them at some point in the day anyway)

19. **OPEN THE WINDOWS.** If you are hot and there is a cool breeze outside, use it to your advantage. There is no need for an air conditioner. I catch people using the air conditioner in my home and in other homes even when there is a free, cool breeze on the other side of the wall just waiting to be tapped into. You know you are probably guilty of this at times. Also, Use the night air to your advantage. At night, temperatures usually fall. I open the windows in my home an hour or so before bed to cool things down fast after a hot day (if there is no air movement outside you might be out of luck). Then I lock the windows up again before bed (for safety reasons). This quick cooling method usually allows us to go the whole night without having to pay for air conditioning.

"The average homeowner spends about $375 on air conditioning" (Shapley).

SAVINGS – $175; TIME INVOLVED – 2 HOURS (open your windows for cool air)
FINAL SAVINGS – $125

20. **REPAIR BLINDS** instead of replacing them. Children and pets can be rough on window blinds. My kids bent and broke off several pieces when they were toddlers. No matter how much I told them to stop messing with the blinds, they still found a way to do it. When they got a little older, I took several slats from the bottom of my blinds and moved them up to fill in where there were damaged pieces. There are usually extra slats at the bottom and if not, you won't be able to notice a few missing from the bottom anyway (it is much better than missing a few slats in the middle).

Depending on what type of blinds you have, you may have to cut a small slit in the blind to remove it from the string. Once in place, you can put a small piece of clear tape across the slit to better secure it. Nobody will see the small piece of tape if you apply it to the underside of the slat.

SAVINGS – $25; TIME INVOLVED – 15 MINUTES (repace slats)
FINAL SAVINGS – $19

21. **GET YOUR GLOW ON.** You heard me. Paint everything you can with glow in the dark paint. Why not paint a walking path with it? How about painting a lantern for use as a porch light? I painted my porch mat as well. Paint a whole room if you like! This is a tactic that utilizes light from the sun. The energy savings is probably not real high, but boy is this a fun idea! Instead of plugging your Christmas lights in during the holiday season, just spray your bulbs with glow in the dark paint. Many people throw away old strands of Christmas lights, you can simply save old strands for this project. I see them in "FREE" boxes and in junk boxes at auctions all the time. There are people who spend $250 or more on outdoor lights each season (not me).

SAVINGS – $250; TIME INVOLVED – 2 HOURS (buy paint, paint lights)
1ST YEAR'S FINAL SAVINGS – $200; **FUTURE YEARS** – $250

22. **LIVE CLOSE** to your family and/or friends. This doesn't sound like an easy one to do, but I've done it without much thought. My Uncle lives less than a block away, my parents live across the street, and my twin sister lives just a few blocks down. My daughter's best friend lives close as well. It wastes no gas to pay a visit to your favorite people. You don't have to take a plane. If you run out of milk, you know who to ask (and vice versa). You can share tools and supplies.

If I need to work on a wood project, I just use my Dad's machinery instead of purchasing my own. If my mom needs to sew, she uses my sewing machine instead of buying her own. It is a community of savings. It's actually a superb and smart way to live. We even share vehicles. We have all different types. Some are better for vacation, some are better for hauling dirty scrap, and some are better for escorting (proms, dances, weddings, and fancy events). We share a garden, chickens, garage space, adhesives, and you name it. You could even share WiFi (wireless internet) if you wanted. I guess you could take things a step further and just live in the same house with everyone! We always wanted to build a castle where everyone shared the same kitchen and courtyard for instance, but each family unit had privacy such as their own wing.

When you live close to family and friends there are countless benefits. Parties and game nights are a snap to put together. I no longer pay for postage to deliver birthday and Christmas cards. I get a slight amount of exercise making the delivery myself. My parents have cable television. So if we want to watch a live show, we visit my parents. My family has Netflix, so when someone wants to watch a past show, we are the go-to people. Sometimes we take turns cooking to give each other a break. If you accidentally leave something at a house while visiting, it is not too hard to go back and get it. But if your family lives far away, things become time consuming if you happen to leave an object behind after a visit. I've heard of people having to return items to loved ones by shipping them. The best reward to living close to loved ones is that you get to see your favorite people more often than not.

SAVINGS – PRICELESS; TIME INVOLVED – 20 HOURS (buy a home that's near your loved ones); TIME SAVED – 52 HOURS (less traveling for visits)
1ST YEAR'S FINAL SAVINGS – $1,000; **FUTURE YEARS** – $1,500

23. **GET A WHITE ROOF.** White will reflect the sun's light (energy) reducing your air conditioning usage as opposed to having a darker colored roof. It makes the most sense to paint your roof white

(or buy a white roof) if you live in a warmer climate (a state such as California, Arizona, Nevada, or Florida for example). On the other hand, if you live in a cold climate, a darker roof may be the way to go. Several cities in the U.S. are even mandating or plan to mandate white roofing. I would only go with a new white roof if my roof was ready for replacement and I lived in a warm climate. Otherwise, *painting* it would be a much more cost effective option than *purchasing* a new roof.

Roofing manufacturers are even producing other aesthetically pleasing colors that reflect the suns energy. If you have a flat roof, white is the way to go because it reflects the best. A sloped roof would probably be more visible to people and you could opt to go with a color instead.

Check out the results of a study done on roof colors and their resulting temperature ranges. The temperature of each roof depends on how much sunlight it is able to reflect. "Different roofing materials were tested side-by-side by Lawrence Berkeley National Lab researchers; their peak temperatures are listed below. Ambient air temperature at the time of the test was 55deg.F" (Robb).

Black acrylic paint	142 degrees F
Galvanized steel	138 degrees F
Black acrylic paint infrared reflecting film	123 degrees F
Common "White" fiberglass/asphalt shingle	118 degrees F
Clay terra cotta tile	112 degrees F
Red acrylic paint	106 degrees F
Light green acrylic paint	104 degrees F
White acrylic paint	74 degrees F
Hyper white acrylic paint	65 degrees F

As you can see, common *white* shingle isn't the best option available, but white acrylic paints are. I do not live in a warm climate (my climate has a bit of everything). I recently replaced my roof with a red metal one which is in the mid-range and beautiful to look at (I used to have a dark gray shingle roof and it was ready for replacement). This summer, my attic was much cooler and we used the air conditioning a lot less.

In summary, "analysis found that . . . over 50 years . . . white roofs save $2 per square foot compared to black roofs" (Chao). For a 1000 square foot roof, that comes to $2000.

Remember, the savings calculations shown in this book are per year unless stated otherwise.

SAVINGS – $40; TIME INVOLVED – 8 HOURS (buy paint, paint roof)
FINAL SAVINGS STARTING ON THE 6TH YEAR – $40

24. **PLACE A BILLBOARD ON YOUR PROPERTY.** I saw the coolest billboard while traveling this year. It jetted up an over a house and even had a walkway. This is a great way to make extra income. Unfortunately, not everyone is going to be able to take advantage of this tip. See, it would only make sense that your house would have to be on a main road visible to traffic. You would also need to check to make sure that a billboard is legally allowed on your property. If you cannot build on your property, you could always purchase or lease land.

With a double sided billboard, you could bring in over $4,000 per month by leasing billboard space. You could have a 10 foot by 40 foot billboard built for $4,000. Vinyl billboard material usually lasts 12 to 18 months. Keep this in mind when making contracts with local or national businesses who wish to advertise with you. Liability insurance would run about $1,200 per year (Group Communications Inc.). Take into account that you will have to pay a printer to print the billboards and then the printed material will need to be wrapped around each side of the billboard. Several printing companies I have found boast printing on vinyl billboard material for lower than a dollar per square foot. So you should be able to get both sides of your billboard printed for about $800. There is another expense to keep in mind. You will need to pay for electricity to light your billboard – using floodlights during the night. This should run you around $600 per year according to my calculations.

There is an easier route to go – lease your property to a billboard company. That way you can just sit back and make some extra money. However, you will make a lot more if you do everything yourself.

EARNINGS – $41,400; TIME INVOLVED – 12 HOURS (have billboard installed on your property, find advertisers, lease for 1 year)
1ST YEAR FINAL EARNINGS – $41,400; **FUTURE YEARS** – $45,400

25. **PAY BILLS ON TIME.** It doesn't normally pay to be late. Late fees and penalty fees stink. It's just wasted money. To make sure I am never late for a bill. I have a list of bills in my computer and the dates that they are due. I check it every day to make sure that I always pay on time. Being late with a payment can also affect your credit score. Another great way to be on time is to have the bills automatically paid using your bank account. I do this for several of my bills (if credit card payments are not accepted). I would much rather use a credit card to pay a bill because then I rack up credit card rewards. You might wonder why I make a list of the bills. Why not just pay the bill when it comes? Well, sometimes they are paperless statements. I sign up for paperless if there is a reward for doing so. Also, I pay my bills close to the due date because I want to make interest on my money for as many days as possible without being late.

So, how much can a person save by paying on time? It is very hard to calculate the savings for this (there are so many variables). My calculations take into account what I consider typical credit card debt and expecting one or two late bill payments per year.

SAVINGS – $800; TIME INVOLVED – 30 MINUTES (make list of bills, pay on time)
FINAL SAVINGS – $788

26. **PLACE A BRICK IN YOUR TOILET'S TANK.** If your toilet uses a lot of water, this will trick your tank into using less water as it will count the brick as part of the volume of water. This should save about half a gallon each time you flush. If a typical family of four flushes 20 times a day, it should save about 10 gallons of water. Compound that by 365 days, and you should see a big savings on your water bill. Place the brick in a zip-closure baggy to protect your toilet tank from scuffs and brick residue that could damage your toilet.

SAVINGS – $22.50/PERSON; TIME INVOLVED – 10 MINUTES (put brick in tank)
1ST YEAR'S FINAL SAVINGS – $18; **FUTURE YEARS** – $22.50

27. **IF IT'S YELLOW, LET IT MELLOW.** If it's brown, flush it down. I'm referring to the inside of a toilet of course. I love that age-old saying. And, as my daughter says, if it's red go to the hospital (she was eight years old when she came up with that cute little adage). My father-in-law taught the motto to my husband and my husband taught it to me. In our house, the toilet is flushed when, um, when there is something in the toilet that is not light in color. We have 4 people in our family and constant guests coming in and out almost every day. So far I have not received any complaints from our guests. However, most of our guests are children who don't flush anyway (and I don't mind a bit).

SAVINGS – $35/PERSON (don't flush after you urinate)

28. **MAKE USE OF DEHUMIDIFIER WATER.** We empty our bucket onto our garden. You can water house plants as well. If you have to empty the bucket anyway, you might as well just pour it over

your veggie or flower garden. If you want to save precious time, just rig up a hose to your dehumidifier – if it has a hookup (most do). Then let the collected water flow right through the hose to your garden. Remember, you only have to set this up once and you can collect the savings year after year. If you use your hose to water your plants and you are charged for water usage, then it makes sense to use dehumidifier water instead.

In the winter, we do not need to water our garden. So I keep a bucket next to the dehumidifier. I dump the dehumidifier water into the bucket and set the bucket next to our toilet. The next time I need to flush the toilet, I remove the lid on the back of the toilet. I flush and then pour the bucket of water in the tank so that we do not have to pay for the tank to fill up on its own. In our house, the water that is used is kept track of by a water meter in order to figure the monthly bill for water usage. However, the water that is leaving is not recorded. So dumping dehumidifier water that was collected from the air into our toilet saves money. Some people just dump it down the drain in their sink (kind of a waste). If your house does not need a dehumidifier, you can check out the next tip instead.

SAVINGS – $15; TIME INVOLVED – 1 HOUR (hook up hose, direct the water flow)
TIME SAVED – 18 HOURS (no need to empty bucket, no need to water plants)
1ST YEAR'S FINAL SAVINGS – $440; **FUTURE YEARS** – $465

29. **HOOK A BARREL TO YOUR DOWNSPOUT.** You can hook up a barrel to your home's downspout to save rainwater quickly. You can use this rainwater instead of using water from your hose. Just rig a hose to the barrel in order to water your garden, flowers, or yard when needed. In our city, they offered free clinics this year on how to do this. The cost of a barrel was just $5 at the clinic.

SAVINGS – $30; TIME INVOLVED – 1 HOUR (get a barrel, hook it up)
1ST YEAR FINAL SAVINGS – $0; **FUTURE YEARS** – $30

30. **DON'T LET BATHWATER GO DOWN THE TUB'S DRAIN.** I personally do not take baths, but my daughter does. For kids, it can be fun to swim around in the tub and play with toys. Some adults find it pleasurable to soak in a hot bath. Anyway, there is no use letting the water go down the tub's drain and into the sewer. You might as well make use of it. Gather it up with a bucket and throw it out the window to water your lawn if you must. You can actually syphon it right out your window using a hose. If you happen to be a shower person, simply plug the drain as you shower to save the water. It will also help to create more steam and heat by letting the hot water collect at your feet while you shower away.

"Since the soap you use in the shower is generally less harmful than laundry detergent (it's mild enough to use on your skin), bath water is the most prized gray water for your plants." In some states, you cannot just pour this dirty/*gray* water on your plants or lawn. A person is required to water plants at the roots through the use of an underground irrigation system. You can collect water from other unique sources as well. For instance, there is a hose on the back of most washing machines that you can lead right out into a barrel if you desire (Clark).

I personally find it to be too much trouble to do all of this. I simply scoop up bathwater with a bucket and pour it in my toilet's tank when we need to flush. In the winter, this is very efficient because the moisture from the warm bathwater also humidifies our dry air.

SAVINGS – $15 (find more uses for used water)

31. **USE DRYER LINT** to start fires. My aunt saves all of her lint and uses it in her fireplace in the winter instead of fire starters that you can buy on the market. You can use dryer lint to start campfires as well. I personally use lint to create art sculptures (but that probably won't help most people who are reading this book). Dryer lint is clean – real clean. You could use it to stuff pillows or even use it like a cotton ball.

SAVINGS – $20 (just keep lint on hand as a fire starter)

32. USE EVERY LAST DROP. Do not throw out product containers. They are certainly not empty. I squeeze every drop out of toothpaste tubes, lotion bottles, and similar items. When I can't get any more out, I cut the end open and scoop out more for another week or so. You can get about an extra 1/15 out of product by doing this. Use a cotton swab to remove every last bit of Chaptick from its container. Add a little water to shampoo and conditioner bottles and shake to get out the product that is stuck to the walls of the containers. You can also do this with cough medicine and similar items such as spaghetti sauce in jars.

SAVINGS – $8; TIME INVOLVED – 1 MINUTE (use every last bit of product)

33. PRINT PHOTOS AT WALMART. Sometimes it makes more sense to have prints made at a *Walmart Photo Center* rather than printing them at home. Ink and photo paper for home use are expensive. If you don't use your color printer often, the ink can even dry up or get clogged (been there). That is a lot of money down the drain. Photo printers can be expensive as well and they take up space in your home. Plus, doesn't it seem like prints that are printed at home get ruined even if a slight drop of water gets on the surface? *Walmart* uses "archival-quality inks and photo paper that last over 200 years". Did you know that you can actually order the prints online at *Walmart.com* from the convenience of your own home? You can get a 4x6 (glossy or matte) print starting at just 9 cents and shipping is even free (Walmart)! Compare that to printing at home which could cost about 40 cents a print after paper, ink, and the cost of the printer are factored in.

You can also order prints and get home delivery from other places such as Shutterfly, Snapfish, and more. I've compiled a list of prices for comparison which is shown on the following page. The pricing is *per-print* on an online order of 100, 4x6 glossy prints (standard shipping included, discounts advertised on main photo site page included, tax is not). In addition, you can order prints online at WalGreens and CVS for pickup in store.

PER PRINT PRICING
$0.09 (Walmart)
$0.10 (snapfish) sale
$0.17 (Shutterfly) 40% off Labor Day sale

SAVINGS – $60 (select photos, order online)

34. **USE A PHOTO FRAME.** At my house, I prefer to display photos using a digital photo frame that I earned for free by racking up reward points on my credit card. This wastes no paper or ink. I can turn it on any time I want. I can even set the device to slideshow mode which allows me to display a photo for a certain amount of time before the photo frame switches to the next photo. I might never have to print another photo again.

SAVINGS – $30 (enjoy a digital photo frame instead of ordering prints)

35. **GET FREE INTERNET PROTECTION.** There are many free choices out there. Do a search online to see what companies are scoring best in reviews. Then, download a version of your choosing when you are ready. Here are some of the better free antivirus programs available for download at the present time – *Malwarebytes Anti-Malware*, *Panda Free Antivirus*, and *AVG AntiVirus*. I have used free protection for many years to protect my personal and business computers. I used to purchase protection for my computers, but I liked the free route better. So far I have seen the same amount of protection as I was receiving when I used to pay for it. You can get free protection for your PC, Mac, Android, or iOS. Do a search online now to get started. Before you download a program, make sure that your system meets the requirements.

I received a free protection offer from my bank yesterday. I'm not sure if I'll try it out or not. I feel safe with what I have. I also noticed that Microsoft offers free protection. You can get it by downloading **Microsoft Security Essentials**.

SAVINGS – $35/COMPUTER (get free internet and virus protection)

36. **WORK WITH WHAT YOU'VE GOT.** For instance, let's talk about remodeling rooms. If you moved into your house and have brown, faux wood paneling that you can't stand; then instead of ripping it out, work with it. That's just what I did. It would be expensive and/or time consuming to tear down paneling and replace it with drywall. Actually, paneling holds up very well! Savor its good qualities. If someone rams something into a paneled wall, it's not going to put a hole in it unless the force was super intense. But drywall is a different story. For one of my rooms, I used thick, textured wallpaper to cover up the paneling. Before I wallpapered, I filled the grooves with spackling paste. In other parts of my home, I simply painted the paneling colors that make me happy (definitely not brown).

Besides paneling, you might have another situation to deal with. Check out the wall in my studio (photo shown on the next page). As you can see, the wall is highly textured. It is composed of several layers of plaster and was falling apart because the house is older; so my parents and I ripped it apart even more to make it look intentional. We sponged on several shades of neutral paint and it turned out great!

SAVINGS – $120/ROOM (instead of replacing walls; wallpaper, paint, or distress them); TIME SAVED – 16 HOURS
FINAL SAVINGS – $520

37. **HEAT OR COOL JUST 1 ROOM.** Instead of heating or cooling your entire house, simply heat or cool the room(s) you are using. To do it most efficiently, close any doors to the room and use a portable electric heater or air conditioner in that room only. If there is no door, you can hang a curtain from an adjustable curtain rod. It is very easy to move the curtain from room to room if

**CREATIVE
REMODELING**

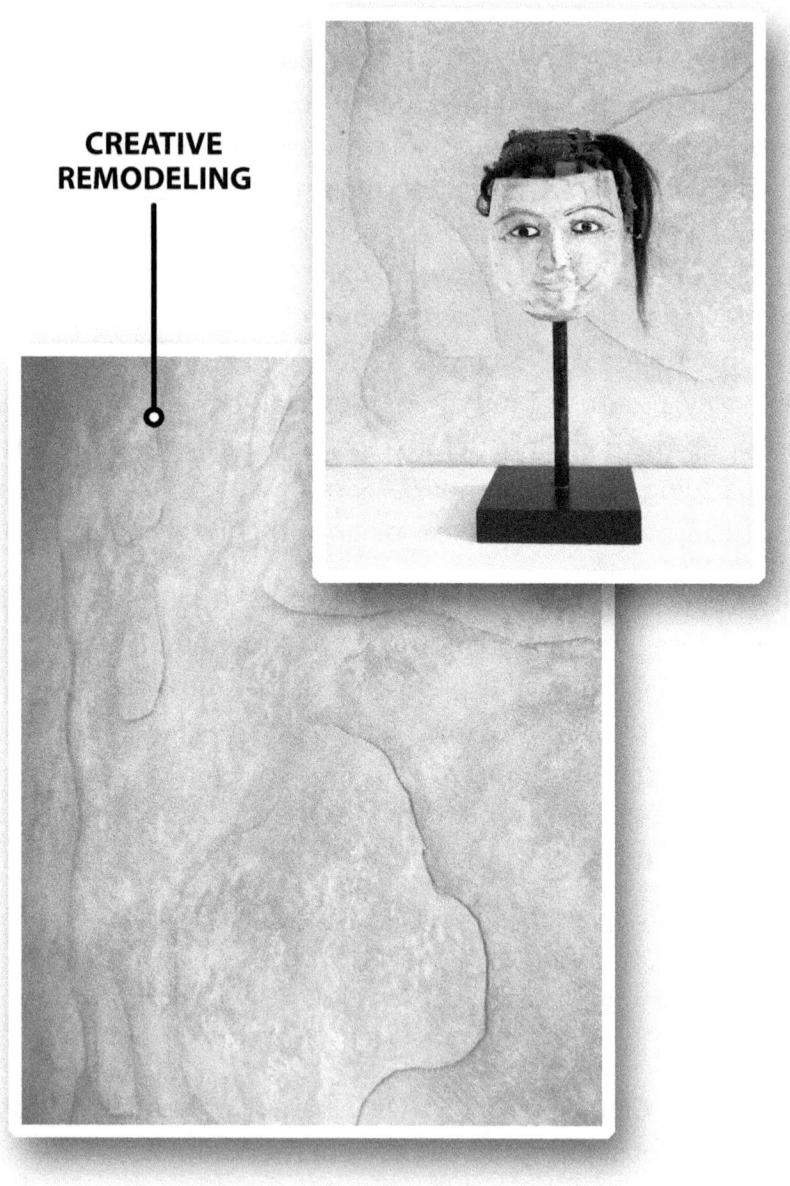

Living Big on a Small Income

necessary. I purchased a pretty curtain and rod for about $13 at **Ollie's Bargain Outlet** this year. You could pick up items like this even cheaper at a local estate auction.

If your annual heating and cooling costs come to $2,300 per year and you have 8 rooms that you usually regulate, you can reduce your costs considerably by only regulating the room you are in.

SAVINGS – $2,000; TIME INVOLVED – 12 HOURS (you may have to move a portable heater throughout the year, so the time can add up)
1ST YEAR'S FINAL SAVINGS – $1,700; **FUTURE YEARS** – $1,713

38. **WATCH FOR OFFERS FROM YOUR ELECTRIC COMPANY.** If you read the flyers that come with your electric or power bill, you can find some pretty cool, free offers that are available. I've taken my power company up on several offers in the past. I've had them install expensive energy savings strips in my house for free. It doesn't let phantom power run wild in your house. If you don't care about some dude coming in your house and going through your rooms, then this is great. I also took advantage of another offer. We had a chest freezer on its last leg and our power company was offering more than the scrap value for old freezers, so we had them pick it up and haul it away. They paid us for it and there was no work on our part. We were going to haul it to a recycling center, so it saved us a trip.

SAVINGS – $160; TIME INVOLVED – 30 MINUTES (sign up for offers, let workers do their jobs); EARNINGS – $35
TIME SAVED – 1 HOUR (1 less trip to the recycling center)
FINAL SAVINGS – $208

NOTES

1. **OBTAIN FREE STORAGE.** A regular storage facility along the roadside averages about $75 per month. I would never pay for storage. My husband and I each have a consignment booth at a nearby antique center. This is where we take items that we don't want anymore. Items that we do still kind of want, but don't want to store at home will get a higher price tagged onto them. If the items sell, then we are still happy. Antique centers usually charge consigners to rent space to sell their goods. But I inquired at one establishment and snagged a smaller space for free (most people do not know that you can make your own offers). In the past, I have inquired at other establishments and snagged free space there as well. I just explain that it is not in my budget to rent a space and ask if they have any space for free (nothing is lost by trying). Regularly a consignment booth space would cost $100 or more in rent per month. I know from experience. I pay nothing and make money all the while.

SAVINGS – $900; TIME INVOLVED – 2 HOURS (obtain 2 booths)
EARNINGS – $500; TIME INVOLVED – 6 HOURS (tag items, collect checks)
1ST YEAR FINAL SAVINGS – $1,200; **FUTURE YEARS** – $1,250

2. **BUY A SECOND CRAPPY HOUSE.** I really need a lot of extra storage space since I run several businesses out of my main home

and I am not fond of clutter. So I bought myself a disgusting fore-closure house to use as a second property. I ripped out the 5 layers of linoleum and carpet that were in each room and now use the house for storing items such our Christmas tree, gift wrap, and toilet paper. I am slowly fixing the house up. I had the house painted and new windows put in. When the house is complete, I can flip it if I desire and walk away with more money than I put into it. This crappy house that we call "The Mansion" (we're sarcastic) is also a great place to store excess food. I'm never afraid to buy in bulk when there is a really good deal on something. The savings here come from the benefits of extra storage space without having to pay for storage units. Did I mention a 4 stall garage came with the property?

Since I got the house so cheap, I don't even worry about the real estate taxes associated with the property and other bills (though I keep track in my Quicken finance program to make sure I make a profit in the end when I resell the place).

SAVINGS – $1,200; TIME INVOLVED – 5 HOURS (look for a cheap property, buy it, store stuff in it)
1ST YEAR FINAL SAVINGS – $1,075; **FUTURE YEARS** – $1,200

3. **UTILIZE A DIGITAL FILING CABINET.** Instead of purchasing filing cabinets which take up valuable space in your home and office, keep a digital cabinet. I always despised filing paperwork until I started filing things digitally. To do this, first gather your weekly pile of receipts, bills, and references. Then take a quick snapshot of each item with your digital camera. Pop the SD card into your computer and name the files by date such as "2014_07_28." By keeping the date in that format, you can search by year, month, and day. Organize the items in folders just like a folder in a real filing cabinet. For example, you might name a folder "utilities". I personally love that I can have folders within folders. So in the utilities folder I can have another folder for electric and gas. I just can't get over how easy it is for me to locate paperwork when I need it and it is all

organized by date. If I need to find a receipt from a specific date, I can locate it within seconds. Things would not be so easy if I were to use a real filing cabinet. After I file the papers, they go to the shredder. By the way, do not shred birth certificates, deeds, and other important papers. Keep them in a safe place. On an added note, if you want to have a backup of your digital cabinet, simply copy your files and store them elsewhere.

SAVINGS – $125 (file things digitally)

4. **UTILIZE YOUR LOCAL LIBRARY.** Do you know how much extra storage space you would have if you got rid of most of your magazines, books, movies, and newspapers? All of these items happen to be available for checkout at my local library and they are probably available at your library too. Make a trip there and see what cool things they have! You can make a bi-monthly trip to the library and get any items that you may need. I only have a handful of useful books that I own and they are books such as this one that are crucial to my life – something that I want to reference on a regular basis. Another benefit of borrowing an item is that you don't have to purchase the item in the first place! Man, I love libraries! If the library is not open and you need info right away, then simply go online to find your answer. Don't forget, you are not only saving money, you are saving space. Doesn't it feel great to have open space in your home? Of course it does!

Our library even has internet service that you can use and movies that can be rented. They even have deluxe kid's toys and a play area; that way your kids can play while you read.

SAVINGS – $250; TIME INVOLVED – 12 HOURS (borrow items twice per month)
TIME SAVED – 12 HOURS (no need to shop for items)
FINAL SAVINGS – $250

5. **SMASH YOUR TRASH.** We share a garbage can with the neighbors who happen to be my parents. Garbage pickup is only about

$2.50 and we only opt for pickup every two weeks. So garbage removal costs about 63 cents per family per week. However, we like to get a good bang for our buck so we jump on the trash bags to reduce them to less than half of the size. This is the main reason that we only need pickup every 2 weeks. When you think you can't fit anything more inside of the trash can, try jumping on top of the pile at your own risk. You'll be surprised at how much you can fit in the can.

SAVINGS – $33

1. **SNAG FREE METER TIME.** When parking at a meter, look to see if there is time left on it. If there is no time left, move to another spot. You are bound to get lucky. We usually snag a free spot on the first try with my husband's *eagle eyes*. My family really takes advantage of this at the beach where meter time is at a skyrocket price. When we park along the boardwalk, an adult jumps out of the car to check the meter. If there is no time on it, we move on to another spot. One time I just walked ahead and pointed to a space if there was really good time on its meter (taking the guesswork out of things). Dollars add up quickly when you live the cheapskate way of life. Okay, so the savings here are minimal, but in regards to dollars per hour, I'm happy with it (plus it's like a game to us).

Did you know that some cities offer free parking during holidays? You don't have to plug the meter. This most likely will not be advertised on the meter (you might need to ask a local passerby or shop owner). Some places also offer free parking after certain hours which should be stated on the meter if you read carefully.

If you travel to the beach off-season, there might even be free parking near the boardwalk. At the beach we are traveling to tomorrow, parking is free after Labor Day (we are taking advantage of that). By the way, I do not book hotel rooms at the beach (they are too expensive). We opt to stay outside of the area using free hotel stays that we have earned.

SAVINGS – $2; TIME INVOLVED – 3 minutes (park at a meter with time on it)
FINAL SAVINGS – $1

2. **NEVER BUY A NEW VEHICLE.** I have never bought a new vehicle. I always buy used and always from family because I know how the vehicle has been treated over the years. I rarely have to put much money into my used vehicles. I still don't know why anyone would want to buy a new one. You are literally throwing thousands of dollars away the minute you make the purchase. But, I'm thankful there are people who will buy new vehicles because I can buy it from them when they feel the urge to have the next new thing to show off. I'll always remember that the things of this world will come to pass. I don't need to show off in a fancy vehicle (although I do own 2 Cadillac models). I personally don't care if people think I drive around in old people cars. My friends have said I drive around in *old granny* cars. I like old people and I feel very comfortable spending time with them. I think many are wise and someday I will be an old person too! From what I have found, old people cars are pretty roomy, and comfortable to say the least!

My husband bought a used truck for $275 many years ago (I talked the owner down in price). It was ugly, but we got 5 years out of it so far. That's really good. We could literally scrap the vehicle and walk away with $230 or more at this point if we remove the catalytic convertor, radiator, and battery. The recycling center we go to gives extra money for those items. Anyway, we use the truck for hauling trash, dead dear, and scrap metal. We also pick up free boxes and furniture items from yard sales when they shut down for the day. I think people thought we were a poor family one time because the truck is a bit beat up. We stopped for a pile of free stuff and the owners came out of the house with even more things for us. They even saw our vehicle in the neighborhood later in the week and brought my husband work pants because they looked about my husband's size. Oh dear. We accepted to be polite, plus the pants did fit him. What nice people. Don't forget to give back by helping others in return (more on this in chapter 9). I donate my time to Vacation Bible School. I used to help with kid writing in school, I've done the yearbook, as well as arranged things such as art programs for a local elementary school. Besides that, I am an active contributor to our local art and historical societies.

SAVINGS – $2,500; TIME INVOLVED – 1 HOUR (find a used car, buy it)
1ST YEAR FINAL SAVINGS – $2,475; **FUTURE YEARS** – $2,500

3.   **SCRAP YOUR OLD VEHICLE.** I use a vehicle until it can't be used anymore or when it no longer makes much sense to fix it (sometimes a newer used vehicle can be bought for less than the repair cost of an older vehicle that needs repair). When a vehicle becomes useless to you, sell off the parts that you can on eBay. Then call your local recycling yard and see if they will tow it away for recycling. You will get a certain amount of cash less the towing fee, the remainder of which you can use towards your next vehicle. Okay, so for this calculation, I'm going to assume that your vehicle needs major repair. Instead of making the repair, you opt to purchase a newer used vehicle that does not need repair and costs the same as the repair would have.

EARNINGS – $500; TIME INVOLVED – 5 HOURS (sell parts on eBay, scrap car, buy new used car)
FINAL SAVINGS – $375

4.   **LIVE NEAR WORK,** or better yet, work out of your home. I work out of my home. My husband walks to work (right up the road). This not only saves a bundle on gas, but saves a lot of time as opposed to if someone had to commute to work. Additionally, you can get exercise each morning and evening as you walk to and from your job. You can even bicycle to work if your distance is just too far to walk. I've seen bicycles passing cars when traffic

is backed up so you might even save time. For goodness sake, I've seen people walking who are faster than traffic. When I was single, I was a package designer in Shillington, PA. I moved in with a friend right across the street from work and we happily strolled across the street to work every weekday morning. Now that's the way to do it.

The savings shown below accounts for a 15 minute commute each way and 1 week of vacation a year.

SAVINGS – $1,750; TIME INVOLVED – 16 HOURS (find a new place, move in)
TIME SAVED – 128 HOURS (less time commuting)
1ST YEAR FINAL SAVINGS – $4,550; **FUTURE YEARS** – $4,950

5. **OBEY TRAFFIC LAWS.** My husband and I are careful to obey the traffic laws. Sometimes it is almost impossible to drive perfect, but we do our best. It pays to avoid getting tickets. Plus, it is safer for everyone!

"Most experts agree that the cost of a speeding ticket varies depending on location and offense, but the average cost is $150 (including court fees)" (Muniz).

SAVINGS – $150/PERSON (obey traffic laws)

6. **CARPOOL.** My family carpools when we can. We carpool to church, shopping, dining, trips, parties, and more. We only carpool with neighbors (usually). That way we don't have to drive to meet up with anyone. I would say that we save 40% on gas by doing this.

The "average American . . . [spends] over $2,000 per year just to fill up the tank" (The Huffington Post).

SAVINGS – $800; TIME INVOLVED – 3 HOURS (set up carpool schedules)
FINAL SAVINGS – $725

7. **GET A VEHICLE WRAP.** You can make money off of your vehicle by allowing it to be used for advertising purposes. There are companies that pay to place catchy advertising on your vehicle in the form of a vinyl wrap. One good thing is that the wrap can protect the surface of your vehicle from the rain, sun, rocks being thrown up, and fingernail scratches.

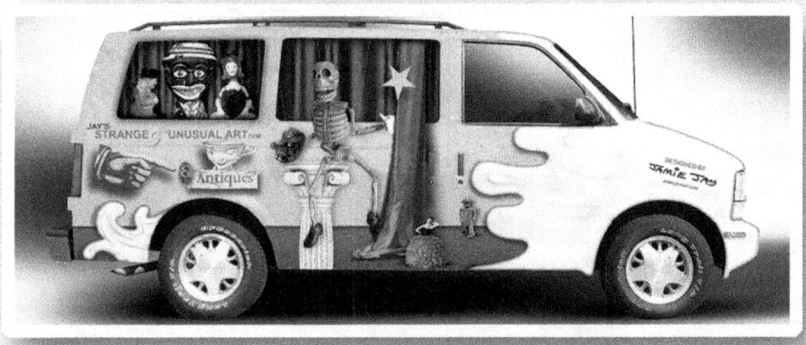

The companies that pay people to have their vehicles wrapped look for several factors when choosing a candidate. They will probably like it when you drive a lot. If you drive more, then more people will see the advertisement. So if you are already driving a lot, you can take advantage of it. You'll have to keep these numbers up if the contract calls for it. I'm sure the companies also look to see where you travel. I went through one of the application processes and it seemed that they were very interested in family life – specifically if your kids are in sports and other activities. If you travel a lot on back roads, it is not as attractive as if you are travelling on major highways. Another factor would be the type of vehicle you own. Will it work well as advertising space? A catchy shape such as the Volkswagen Beetle would be very appealing.

Carvertise.com allows you to apply if you meet these requirements – you own a vehicle with insurance, have a clean driving record, and drive often in high traffic locations (Carvertise LLC.).

If you qualify and get accepted, you can expect to make various different amounts depending on what company you apply with. **Myfreecar.com** pays about $700 -$900 per month (Dempsey). Hey, you can put this towards your gas money.

Here is a list of several companies where you can apply to have your vehicle wrapped with advertising (the application process is free):

carvertise.com
freecarmedia.com
myfreecar.com
autowrapped.com

EARNINGS – $9,600; TIME INVOLVED – 2 HOURS (apply, get interviewed, let them wrap your vehicle)

8.   **MAKE YOUR VEHICLE YOUR HOME.** Yes, I am telling you to live in a vehicle. Because I have accumulated too many belongings, I am not at the point to do this myself. I am slowly selling everything off and someday I hope to live in a *Roadtrek* along with my husband. A *Roadtrek* is a class B motorhome that looks like a van. They are easy to maneuver and you'll fit right in with traffic. You can get a used one for a few thousand dollars complete with toilet, sleeping for 4, table, sink, shower, closet, microwave, oven range, and television.

There are many benefits to living in a moving home. The first benefit that comes to my mind is that you have fewer belongings to clean and care for. That is one less headache to deal with in life – one less stress. Living with only the essentials can create financial freedom. Having more wealth can allow you to do more of the things that you really enjoy. Things take up a lot of time! As a materialistic society, we purchase, move, clean, organize, fix, and re-arrange things. We could be using that precious time to do things that are more productive and meaningful. And the best part – the fewer things you own, the easier it is to find the things you need. I'm very excited about setting out on a new adventure with minimalism being center stage. I've been a hoarder for decades and I can tell you firsthand that things do not create happiness. To me, they are headaches.

Another great benefit of living in an RV is that you do not have to pay property tax. If you choose Alaska, Florida, Nevada, South Dakota, Texas, Washington, or Wyoming as your home base state, you won't even have to pay state income tax.

When you live in an RV, there is no home insurance to worry about, less bills to pay, no lawns to mow, and no weeds to pull. There are no trees to trim, leaves to rake, sidewalks to sweep, or driveways to upkeep.

There are many places where you can park and stay for free including many **Walmart** and **Cracker Barrel Restaurant** parking lots. For free campsite locations, check out ***freecampsites.net***. A search online will help you to discover many of the possibilities. You might even be able to park on a friend or relative's property temporarily as not to intrude.

There are some factors to consider when living in an RV. Where will your mail go? When I live in an RV, I plan to use email for as much as I can and pay my bills online. I will have things such as vehicle registration sent to a PO Box or to a family member who has a permanent address. I plan to have wireless internet which is very easy to set up. I will have Netflix service in order to watch television episodes at a very low cost. Additionally, my husband and I can watch the news right on our laptop using the wireless internet.

Even if living in a vehicle seems too drastic to try, you can always add a little minimalism to your current lifestyle. The less you have, the more you save. I would like to elaborate on this and add that if you buy smaller things you can also save money. For instance, if you buy a smaller couch it should weigh less and cost less. You will not have to hire a moving company if you have to move it someday. You can move it easily with a friend. Same thing with a smaller refrigerator, stove, and table for example. Sometimes it is not so much the size, but the weight that matters. My husband and I made a pact that we would not buy anything that we couldn't lift together because we never want to have to depend on others for assistance.

If you plan to purchase an RV, your savings can be tremendous. Be sure to purchase a used one to save thousands of dollars. If you sell your home, you should have thousands extra to stow away in the bank. The savings calculation includes the cost of the RV which should pay for itself within the first year if you allow a $12,000 budget for it. The calculation also factors in the savings of not having to pay home insurance and property tax. It doesn't include not having to pay state taxes, but if you wish to live in a state that does not charge state tax, then figure on saving an extra $3,500 per year if you are working full time while living in an RV.

SAVINGS – $4,000; TIME INVOLVED – 60 HOURS (sell non-necessities, purchase RV, sell home); TIME SAVED – 380 HOURS (less things to care for each year)
1ST YEAR FINAL SAVINGS – $0; **FUTURE YEARS** – $13,500

9. **SKIP USING WINDSHIELD WASHER FLUID.** I never put fluid in my reservoir. It takes too much time and I don't feel like shopping for windshield washer fluid. I've gone 36 years without doing it. If I'm in a pinch, I use the free window washing

tool at gas stations. I rarely even need that though. A bug splat here and a splotch of bird poop there on my windshield doesn't bother me.

Don't think that you can get by with water alone. In the winter it can freeze rendering it useless. Also, according to BBC News, bacteria can grow in your windshield washing system spreading bacteria that can cause pneumonia and Legionaires' Disease (Bowman).

SAVINGS – $5; TIME SAVED – 1 HOUR (no need to shop for fluid or fill reservoir)
FINAL SAVINGS – $30

10. **USE YOUR TURN SIGNAL LESS OFTEN.** When I am at a red light and plan to make a turn, I do not turn my signal on until the light changes to green. Some people sit there for a minute letting the signal click away. That could add up to 70 flashes or more. That is a waste of the bulb. As soon as I have turned the corner, the signal is switched off. Remember that all of the little things add up. Plus, what else do you have to think about while sitting at a light. Make it a mission to save that bulb!

SAVINGS – $20

11. **STEAR CLEAR OF AUTOMATIC FUNCTIONS.** When you purchase your next car, look for things such as manual windows, manual seat adjustments, and manual door locks. If you were to opt for electronically controlled functions instead, and they were to go bad, it would be more expensive to fix the problem. My husband has always been able to fix things himself if a manual item needs some adjusting on one of our vehicles. The savings shown at the end of this tip are based on parts going bad over a 15-20 year period. I divided the savings out showing the average you will save per year by going with manual car options instead of choosing the more expensive upgrades. One thing that I did not factor in is that

you will usually get your car for cheaper to begin with because most people think that manual functions are undesirable. You're not one of those lazy people that think that way, are you?

SAVINGS – $145

12. **DON'T PAY TO PUT AIR IN YOUR TIRES.** There are gas stations that supply free air. Take advantage of it.

SAVINGS – $10

13. **GET GAS FOR LESS.** Check with your local grocery stores. They may offer a program that allows you to save big on your auto fuel. You'll probably have to sign up for a free shopping/club card. At my grocery store I get 10 cents off a gallon for every $50 purchase I make. I always strive to spend as close to $50 or $100 as possible. If I go over the amount, I receive no extra gas reward points. If I am under $50, I don't get any gas rewards. Another thing I keep in mind is that they do not count milk purchases towards the $50 amount. So when I am adding the total in my head as I shop, I never count the cost of milk. Gas rewards add up quickly, so I am able to save about $8 every time I go to the pump. My husband and I used to fill up two cars in a row plus a gas can using the same rewards until they made a new rule that there was a 20 gallon limit.

SAVINGS – $208

14. **WASH YOUR VEHICLE IN THE RAIN.** Just slip on a raincoat and head outdoors. Wear flip flops and a bathing suit if you prefer. Not only is this fun, there is no need to hook up a hose. You can even set your bucket right under the rainspout to collect water for rinsing your sponge. I wouldn't recommend washing your vehicle in a thunderstorm due to that nasty thing called lightning.

SAVINGS – $80 (no need to visit a carwash)

1. **GET MARRIED OR FIND A ROOMMATE!** Marriage is awesome. Not only do you have a friend for life, you get to split all of the bills! You just saved 50% on your water, electric, gas, phone, sewer, and real estate bills (maybe more)! Even the price of things like decorations, dishes, furniture, and appliances get cut in half. Say goodbye to 50% of the chores as well! You also get to share all of your cheapskate experiences together! Everyone has fights. Overlook that. It doesn't matter. If you are not interested in marriage, try a roommate! One time I slept on a cot in my friend's dining room for half a year saving me over $500 a month on rent. This really helped me to save up for my first home. In a situation like that, it helps to have open-minded, nice, fun friends like mine (that happen to cook really awesome meals to boot).

SAVINGS – $10,000; TIME INVOLVED – 24 HOURS (get married, move in)
1ST YEAR FINAL SAVINGS – $9,400; **FUTURE YEARS** – $10,000

2. **PROPOSE WITH A PLASTIC RING.** When my father gave my mother a *going steady* ring (in his college years), he used a cheap, penny ring from a toy vending machine. If you want to see if someone really loves you and you want to save a load of money, try this tactic for a wedding proposal. Real love does not need a fancy metal ring. Besides, you can use the savings to pay for a fun honey-

moon or towards getting your first home together. A replacement ring could always be purchased on the 5 or 10 year wedding anniversary (when you have extra money saved up)! Yay for plastic.

Most people in the United States spend $2,492 to $4,154 on an average engagement ring (The Wedding Report, Inc.).

SAVINGS – $3,323; TIME INVOLVED – 10 MINUTES (buy toy ring from machine)
TIME SAVED – 1 HOUR (no need to pick out ring, what comes out is what you get)
FINAL SAVINGS – $3,344

If you want to be clever, you could propose in a store right at the toy vending machine area. When you are leaving the store, tell your partner that you would like to get a toy from the vending machine (if there is a ring machine around). They will probably think you are a bit odd. Just say it is for a niece or a cousin. Then when the toy falls out into your hand, immediately get down on one knee and propose in your own unique way. Your partner might think that the ring is a joke for now, but you'll have to explain that you are using the money that you saved to go on a nice honeymoon or to put towards a future home together. They can tell the story to everyone who asks. I'm sure it will get a lot of laughs or at least some sort of reaction.

3. **SNAG A FREE RIDE.** Being anti-traditional with your wedding could save you a bundle. Start by catching a free ride. I surprised my wedding guests by arriving at my wedding in a cop car instead of the traditional limo (price of rental – free). At the time, I worked at the local police station as a meter enforcement person (meter maid). I asked the chief if one of the officers could drive me to my wedding. He agreed with the idea and I really scared the older guests when I came bursting through the woods with the sirens blazing. I wish I had a photo of the look on their faces! Of course, things settled down pretty quickly when they saw me get out of the vehicle. The officer gave me a kiss on the cheek and off he went. By the way, if your parents are paying for the wedding, it still makes

sense to save them money. My parents gave me a couple thousand dollars to put towards buying a home since I barely spent a couple hundred dollars on our entire wedding. I'm sure you can work out your own special deal. I had a twin sister who got married previously, so whatever they spent on her wedding, I received the difference to use as I wished.

The average amount spent on transportation or a limo rental for a wedding in the United States is about $483.25 (The Wedding Report, Inc.).

SAVINGS – $483 (ask around for a ride)

4.   **MAKE YOUR OWN WEDDING CAKE.** I made an individual cake for each guest at my wedding. I thought this was really classy. I used fondant to cover each mini cake. My mother, sister, and I made floral decorations out of fondant for the tops. If you do not know anything about baking or icing a cake, you can learn some tricks and tips by watching YouTube videos online. However, I just followed the instructions on the cake and fondant boxes. You can cut your time and expense by faking some things. You can use Styrofoam for the first couple of tiers. You can still cover it in icing if you wish. Instead of creating flowers out of icing which is time consuming, you can use artificial flowers from a craft store. Just poke them right into different parts of the cake.

Americans spend an average of $419 on wedding cakes/dessert (The Wedding Report, Inc.).

SAVINGS – $390; TIME INVOLVED – 4 HOURS (plan/sketch cake, buy supplies, bake, decorate); TIME SAVED – 2 HOURS (no need to shop for a cake)
FINAL SAVINGS – $340

5.   **CATER YOUR WEDDING YOURSELF.** Because I did everything myself (with some extra help from my wonderful mom), my wedding did not cost much at all (we are talking a puny amount). We had the wedding in my grandfather's field. My mother cooked up

some fancy steaks on the grill along with some other great sides. I purchased a table with an elegant umbrella and padded chairs on clearance at Kmart so that the guests of honor (bride, groom, matron of honor, and best man) had a special place to sit. (We still have the table and chairs in our yard for use during outdoor picnics.)

"According to the Bridal Association of America's 2006 wedding report, the average catering bill is $12,247, which includes just the food and the beverages. This is based on an average of 150 people, so you can expect to spend approximately $82 per person" (Zisko).

So feel free to cook up whatever you desire! I'm sure you are not going to spend $12,247. Keep in mind, the fewer guests you invite, the less you have to cook. My husband and I only invited very close family members to our wedding, but they ate well on fancy, red disposable plates (no dishes to be washed). Who wishes to do dishes when a honeymoon is on the horizon? By the way, you could have each guest bring a covered dish to your wedding! Now isn't that a fab idea?

SAVINGS – $11,500; TIME INVOLVED – 10 HOURS (plan the meal, shop, cook)
TIME SAVED – 2 HOURS (no need to find and meet with caterer)
FINAL SAVINGS – $11,200

6.   **BE YOUR OWN DJ.** I took care of the music at my wedding. Just call me "DJ Jamie Jay". I had all of the music set up. I purchased a complete wedding music CD set on deep discount and simply pressed play on my boom box to start the ceremony with the "Wedding March". If you have musicians in your family or circle of friends, they can be invited to play a piece at your wedding so that you have some live music (I'm sure they would be honored and flattered by the request).

Most wedding couples in the U.S. spend an average of $699 on a typical DJ. A run of the mill live band would cost around $1,633. A musician, soloist, or ensemble could be hired for about $593 (The Wedding Report, Inc.).

SAVINGS – $970; TIME INVOLVED – 30 MINUTES (order music, get playing device ready); TIME SAVED – 30 MINUTES (no need to find or talk to a DJ)
FINAL SAVINGS – $970

7. **MAKE YOUR OWN BOUQUET.** I still have my bouquet and it decorates a valance in my living room. To make it, I purchased artificial flowers at a craft store and bound them into a bouquet that was just perfect for me. I made a matching bouquet that was a little smaller to throw after the ceremony which my matron of honor held. I even crafted matching boutonnieres for the men. Any arts and crafts chain store should have artificial flowers, ribbon, pins, and other accessories just right for this project.

According to The Wedding Report, Inc., typical costs for boutonnieres and corsages comes to $134.50, the bridal and bridesmaid bouquets amount to $313.50, and the flower girl flowers average out to $87.

SAVINGS – $500; TIME INVOLVED – 3 HOURS (get reference photo, purchase supplies, create); TIME SAVED – 2 HOURS (no need to pick out real flowers)
FINAL SAVINGS – $475

8. **DECORATE ON YOUR OWN.** For my wedding, I purchased a cheap, lightweight metal arch. I covered it with free, sheer white curtains that I had stockpiled (I save almost everything. I might be considered an organized hoarder). Then I wove a garland of roses around it. It looked beautiful. My husband and I stood under it when we got married in my grandfather's well groomed field. I also purchased an inexpensive, long red carpet to lay on the ground so that we looked important and regal walking to be wed. It created a faux isle in the field. After the wedding, the rug could serve another purpose in our hall.

In the United States, typical couples spend an average of $434.50 on event decorations, $460 on flower arrangements (not including bouquets and such), $327 on centerpieces, and $95 on flower petals (The Wedding Report, Inc.).

SAVINGS – $1,250; TIME INVOLVED – 4 HOURS (decide on a look, shop, arrange)
TIME SAVED – 3 HOURS (no need to meet with decorator)
FINAL SAVINGS – $1,225

9.   **BORROW THE DRESS** and/or suit. If you have a friend or relative of similar size, you can borrow their dress or suit for your wedding. I even borrowed the veil for mine. Items can be pinned or tacked in to fit better if needed. Another great option is to visit a secondhand store. At our local thrift stores, there are an abundance of suits and wedding dresses. If you go with this option, you can keep your dress On the other hand, if you borrow it, you have nothing to hold on to.

U.S. couples typically spend $1,211 on the wedding dress and $203 on the suit (The Wedding Report, Inc.).

SAVINGS – $1,414; TIME INVOLVED – 1 HOUR (ask to borrow a dress and/or suit, try it on); TIME SAVED – 3 HOURS (no need to search for the perfect dress at a boutique or two or three)
FINAL SAVINGS – $1,464

10. **DO YOUR OWN HAIR** or have someone else do it. If you don't have any ideas on how to do your hair, look online. You can search for ideas by visiting google.com. Type in your search phrase and then click on "Images". If you are going to do your own hair, then you might as well do your own makeup (if you are the type of person who would wear makeup). Don't forget to do your own manicure and pedicure as well.

The average amount spent in the U.S. on wedding hair service is

$65, makeup service is $53, and manicure and pedicure is $43(The Wedding Report, Inc.).

SAVINGS – $161; TIME INVOLVED – 1.5 HOURS (look for styles, round up supplies, get ready)
TIME SAVED – 2 HOURS (no need to schedule and attend appointments)
FINAL SAVINGS – $174

11. **ONLY HAVE A BEST MAN AND MAID OF HONOR** (no extras). That way you won't have to match the outfits. Such would be the case if you had more people in your wedding party including bridesmaids, groomsmen, ushers, flower girls, and ring bearers. You also don't need to buy more bouquets for each of the bridesmaids if you don't have any bridesmaids to begin with. For our wedding, my husband had his best man wear a dark suit. We bought him and my father matching ties. My sister wore a prom dress (I think. No, I'm pretty sure she wore a dress from her closet). I wore a prom dress as the maid of honor in her wedding though (it was classy).

Now, I know that it is traditionally expected that the wedding party pay for their own outfits (so it might not be any money out of your pocket), however, I also know that they do not enjoy shelling out the money. So I did not ask for my wedding party to pay for their own outfits. I simply asked them to get something out of their closets! Then I simply bought some accessories for them to wear for the wedding which they could keep as gifts.

So, for the savings in this tip, I'm going to assume that you do not have to pay for any outfits anyway since that seems to be traditional. The figure will only include savings on boutonnieres, corsages, flower girl flowers, and bridesmaid bouquets. According to costofwedding.com, here is the average amount spent on these items in the United States.

Boutonnieres, Corsages	$101 - $168
Bridesmaid Bouquets	$131 - $219
Flower Girl Flowers	$65 - $109 (The Wedding Report, Inc.)

SAVINGS – $320 (keep your wedding party small)
TIME SAVED – 12 HOURS (a lot less people to contact and explain things to during the whole process)
FINAL SAVINGS – $1,200

12. **WED AT A FREE LOCATION.** You don't need to rent a fancy space at restaurant, country club, park, catering hall, or hotel. I've known people who were married in their own yards. If you don't want to rent chairs for your yard, have guests bring folding chairs. I chose to be wed in my grandfather's field. My wedding was short and sweet, so the guests stood. Later we ate at picnic tables and other miscellaneous tables that were scrounged together by my family. I purchased cheap silver colored, vinyl tablecloths at our local party outlet to spruce everything up. The silver tablecloths tied everything together nicely.

There are many free venue possibilities to choose from if you ask around. Your church or synagogue might let you use the facilities at no charge or for a small fee. I could have done that, but my husband and I preferred to have an outdoor wedding. As an added note, if people who come from families with two different belief systems are marrying, it might be hard to choose which religious site to go with.

The typical cost of renting a wedding location in the United States ranges from $2,711 to $4,518 (The Wedding Report, Inc.).

SAVINGS – $3,615 (find a free location)

13. **HAVE A FAMILY MEMBER OR FRIEND TAKE THE PHOTOS FOR YOU.** If you skip hiring a wedding photographer, you can save a bundle. Just have your prints made at *WalMart* for a very small fee; or better yet, simply display your photos on a digital photo frame. If you don't have a digital photo frame, add one to your gift wish list. You can also opt to display your wedding photos on your

computer monitor or television set.

Typical U.S. couples spend money on a photo cd/dvd, an engagement session, prints and/or enlargements, and a wedding photographer. The average cost of all of this comes to $2,642 (The Wedding Report, Inc.).

SAVINGS – $2,610; TIME INVOLVED – 1 HOUR (have a friend take photos)
TIME SAVED – 1 HOUR (no need to hire a photographer or meet with them)
FINAL SAVINGS – $2,610

14. **MAKE YOUR OWN INVITATIONS AND MORE.** Instead of ordering custom wedding invitations, you can make them yourself. I purchased a fancy invitation kit from **Staples** back in my wedding year. I printed my invitations and response cards using my printer. I know people who order clear custom craft stamps from **StampsByDesign.com** for use in making their wedding invitations. The prices are low for a custom stamp and the shipping is free. The invitation will look like it was printed by an expensive print shop boasting special heat embossing effects or fancy ink accents in colors such as gold or silver. Stamping takes a little skill if using a large stamp, so I would suggest just adding a special little touch to your invite – such as gold or silver stamped names, initials, or the wedding date.

Most couples order ceremony programs for an average of $104, engagement announcements for $96, a guest book for $54.50, invitations and reply cards for $225, reception menus for $101, save the date cards for $107, table place cards for $77, and thank you cards for $84. The postage amount for all of this usually totals $101 (The Wedding Report, Inc.). If you can skip a bunch of the paper mailing and limit the amount of people you invite, all of these costs can be reduced. I kept things simple for my wedding with handmade invitations, response cards, table place cards, and thank you cards. We didn't have a guest book and didn't' need one. My wedding was so small that I can remember everyone who was there (my nearest and dearest). We didn't have a menu. Everything we served rocked, so why have a menu. I didn't need to send *save the date* cards because if someone didn't choose to save the date on their own, then they really didn't care enough in the first place. I don't need people like that in my life.

If you want to be super cheap and maybe a bit tacky, email your invitations and thank you cards instead of mailing them.

SAVINGS – $915; TIME INVOLVED – 2 HOURS (make invites; reply, place, and thank you cards); TIME SAVED – 2 HOURS (skip announcements, guest book, menus, and save the date cards)

FINAL SAVINGS – $915

1. **ENROLL KIDS IN LOCAL PROGRAMS.** Children can take part in locally funded programs and government funded learning programs throughout the year. My children enroll in several free programs every year (math, science, reading, vacation Bible school, Good News Club, and more). That is education and entertainment for them at no cost. They get to take part in things such as field trips and outings including cave tours, train rides, nature center visits, lake visits, and bowling. Other benefits include food, snacks, beverages, and other fun rewards that are offered. Usually there is free swimming, skating, pizza parties, or similar; and the parents are almost always invited as well. That's free entertainment for the entire family. We're talking about no-fee education, fun, socialization, and free child-sitting during the actual running of the program. My husband and I stay young and fit by participating in what we can. Why join a gym when you can stay active by swimming, roller skating, and more for FREE!

SAVINGS – $1,400; TIME INVOLVED – 30 MINUTES (enroll kids, attend free events/parties)
FINAL SAVINGS – $1,388

2. **ATTEND FREE WORKSHOPS FOR KIDS.** Over the years, I have taken my children to free workshops at many places including

Michaels arts and crafts stores where they have created greeting cards, worked with clay, and more; ***Lowe's*** home improvement center where they have built many wood toys and useful items; our local library where they have made jumbo chalk, soap bubbles, jet packs, and more. Some places even have free Lego building workshops. Our library supplies thousands of Lego building blocks for the kids to play with during sessions throughout the year. If you live near a ***Toys "R" Us*** store, check it out. They may offer free events for kids as well.

SAVINGS – $90/CHILD (attend free workshops, shop while your kids craft, play, and learn)

3. **MAKE USE OF SCHOOL PROJECTS.** When a child brings home a school art project, hang it on your fridge. In time, think about how you can recycle the project. Here is an example. If a project has cotton balls, I harvest them. I can use a cotton ball to clean my face with astringent. After I clean my face, I may decide to use the cotton ball to clean my bathroom sink, baseboard, or garbage can. We're talking triple usage on these cotton balls! Since I am an artist (often times a junk artist), I even cut off pieces of construction paper from the school projects for use in my own art projects. It beats throwing the projects directly into the garbage can.

SAVINGS – $10; TIME INVOLVED – 2 MINUTES (hang on fridge, harvest materials all year long)
FINAL SAVINGS – $9

4. **NEVER HIRE A BABY SITTER.** I have never paid for child sitting. Take your children everywhere with you. Work from home if you must. Think about it. If you have a job, you can save thousands of dollars on child care by quitting your current job and working from home. Be your own boss (even if you have a good paying job). Do the math first. It might actually make sense for you to work from home if you consider the cost of childcare.

"The average cost of center-based daycare in the United States is $11,666 per year ($972 a month), but prices range from $3,582 to $18,773 a year ($300 to $1,564 monthly), according to the National Association of Child Care Resource & Referral Agencies . . . (BabyCenter)."

It is advantageous to watch your own children. It should give you a closer bond with them (and make you tougher). Work together and play together. If you clean houses, take your child or children with you. Same thing if you run a vegetable stand. On the other hand, if someone asks you to watch their children, say *yes* to that. You can make some extra bucks; and if you have children, they will have a friend or two for the day.

SAVINGS – $12,000/CHILD (multi-task, watch kids and work, it seems to take just as much time to call a sitter, pay the sitter, and chat with a sitter as it does to multi-task and watch your own kids)

5. **PLAN THE BIRTH DAY.** Give birth to your children on the same day of the year (or talk your wife into it). I did. My children were both born on July 1st. Not only is this cool, it can save you money by allowing you to have one big party. Sure, you can have a simple party at home, but the savings really show when you rent a facility. For instance, one year I rented the swimming pool for my kids' party. So, doing this sort of thing can save you $150 or more per year just on the facility rental. Besides that, you can save on decorations and your time (you only have to plan 1 party instead of 2). Having one party is a win! You'll just have to take care to time things right. I planned to conceive another child 3 months after my first was born. This puts things very close since they grow in a stomach for about 9 months. Luckily I was able to get pregnant on the day I desired (not everyone has that option and some people may have fertility issues). You can get the date pretty exact if you have a planned C-section which was my case since I am very petite (4' 10"), and my husband is 6 feet tall. My babies were 8-9 pounds each (too big for my body). In conclusion, I happen to be a twin

and I never minded sharing a birthday with my sister. It makes for a big, fun party! If you want to go to super, extreme lengths, you can have your children on your birthday as well! Why not make it a family affair?

SAVINGS – $175; TIME INVOLVED – 5 MINUTES (calculate the day of conception)
TIME SAVED – 13 HOURS (plan and throw one less party per year)
1ST YEAR FINAL SAVINGS – $498; **FUTURE YEARS** – $500

6. **USE A FREE PARTY VENUE AND MORE.** Either have your party at home or rent a free space such as a local playground. I have reserved picnic tables at our local water playground several times when my kids were under the age of 8. The playground was geared towards younger children. To reduce the costs of the party further, you can make your own cake or cupcakes, bring small cups (very small) because children forget which cup is theirs, make your own punch (two kinds to be classy), and place the punch in pretty dispensers that you will use every year. I don't use disposable tablecloths. I use pretty vinyl ones that I can wipe down and use again. Make fun games so that the party will be a blast. Give away cheesy little prizes that you keep from other kids' parties. Buy penny candy for the goodie bags or fill them with things that you can get at a discount such as items from your work or your own business.

If you really don't have time to bake your own cake, then buy one on discount that is about ready to go out of code and jazz it up at home with some cool decorations. One year, there were only small discounted cakes available for a birthday party I was hosting, so I got three small cakes. I remember one being shaped like a sitting puppy dog. The party guests liked the selection because there were a variety of flavors to suit any taste.

I just love making cupcakes, but then you have to buy wrappers. If you can get some wrappers in a dollar box of goods at an estate auction, then good for you. I actually have gotten some at estate auctions. They were even in the original packaging. I'm not so sure I would use cupcake wrappers if they were bought secondhand in an unwrapped fashion.

SAVINGS – $190 (use a free party venue, supply the food, think smart)

7. **NEVER BUY CANDY AGAIN.** If you have children, you should never have to buy candy. Actually, you should not be buying candy to begin with. It is not good for you. But I have to admit that I enjoy a free chocolate treat now and then (I also used to make a living designing candy packaging and displays so I don't want to knock candy too much). Your children will bring home so much candy during the year that you will not know what to do with it all.

There is Valentine's Day candy that they can get at school and club parties. We go to several Easter egg hunts each year. Don't forget to train your kids for the hunt. You don't want them to be the kid with just one egg in their basket at Easter time. Do you? Train your kids with manners as well so that the hunt is enjoyable for everyone! Then there are Halloween and Christmas parades to attend. Don't forget about trick-or-treating. We go to several neighborhoods to really load up. After all of this you should end up with several grocery bags filled with candy. Never leave the candy unattended in your home or it will disappear quickly. I lock it up in a buffet cabinet because I don't want fat, sick kids or spouse for that matter. The kids are allowed to pick out 1-3 pieces a day, eating the short shelf life products first. Chips and pretzels are consumed first, followed by chocolate which actually could be frozen to prolong the life; and then finally the hard candy and taffy are the last to be consumed. We usually never get around to eating the last bit of stuff. It seems to be pretty common candy anyway. This common stuff could be given away. Stick it in a bowl for guests or give it to friends at work. If you set a bowl on your desk at work for all to enjoy, I think your co-workers would really appreciate it. It's a good way to get rid of extra candy fast.

Another place where you can pick up free candy is at fairs and events. The booths usually have bowls of candy. If you act interested, you can pocket a piece or two for yourself and maybe you'll even learn something new. You have to admit, going to all of these events such as parades and Easter egg hunts is much more fun than shopping for candy. Be sure to never give in when your children want candy from convenience stores, restaurants, vending machines, or at store checkouts. You have plenty of candy at home, always keep some with you when you are out and about which will keep you from buying candy at the store.

Americans spend an average of $146.77 per person on candy each year (Bureau of Labor Statistics).

SAVINGS – $147/PERSON; TIME INVOLVED – 4 HOURS (gather candy at events)
TIME SAVED – 2 HOURS (no need to shop for candy during the year)
FINAL SAVINGS – $97

8. **DO NOT BUY TREATS ON THE BOARDWALK.** When you go to the beach, does your kid beg for the $6 marshmallow lollipop at the corner candy store or the $8 jumbo jawbreaker on a stick? Yeah! So do mine. But we just purchase a dollar bag of marshmallows at that local grocer a few blocks down. It helps to keep a stash of Easter or Halloween candy in your purse or pocket in case the kids (or even you) get tempted by the boardwalk fare. It is way too easy to spend $20 on a bag of candy on the boardwalk. If you don't hoard candy throughout the year, one place you can pick up candy for a very reasonable price is at the *Cracker Barrel Old Country Store and Restaurants*. You can usually get the same or similar candy that you find in the expensive tourist stores, but for a fraction of the price.

SAVINGS – $14; TIME INVOLVED – 10 MINUTES (take a short walk to the local grocer to shop); TIME SAVED – 10 MINUTES (no need to stand in the long line at the popular tourist candy store)
FINAL SAVINGS – $14

9. **STEER CLEAR OF VENDING MACHINES.** They are a rip off in my book. I will never give my children money for a vending machine, bubble gum machine, candy machine, or similar. It is a novelty. I will however, let them look for coins behind and around the machines. If they find a coin, by all means use it. I also let them jiggle the handles (after wiping them down with free hand sanitizer wipes). If fresh candy falls out, they may have it. If candy was already lying in the machine, they may not have it (it could be poisoned or germy).

The last vending machines I looked at priced water, soda, and candy bars at $1.25. I think it pays to buy in bulk at a grocery store instead. A big bag of candy bars, a gallon of spring water, or a 2 liter of soda would be a much better deal than if you made a purchase through a vending machine.

Think about how much money would be wasted if you gave your child a quarter every time you went out and they wanted a gumball. You can buy a large bag of gumballs at the grocery store for about a dollar and keep them in your purse if that makes things easier. You could save $24 a year on gumball purchases alone (even if you have to splurge and buy two bags at the store).

SAVINGS – $250 (exert self-control, don't use vending machines)

10. **MAKE A SLIDING BOARD.** If you have stairs in your house, you can easily turn the stairs into an awesome sliding board! Where do you know of where you can buy a slide this long that can be used in any type of weather? Use your own judgment when it comes to the issue of safety. Maybe you want your kids to wear a bicycle helmet and knee pads. You can either tape pieces of cardboard together to make a slide and let your kids slide down on a blanket (not my favorite choice). Or, you can use cardboard as if it were a sled. Better yet, just use a plastic sled if you have one. Again, keep safety in mind. My kids have not gotten hurt doing this, but yours could. Supervision is a must. One good thing about this idea is that cardboard folds up flat and can be stored easily under a bed or couch.

Living Big on a Small Income

SAVINGS – $150; TIME INVOLVED – 5 MINUTES (make cardboard slide or find sled)
FINAL SAVINGS – $148

11. **SAVE YOUR TOYS.** It might be too late for you, but I saved my childhood toys and passed them down to my own children. Things come back into style (Care Bears, Transformers, Strawberry Shortcakes, G. I. Joes, Legos, board games, video games and more). Actually, do they ever really go out of style? You can give your kids a few toys on each birthday or at Christmas time.

In 2013, the average amount spent on toys (per child) in the U.S. was $371. The United Kingdom surpassed the U.S. at $438 per child (Statista).

SAVINGS – $371/CHILD (give your child a few toys each year)
TIME SAVED – 3 HOURS (say goodbye to time spent toy shopping)
FINAL SAVINGS – $446

12. **SELL YOUR TOYS.** If you don't feel like saving toys like in the previous tip, then sell them. You can sell your toys or your kids' toys through online outlets such as eBay or Listia, through consignment, or at your very own yard sale. If your child outgrows a swing set, sell it in your local shopper or newspaper. We actually bought ours from an ad in the shopper. Now we are ready to sell it to someone else. One time we had someone offer to barter for it. They owned a drive in theater and wanted to exchange free passes for our swing set. However, I have only been to the drive in theater a few times in my life, so I didn't think it would be worth it to me.

EARNINGS – $100; TIME INVOLVED – 3 HOURS (gather unwanted toys, sell them)

13. **MAKE DOLL CLOTHES.** My daughter received a rather large, expensive doll for Christmas the other year. The clothing for the doll that is available for purchase is pricey so I chose to make my own. My little girl literally wants every outfit from the doll catalog. Instead, I let her go through all of our old, outdated clothing. Then I

reduce the size down easily to fit the doll. The cost for this project is nothing since I already own a bunch of thread that came from box lots at estate auctions. It is fairly quick to make the clothing since things like cuffs, collars, and waists are already created. I just have to turn the item inside out and scale it down by sewing it smaller and then cut off the excess fabric. My daughter can't get enough . . . of course! In addition, she now has one-of-a-kind doll clothing. I do not have that much sewing experience, so this is something that everyone should be able to do or learn to do fairly easily. Always save old underwear for the elastic band. Elastic is not cheap. I used elastic to turn an unwanted shirt into a doll skirt. The elastic keeps the skirt snug on the doll's waist.

SAVINGS – $150; TIME INVOLVED – 5 HOURS (gather old clothes, sew them smaller); TIME SAVED – 2 HOURS (no more shopping for doll clothes)
FINAL SAVINGS – $75

14. **MAKE SLIME.** This is a really cool project! It turns out looking like the slime you can buy in toy stores. You just mix half a tablespoon of borax with 1 cup of water and set it aside. Now take half a cup of water and mix it with 1 regular container of Elmer's Glue. Add a little food coloring to your liking if you wish. Now add the borax mixture that you had set aside previously. Mix it quick -- it will thicken into slime fast! Make sure your kids are old enough to handle this safely and are supervised. This is a popular project, however, borax can be absorbed through cuts and you should not place your hands in your mouth after handling borax because it is toxic to eat.

A safer project to make would be goop. Place some cornstarch in a bowl. Add water slowly until you like the texture. Then simply add a few drops of food color if you desire. For the savings calculation shown below, let's assume you make four small jars of *slime* (not *goop*) per year. This project is quick to make, but for the time calculation, I assumed you will have to shop for supplies. The cost of supplies is also factored in.

SAVINGS – $20; TIME INVOLVED – 1 HOUR (gather supplies, have fun))
TIME SAVED – 1 HOUR (no need to shop for slime)
FINAL SAVINGS – $20

15. **CREATE A FREE PHOTO SESSION.** Instead of taking your kids to a fancy photo studio to have their portrait taken, take them to a dressing room. Let your children pick any extravagant clothes they want for the session, even fancy hair clips, hats, ties, and other accessories (only if the store allows smaller accessory items in the dressing room area). Train your subjects ahead of time to keep quiet in the dressing room as you do not want the staff to get tipped off as to what is going down (at least I wouldn't want them to know). From my own research, this is not an illegal act unless the person you are photographing does not give you permission to photograph them. Once in the dressing room, whip your camera out of your purse and get creative! The lighting is already set up for

Living Big on a Small Income

you, so there is no real need for a flash. It's up to you really. This project should cost nothing except for time and gas. The full wardrobe and location are free. Plus, you don't need to pay the photographer. Hmmm…this tip doesn't seem too classy, but the end photo result should be. Check out my dressing room photo results over there on the left! I used my art program to blur the edges and then added a few other decorative swirls; and even some fake snow.

SAVINGS – $187.50/CHILD; TIME INVOLVED – 1 HOUR (go to store, try on clothes, snap pictures)
TIME SAVED – 2 HOURS (no photography appointment necessary)
FINAL SAVINGS – $213

16. **LIFT YOUR CHILDREN.** Save yourself a gym membership and the drive to the gym. When I had young children, I built my muscles up large without even trying. No exercise classes or gym memberships needed here. I carried my children around – one on each hip. I think I did this up until they were 6 years old (not constantly of course, just here and there). I still give my kids piggy back rides even though their weights are surpassing mine. I used to pick my son up and say, "You're heavy." I must have said it so much that when I asked him his name one time he said it was "Heavy". That cracked me up. I totally confused the poor little guy.

SAVINGS – $350 (don't drive to a gym, carry the kids around)

17. **CONVERT PANTS INTO SHORTS.** Isn't it annoying when kids wear out the knees in their pants? They're always crawling around on the floor and falling all over the place. Instead of adding an embarrassing patch to the knees or throwing the pants out, simply cut the legs off converting the pants into shorts. If you don't know how to sew a nice hem, just purchase a roll of no-sew tape. You can roll the pant leg under to hide the *rough cut edge*. Apply a piece of no-sew tape under the rolled up fabric edge and iron to create a finished look.

SAVINGS – $100; TIME INVOLVED – 1 HOUR (convert pants into shorts)
TIME SAVED – 2 HOURS (no need to shop for new shorts)
FINAL SAVINGS – $125

18. **PURCHASE NUETRAL COLORED ITEMS FOR YOUR KIDS.** I have to admit that I have purchased nuetral colored items so that I could pass certain articles of clothing down from one child to the other even though my children are of different genders. I do not go to extremes with this. For example, I do not have my daughter wear hand me down underwear from my son. I think it is totally cool to hand down items such as snow pants, gloves, and boots though. Oh, and I have also handed down socks – so I usually buy classic white.

Some non-clothing items that you could buy in gender neutral colors include a car seat, stroller, diaper bag, bibs, playpen, highchair, and toys to name a few.

What happens if your little girl just has to have pink, purple, or teal on her garments? To deal with this dilemma, simply use fabric paint, gems, or a cool patch to jazz things up. If you purchase a white snowsuit for your son, you could always dye it pink for your daughter. A red snowsuit could be bleached to create pink. Things can be altered – just do a little creative thinking. Think in reverse if you have an older daughter and a younger son. A pink snowsuit can be dyed red at a low cost. In the end, I would really just rather force my children to wear a white or black snowsuit and then compliment the suit with colorful hats, gloves, and scarves. That way I don't have to pay anything more to dye an item or spend time to alter the outfit with colorful patches and other fun elements.

SAVINGS – $200; TIME SAVED – 2 HOURS (no need to shop for certain items)
FINAL SAVINGS – $250

19. **SAVE ALL CAR SEATS.** Even if the car seat is torn and stained, there are usually events at local malls or the YMCA which allow you

to trade your old car seat for a gift card. I recently traded a dilapidated car seat for a $5 Wal-Mart gift card. Nobody would have wanted the car seat (it was in rough condition). Health fairs usually collect up car seats because they want your child to use a new car seat that is up to current standards. If I see an ugly car seat lying alongside the road for free, I'm sure to pick it up. It's like a five-dollar bill slapping me in the face! And don't forget, you do not have to pay for the disposal of your car seats either (you are getting paid for someone to take them away).

EARNINGS – $10; TIME INVOLVED – 30 MINUTES (get car seats, exchange them for gift cards)

20. **CRAFT YOUR OWN HALLOWEEN COSTUMES.** You don't have to have great skill to do this and you don't need money. When I was a kid, my sister and I made our own costumes out of cardboard, old clothes, and more. It makes for a unique, one of a kind costume that is sure to get attention. One year, my sister was a walking toilet complete with a toilet seat and plunger. Another year my mom made the whole family grape costumes. She blew up purple and green balloons so that we looked like bunches of grapes. Here are some other costumes that we have created over the years: scarecrows, table with a head in a bowl (cut a piece of cardboard and a tablecloth or sheet so that your head can stick through), character costumes that don't look cheap and cheesy like the ones in the stores, and a cute cat costume to name a few.

If you don't like to make costumes, you can always opt to buy costumes a year in advance after Halloween is officially over. You can save 75% or more by doing this.

SAVINGS – $35/COSTUME (don't shop for a costume, make one)

21. **BUY NAME BRAND CLOTHING AND RESELL IT.** Up until about a year ago, I purchased *Gymboree* brand clothing for my children.

This is a brand that is up there in price. I practically got the clothing brand new and for free though. I'll tell you how. I would buy a year in advance for the next season. So the prices were super low to begin with because I was getting end of season sale prices. When I made purchases, I would also earn *Gymbucks* which gave me a further discount on my next purchase. I also signed up for a Gymboree credit card which gave me an extra 5% back. Plus, when I signed up, I got an enrollment bonus. That tempted me so I had my husband sign up for a card too so that he could get an enrollment bonus that I could spend. On top of all that, I also watched for extreme sales always shopping from home and making my order big enough to receive free shipping. Finally, when my kids outgrew the clothing, I sold it on eBay. Gymboree clothing is sought after on eBay, so I had no trouble selling it for a good price. In the end, I got top of the line clothing for free or close to practically free making thrift stores seem expensive.

SAVINGS – $2,200 (buy name brand clothing cheap, sell it later on)

22. **DON'T GET THE KIDS' MEAL.** Kids' meals at fast food restaurants are a rip off because you have to pay for a toy and a drink that are not necessary. If my kids want a toy, I carry some wrapped toys in my purse that I saved from my childhood or picked up for free at yard sales. Themes are repeated through the years, so I usually have something cool. So anyway, if you order tap waters, that takes care of the drink. Then all you have to do is order fries and chicken nuggets off of the dollar menu and you just saved a couple of dollars per child. We only visit fast food restaurants occasionally since we prefer home cooked meals so we don't really have to deal with this situation all that often.

SAVINGS – $150

23. **BONUS TIP – SAVE YOUR CHILDREN'S TEETH.** If you have children, save their teeth. I have them arranged perfectly in fake gums made of silly putty as you can see below. They could be rare someday. Who has a whole set of children's teeth lying around? Hey you're the tooth fairy and you paid for those teeth. Don't let that investment go to waste! I keep the teeth in a closed cupboard with a cup of water so that they don't dry out. Okay, I am eccentric, but it's all cool. My kids love it when I stick one of their teeth in the holder.

As you can see, my kids are still losing teeth since all of the slots are not filled. I even saved one of my cat's teeth that I was fortunate enough to find. Did you know pets have baby teeth that they lose just like us?

EARNINGS – $4 (you'll have to save up for several years to see a good payoff)

Seriously though, I'm never selling my children's teeth. They can pass them down to their kids as a novelty item.

24. **MAKE YOUR OWN VALENTINES**. Don't pay premium price for kid's valentine kits. If you don't want to go through the trouble of cutting out hearts or handwriting messages, try my approach. We usually just buy boxes of pre-packaged gummies on sale for like 75 cents a box. Then I just print out sticker labels and have my kids slap them on. Kids are usually very happy to receive something like this. Who cares about the valentine card? It's the yummy snack that counts. I just type the names into the computer and print out the sticker labels. If you don't have sticker labels, just tape them on. I keep the computer file so I have it easily accessible for the following year. The labels look nice and neat and it takes less time than having your kids handwrite their names on a card 20-30 times. My kids give out Valentine's in school and in their clubs. So the savings adds up.

SAVINGS – $7; TIME INVOLVED – 10 MINUTES (make labels for on treats)
FINAL SAVINGS – $3 / CHILD

1. **BE AN APPRENTICE.** College is overrated in my opinion. What happened to the days of apprenticeship? You can still learn on the job. Get a job in the field you like, start low, and work your way up to the top. If you have to go in debt to go to college, I would personally skip it. You might start your career making a tinge less than a college graduate (or not), but you are getting a big head start! By the time your competition graduates, you may be making more than their starting wage.

"In its most recent survey of college pricing, the College Board reports that a 'moderate' college budget for an in-state public college for the 2013–2014 academic year averaged $22,826. A moderate budget at a private college averaged $44,750" (COLLEGEdata).

SAVINGS – $33,788; TIME INVOLVED – 5 HOURS (prepare resume, dress nice, go on interviews)
TIME SAVED – 5,250 HOURS (avoid class time and study time)
1ST YEAR FINAL SAVINGS – $164,913; **FUTURE YEARS** – $165,038

2. **LEARN BY WATCHING.** When I wanted to learn more about becoming a videographer, I signed up for a job as an actress/presenter. It was no pay, but the videographer came to me (in my own town) and I presented one of my businesses for the video. I demonstrated skills related to my business which resulted in free advertising. This

is a real bonus because I was learning and advertising at the same time at no cost to me. I watched and learned how to do the job without the videographer being the wiser. This was a great opportunity to spend the day with a videographer to learn the ropes. Afterwards I purchased the same equipment and got started doing some video work on my own. I learned even more by watching **YouTube** videos online. I educate myself often in this way. I don't want to pay for a college course on just one subject. First of all, I don't like to spend my hard-earned money on education when I can get it for free and second of all, I don't like to commute. I'd also like to add that I think a lot of time is wasted in college (chit chat, filler, overview of things some of us already know, but it is taught because someone might not know it). I think it is smart to learn *specifically* what *you* need to know through research and first-hand experiences. For this savings scenario, let's assume a college course is about four credits and each credit costs $300.

College courses usually require more at-home study time than actual class time anyway. So why not just study at home for everything. "For every one credit hour in which you enroll, you will spend approximately two to three hours outside of class studying" (Universtity of Michigan-Flint).

Watching and learning is a great tactic. Another firsthand example of watching and learning involves my husband. He was one of the worst artists I knew. I told him to try his hardest to draw a subject. It didn't turn out well at all. Then I had him watch me draw the same subject. I talked him through my thought process. Then he tried again and I was thoroughly impressed with his work. It was amazing to see such an incredible improvement in just 10 minutes time. That beats taking a paid course anytime.

SAVINGS – $1,200; TIME INVOLVED – 10 HOURS (find a free learning outlet, watch and learn, take notes)
TIME SAVED – 135 HOURS (less class time, less commuting)
FINAL SAVINGS – $4,325

3.   **LEARN BY READING.** Get some books *"For Dummies"*. It is like taking a fast, straight to the point, and super cheap college course right in the comfort of your own place, at your own pace, and on your own schedule. I am a web designer. Did I go to school for it? No, I did not. When I began to learn web design using the manual for the web design program that I had, I was a bit lost and confused at certain points. I was almost ready to give up or pull my hair out (not literally). But when I turned to the books *"For Dummies"* version, I caught on quickly. It didn't take long before my first website was up and running. I highly recommend starting with a book from the books *"For Dummies"* series before purchasing another type of educational book and before considering taking a college course on a subject. Check out your local library, you might be able to borrow just the right book for free.

SAVINGS – $1,200; TIME INVOLVED – 12 HOURS (purchase or borrow book, read, take notes); TIME SAVED – 135 HOURS (less class time, less commuting)
FINAL SAVINGS – $4,275

4.   **DON'T TAKE PART IN FUNDRAISERS.** I'm talking about the kind that help to raise money for sports and school activities where kids are expected to sell things such as chocolate, candy, gift wrap, and candles. First of all, it's fine and dandy that an organization wants to raise money for the kids. But these items are jacked up in price. I don't find it pleasurable to have to try to sell this stuff. I actually feel guilty that someone else has to pay out the wazoo for something they don't really need just to pay for my child. It feels like a pity party. I would much rather save our time that we would have spent reading over the paperwork, selling the goods, filling out forms, collecting money, and then delivering the goods; and use that time to work for money and pay for my kids' activities myself. I think that sports should charge the real fee and not depend on a child to sell a bunch of junk. When I see fundraiser packets come home, they

go straight in the trash can or scrap paper bin. I used to take part in fundraisers by purchasing a bunch of stuff myself so that my kids wouldn't have to beg people for help, but no longer. Some sports offer a *fundraiser opt out* where you can pay a certain amount up front to get out of the fundraiser. I have done this. But one time when the fundraiser rolled around, they still gave me the tickets to sell. I told them I paid to opt out and then I was free of the headache. What a relief.

You might wonder how this could possibly save you money. Why not let other people pay for your children's activities? It's because you are saving so much time. Don't even browse the catalogs. Barely even skim over the paperwork. Everything should go promptly into the trash. Admit it, your kids don't do much of the work, you do.

SAVINGS – $75; TIME SAVED – 6 HOURS (no need to deal with various fundraising activities including paperwork, selling, collecting money, and delivering) **FINAL SAVINGS** – $225

1. **START UP A HOME BUSINESS.** If you don't own a business, don't let the idea of starting one scare you. Here is a great verse from The Holy Bible. Philippians 4:13 states, "I can do all things through Christ which strengtheneth me" (*King James Version [KJV]*). When I was a child, I had a t-shirt that displayed a modern version of the quote. I think anything is possible. Because I believe this, I have accomplished many great things in my life and you can too. If you don't try, how will you know what is possible? If you apply yourself, a good business idea can become a success.

If you are wondering how starting a home business can be a savings, I will tell you that answer right now. I have found that my home businesses bring in more money per hour than average jobs. I am making as much as my husband per year (he has a regular full time job), but I am putting in about a fourth of the hours he does. So what I am really saving is *time*. That is one reason I am able to raise my children, obtain flexibility with my schedule, and keep up with household duties all while bringing in a full income.

When starting a business, keep in mind that it helps to have a demand. Most of my businesses were started because someone or several people were asking for something, and so I provided what they wanted or needed. Nobody ever asks me for dirt, so it probably isn't going to make much sense for me to start a business where I dig up dirt from my yard and sell it by the pound, unless I can come up with some awesome gimmick to sell it.

Actually, my father is good at coming up with gimmicks. Back in the 1970's, he used to collect moose poop from the fields in Idaho. Then he would take a single moose turd and create a caricature out of it by adding wire for the arms and legs, feathers for the hair, and other great details. The poop was kind of clean like that of rabbit poop when it dried (just bigger). There is a town called Tetonia where he sold "Tetonia Terd Birds" in an art gallery. They were bird sculptures constructed of excrement as the name suggests. He may have started a trend because if you do a Google search, you can even find earrings for sale that are made out of moose poop; or maybe moose droppings are just an interesting medium for artists to work with.

If starting a home business, you'll also want to make sure you are not breaking any rules or laws. Check your zoning. Is it residential, commercial, agricultural, industrial, or mixed? Check to see if you need any business licenses. I called my city hall when I had questions. If rules stress you out, don't worry – you won't

be the only one who has had to deal with them. "According to the SBA, home-based businesses make up roughly half of all U.S. businesses" (Rampenthal).

EARNINGS - FLEXIBILITY; TIME INVOLVED – 540 HOURS (plan a business, name it, take action, enjoy being your own boss)
TIME SAVED – 1400 HOURS (work less while keeping the same income)
1ST YEAR FINAL SAVINGS – $21,500; **FUTURE YEARS** – $35,000

SAVE AT THE GET-GO WHEN STARTING A BUSINESS. As I stated in the introduction of this book, all of my businesses have been started for under $100. So funds should not be an issue for most people wishing to start a business. I managed to keep the start-up spending low in many ways. I designed my own logos and websites, purchased products only when they sold, used what I already had, purchased only the bare necessities, borrowed tools, and even made my own machine (which I have been using for almost exactly a decade now).

2. **DESIGN YOUR OWN BUSINESS LOGO.** Start by looking at other business logos to get a feel for what is involved. Your logo can be text or text with additional art. Some logos are strictly just a symbol. Sometimes the simplest logo is the most effective. Take a look at the signs of chain stores and restaurants and you should get a pretty good idea of what works. Wendy's logo includes art which is more elaborate than most. In fact, on their website, they seem to prefer just the use of the girls face as their logo (Wendy's).

If you are using a computer program to design your logo, be careful about what font(s) you use. Check for copyrights and/or get permission to use the font. It is safer to create everything yourself. Avoid plagiarism and likewise look to see if there are business names online that are similar to yours. You should try to be as original as possible.

Coca-Cola did not hire a designer to create their logo. "The famous Coca-Cola logo was created by John Pemberton's bookkeeper, Frank Mason Robinson, in 1885. Robinson came up with the name and chose the logo's distinctive cursive script" On the other hand, some companies spend a fortune on a logo design. One million dollars was spent on a complete branding package for Pepsi which was designed by the Arnell Group back in 2008 (Stock Logos).

If you were to hire a graphic designer with years of experience, you can look to pay about $800 for a well thought out logo design for your business. To get the job done for less, a business that is just starting out may look to a practicing designer for help (such as a student from an art or design school) where the total cost might come to something like $200. Take it from me, I am a designer. I charged less when I was designing logos in my school days because it gave me experience and added to my portfolio.

SAVINGS – $800; TIME INVOLVED – 5 HOURS (design your own logo)
FINAL SAVINGS – $675

3. **MAKE YOUR OWN WEBSITE.** If you do not have your own web design program, maybe it is for the best. Designing a website is not easy when you are starting from scratch. For me it takes hours upon hours of technical and design work. A Simpler method of creating a website would be to work directly online. For example, it is very inexpensive to use *WordPress* where a lot of the technical work is done for you. Simply visit *wordpress.com*. Get yourself familiarized with things by creating a blog website for free. If you opt to upgrade to a business website in the future with e-commerce options (to be able to sell goods or services on your website), the price is still awesome! Plus, you don't have to pay a web designer to update your website every time there is a change or additional information to add. You are in charge of doing the updates and can do so at your leisure.

Just to make sure that WordPress is manageable and worthy of mentioning in this book, I went and created my own free website! I really like the whole process. Since I didn't read the tutorial, it was a tinge confusing at times (just a tinge). But if I needed an answer to a question, I just did a Google search. If you have the time to spare, there is a complete tutorial that can walk you through the whole process. To get my website looking complete, it took me about 3 hours (but I'm pretty computer savvy). I completed the basics of my website including photographs. I can add new content as needed. Come visit me anytime online at *classy-cheapskate.wordpress.com*. I've added links to my favorite freebies! I also made sure that things were aesthetically pleasing and clutter free.

Hey! If you are reading this and WordPress no longer exists (I doubt it though), then get out there and search for another solution. You can do it!

SAVINGS – $1500; TIME INVOLVED – 4 HOURS (create your own website)
TIME SAVED – 2 HOURS (no need to tell a designer what you want)
FINAL SAVINGS – $1,450

4.   **DON'T CARRY AN INVENTORY.** I sell things that I don't even have in stock. I just love this method of mine. I don't need a storage room, nothing goes bad, and I'm not stuck with goods that may never sell. How? I sell things on the internet instead of in a brick and mortar store. With a *virtual* store, you do not *need* to have the item until it actually sells and needs to be shipped. In a *retail* store, people expect to walk away with the item right away. When an item sells on one of my websites, I either purchase it from a distribution warehouse, make it, buy it from a store, or have it drop shipped. Drop shipping is when you sell an item, and then another company ships it direct to the customer for you. I try to make my rounds every day to buy up goods and produce products promptly so that my customers receive their item in about 1 week or less. A happy customer could be a returning customer.

So, by not needing a storage room to stock my goods or a retail establishment to sell my goods and services, I am saving a load of money! On top of that, I have no wasted product. Better yet, I have flexibility. I do not need to open my store every day at a certain time – it's always open, even when I am sleeping!

I allow for a half hour of shopping each day. I make sure that anything I sell is either available locally, can be drop shipped, or produced by me.

If you were going to open up a retail store, "a 1900 sq. ft. store in a popular shopping center located directly in front of a busy highway may run $13 per square foot. This retail store would cost approximately $2058 per month" (Waters).

SAVINGS – $24,696; TIME INVOLVED – 125 HOURS (purchase or make goods as needed, try drop shipping)
FINAL SAVINGS – $21,571

5. **MAKE YOUR OWN MACHINE.** I felt like a genius when I made my own production machine back in 2005. My grandpa built his own airplane back in his day. He used to take me for rides in it (I even got to steer it). So, the thought of me building a machine seemed achievable even though I had no knowledge of how to do it. Can you imagine how nerve racking it would be to build an airplane and then have to trust your workmanship when the time came to fly it? My grandfather was so confident in his work, that he would take his dearest loved ones for rides in it. How awesome.

The reason I built my machine is because I didn't want to purchase one. A production device was available on the market, but it cost over $1,000. I had no idea if the business I was starting would be a success or not, so I didn't want to invest the money. Instead, I researched how the machine functioned by doing some digging online (that was the most time consuming part). Then I acquired the parts I needed and built the machine at home. I spent just about $30 for materials (probably less) and I had it assembled in no time. The housing is made out of scrap wood I found in my garage. The contraption is actually pretty ugly. I got the job done fast and crude (but customers care about the product, not how pretty the process is). I don't have to be all glamorous and give factory tours. I bought one part for the machine at Kmart. It was an everyday item that I converted for another use. I had a local electronic store order a part special for me (it was cheaper than ordering the part online), a glass shop cut some glass, I bought some magnets at a craft store using a percent-off coupon, and I used some electrical tape that I had on hand at home. And there you go! Things were up and running.

If you are going to build a machine, don't do anything dangerous. I felt confident in what I was doing. Also, don't do anything that could harm the environment. If you have neighbors, steer clear of devices that make loud noises.

SAVINGS – $1,070; TIME INVOLVED – 8 HOURS (make your own contraption)
TIME SAVED – 1 HOUR (no time spent purchasing a machine on the market)
FINAL SAVINGS – $895

6.   **SHIP FOR LESS.** If you ship packages for your business, try shipping using **FedEx SmartPost**. This is usually a good cost savings compared to other similar services, however it can be slower. The system typically works in the following way. FedEx transports the package to USPS who then completes the delivery. It is a team effort in the delivery process in order to keep shipping rates low and competitive. It is a service worth looking into for the shipping needs of your business.

UPS also offers a similar service called **SurePost** where USPS typically completes the final delivery. I have not used that service, but I know it is currently out there and available. Keep your eyes open, looking at all possible shipping options. The shipping industry is constantly changing. Who knows, in a year or two, some of these services might not exist anymore (it could be that way with anything really). So, look at what's available each year.

When I get ready to ship a package, I easily compare FedEx rates with that of USPS. It only takes seconds. I have both programs open and simply enter the zip code of the receiver to see which option is cheapest. If your business ships 5000 packages per year and you compare rates going with the least expensive shipping method as opposed to using a middle range shipping method for each package, you can save a bundle as shown in the example below.

SAVINGS – $10,000; TIME INVOLVED – 6 HOURS (compare rates when shipping)
FINAL SAVINGS – $9,850

Please visit chapter 18, tip number 27 for more ways to save on shipping.

7.   **NEVER THROW A BOX AWAY** (unless it is damaged). Cardboard boxes are expensive. Did you ever look into buying one? I have never bought a cardboard box for shipping purposes. I always save boxes that I receive in the mail if they are descent enough to reuse. I also save boxes for storage purposes to keep things organized. There are companies who simply throw boxes away. Check around your community to find out where you can obtain some at no cost (hint – grocery stores). I use over 5,000 boxes per year and they are all free. See my savings below.

You can save packing material too. Save cushioning, air bags, and packing peanuts. If you find a packing peanut or two on the ground, don't throw them out. It would be like throwing away pennies. Those little buggers are expensive.

SAVINGS – $8,500 (instead of shopping for boxes, save or ask for them)

8.   **USE NEWSPRINT AS CUSHIONING.** I ship a lot of items through the mail for my business. Plain newsprint paper is my choice of cushioning. It is cheap and takes up very little space. I can cushion a package for just a few pennies. I don't use packing peanuts due to its expense and bulkiness. I simply don't have the space to store huge bags of that material. Newsprint is clean – it doesn't break into pieces and fly all over the room like packing peanuts do. It lays flat and I can just crinkle it to use as filler as I pack my orders. Some people use actual newspapers, shoppers, and flyers as packing material. I think that is fine for a person to do, but not a business. It gives the impression that the business is not doing well financially if they have to go around and scrounge for pieces of newspaper to pack their orders. I could never find enough free material to cushion all of my orders anyway. Plus, newspaper pages leave black residue behind when they are handled. It seems unclean. So plain newsprint

is the option for me. I've been using the material to pack my orders for over 10 years now.

You could obtain a reduced price if you ordered packing peanuts in bulk (10 bags). These 20 cubic foot bags would take up the rest of the space in my office making me unable to even move. Each bag would cost about $33 including shipping. If I ordered just one bag it would set me back nearly $100 due to the high price of shipping (it would pay to buy in bulk in this situation). On the other hand, if you order newsprint paper in bulk, you can get about 25 bundles for approximately $35 per piece including shipping; and all 25 bundles would take up just about the same amount of space as one large bag of packing peanuts. I use 10 bundles of newsprint per year to ship roughly 6500 packages. I only have to order newsprint about every 2 ½ years. If I opted to go with packing peanuts, I would have to re-order every 2 weeks since I just don't have the extra space to store this type of item. Ordering that often would be a waste of my time and is something that I do not enjoy doing. I would have to order 700 bags of packing peanuts if I wanted them to last 2 ½ years like my newsprint does. That would take up 16 offices packed to the brim.

SAVINGS – $8,890 (use newsprint instead of packing peanuts)
TIME SAVED – 10 HOURS (only order 1 time instead of 31)
FINAL SAVINGS – $9,140

9. **MAKE USE OF THE RESOURCES AROUND YOU.** It pays to think outside of the box. I think outside of the kitty litter box. For example, I recycle used cat litter, making art sculptures out of it. I came to realize this was possible when I was looking for alternative ways to get rid of our used cat litter. I didn't want to pay the garbage man to haul it away. I researched online to see what people do with their litter. It turns out that you cannot throw it in your compost pile because the main ingredient in cat litter is clay. That is why it clumps so well. It will turn to mush in your yard and it will stay mush. I checked the ingredients on the

litter box and it was true, the main ingredient in clumping cat litter is clay. So regular people have to pay their garbage man to haul their used litter away. But a light bulb went off in my head. I am a sculptor, so I know that clay is expensive. For 50 pounds of clay to be shipped to me I am looking at over $70 in expenses. I decided that I would use the cat litter just as I would use clay by adding water to it. The consistency becomes that of actual clay (I avoid the brands with scent crystals unless I am looking for a little texture).

Another way that I collect clay is by digging it in nature. Luckily I have permission to dig on my father in law's land where clay is plentiful along his creek. As a junk artist, I look to repurpose anything I can.

When I create cat litter art, I wear gloves, usually a mask, and remove the clumps first (well most of them). The clay shapes up nicely. When I finish my cat litter masterpiece, I fire the art in a kiln to over 1000 degrees Fahrenheit. At that point it is ready to hit the art market. In summary, I save by not having to purchase clay and by not having to pay for garbage removal. Obviously, you may have another resource that works for you. This is just an example of one year's savings that result from finding another use for something considered garbage (used cat litter transformed into a clay masterpiece).

Maybe you are not an artist. You can find free resources all around you. If you live at the beach, maybe you want to use sand as cat litter. I don't know if you are allowed to take sand unless it is on your property though. You can check into that if you are interested. Some people forage for food picking leafy, wild greens for salad. I don't know much about wild, edible food, but I wouldn't mind looking into it someday. Let's talk about dirt. Why do people buy it? There is dirt in our yards. If you want richer dirt, start a compost pile in your backyard. It will save on trash removal and save you from having to buy soil.

SAVINGS – $450; TIME INVOLVED – 1 HOUR (find another use for something)
TIME SAVED – 1 HOUR (no need to shop for an item, you have a replacement)
FINAL SAVINGS – $450

10. **FIND MULTIPLE USES FOR ONE ROOM.** Be flexible. Find ways to incorporate your business into your home. At night I use my living room to watch television shows. Flip that around and on another occasion I might be in my living room being recorded for a television show. On the weekends the room might serve as an art studio with students painting. All I need to do is have my folding table and chairs set up with supplies at hand. My business is conducted out of my home and I have never had a problem with that. It is a big money savings when you don't need to rent a space or keep another facility in operation. You don't have to travel to another facility either (a big plus).

SAVINGS – $4,000; TIME INVOLVED – 1 HOUR (plan how a room can serve double-duty); TIME SAVED – 128 HOURS (skip the commute)
1ST YEAR FINAL SAVINGS – $7,175; **FUTURE YEARS** – $7,200

11. **GET CREATIVE WITH FREE ADVERTISING.** For example, I am an artist (actually almost my whole family consists of artists), so when we dine out, we often times sketch on napkins while waiting to be served. People get curious, see the great art, and word gets around. Sometimes the wait staff will ask for the drawing (mostly if it is a likeness of them) and we always sign our art pieces. So when someone needs art or design work done, they know who to call locally.

I have never paid for advertising because I do not want more work than I already have. My businesses are actually a little too big for me to handle right now. I'm glad my children are getting older because someday I can pass a business or two onto them.

If you want your business to grow, try using *Groupon*. It is a website offering extreme deals. *Groupon* can really help to reach an audience quickly, helping to rack up business right when you want or need to reach more customers and gain exposure.

From what I've learned, the general rule of thumb is that businesses spend about 5% of their gross sales on advertising. Let's go with $100,000 for the gross sales figure for this savings scenario and you'll see how much you can save by not paying for advertising.

SAVINGS – $5,000 (keep your mind open to free advertising options)

12. **SAVE YOUR TONER CARTRIDGES.** Even when my printer says the toner is all, I hold onto the cartridge because there is always some left inside (the printer just can't grab at it). When I get several cartridges saved up, I remove each plug and dump the toner out onto a sheet of paper. I take the leftover toner from the used cartridges and dump them into one to create a full cartridge. Toner is not cheap, so this is well worth it to me. Be careful, I'm not a toner expert. Not all printers are created equally. Oh, and you might want to wear a dust mask for this project. I personally do not wear one because the powder dust in the air seems minimal. It also appears to be heavy, falling downward instead of floating upward. However, to be safe, I probably should wear one.

The toner cartridges that I deal with all have a plastic plug. It is usually covered by a label that says if I remove it, I may void the warranty. I don't care. I remove the label and then use pliers to pull the plug out *(see photo on next page)*. Sometimes they can be a bugger to get out if I try to use my fingers alone to do the job. You will be amazed at how much toner comes out! Believe it or not, what you see in the photos is from one single *empty* cartridge – EMPTY . . . yeah right. I know that I was surprised when I emptied my first cartridge. I actually thought I had made an error and accidentally cleaned out a new one (but I had not). I didn't even have a new one on hand. Anyway, really pound away tilting the cartridge this way and that until you can't get much more out. When you have

enough toner collected, roll up a sheet of paper to create a funnel and then use it to easily pour the toner back into a single cartridge. Complete the process by gently swishing the toner cartridge on an even level from side to side. This will help to distribute the toner evenly inside the container.

Here is a bonus tip for you. Sometimes there is a shipping label in the toner cartridge box which allows you to ship the empty toner cartridge back to the factory at no charge. You can drop it off at the post office or hand it to a mailperson. That way you do not have to pay to dispose of the cartridge and the company can refurbish it. It keeps a bit of trash out of the landfills and gives your mailperson more work (more work means job security). It's a winning situation. If there is no return label, then at least save the toner box to use for shipping purposes or storage.

SAVINGS – $250; TIME INVOLVED – 10 MINUTES (keep your cartridges, combine the leftover toner to refill a cartridge)
FINAL SAVINGS – $246

13. **REUSE PAPER.** If you print an error page, stick it back in the printer so that it prints on the opposite side next time. You can place an "x" across the unneeded side of the page so that you know it is not important anymore. Also, when printing a document, if you see there is unimportant information on page 2 for example, click to only print pages 1 through 1. That will save you an extra sheet of paper. Doing this type of stuff is only going to save you about $5 or less per year. Let's move on to a bigger and even cleverer idea.

Elementary schools and other educational systems accumulate a lot of paper trash which is a real nuisance. Ask your local school or another source if you can have unwanted used paper. Get a bunch so that it lasts for the whole year or simply keep your own children's homework papers and use them. My business prints out packing slips for in packages that we ship. By using school papers, I could save a bundle of money each year and save a tree or two. Since I just thought this idea up, I have not implemented it yet. When I do, I plan to have an automatic notice print out on the packing slips stating that we recycle paper from local sources in an effort to save trees and be more resourceful. I actually think the customers would enjoy reading the other side of the paper.

Maybe they will learn something new or get some entertainment out of it.

Please do not put papers with crayon markings through a laser printer. I think the high heat would melt it which could possibly cause damage to your printer. The good thing is that the crayon marks would be on the opposite side of the paper which won't have contact with important, expensive elements of the printer such as the drum. You might want to avoid getting used paper from nursery schools or kindergarten classes for this reason.

SAVINGS – $70; TIME INVOLVED – 30 MINUTES (ask a source for some used 8 ½" x 11" paper); TIME SAVED – 30 MINUTES (no need to purchase paper)

FINAL SAVINGS – $70

14. **BE YOUR OWN STAFF.** I try to do everything myself. I am the owner, secretary, manager, shipping department, artist, cleaning lady, tech support, customer service representatives, and more for my businesses. Did you notice I wrote *representatives* – plural? For email correspondence, I am Jamie by day, Nathan (my husband, who gives me permission to do this) by night, and Renee (my middle name) on the weekends. What staff works 24 hours a day? I want my business to be believable and taken seriously by my customers, so I change my email signature throughout the day and week. I don't have the typical business setup, but I get a lot of compliments on my customer service, so I must be doing something right. If a customer calls or emails, I know exactly what is going on because I handle everything and I usually have an answer right at my fingertips. I need no permission from the owner or manager for any decisions. There is no ladder to climb and I never need a raise because I already reap all of the profits.

One reason that I don't want employees at this time is because I value my freedom and the flexibility in my schedule more than I value the extra cash that I could possibly make if I had employees. If I decided to hire employees, taxes would become more difficult, I'd have workers who expect steady work, and if there is not quite enough work for a particular day, I'd need to pay them anyway. If there is too much work, I'd need to pay them overtime or higher temporary workers. I'd have to fix up one of my properties to use as an office space. I'd have to wake up early to go to work and work regular hours. In my life right now, I can work on what I want, when I want (to a great extent). I value flexibility so much! It is a great treasure.

I have children that I am raising. If I had an office space with employees, I'd have kids running around making noise (remember, I do not pay for child care and I'm not sure employees would appreciate kids making a ruckus).

So, if I intended to build my businesses up, I could, but I choose not to at this particular point in my life (I might never want to). This subject has so many variances that I am going to say the savings here are *FREEDOM* as well as *FLEXIBILITY*. In my situation, there are *monetary* and *time* savings as well because employees would not work at my speed. I think they would get 1/3 of what I get done in an hour. Plus they would be asking what to do next and how to do it – taking up my time. I might as well just do things myself. Training takes time and employees don't have the incentive that I do. Being the boss, the faster I work, the more I make. Most workers get paid hourly and do not have much to work towards. If they work faster, they probably are not going to get paid more. If I ever required additional help (labor), I would consider paying a worker for what they do and not by the hour (like contracted labor). That is a good incentive for the worker to be able to make more per hour by working faster. If I was a worker, I would like that. If a person would work fast and sloppy, they would not be hired again.

SAVINGS – FREEDOM, FLEXIBILITY (be a one man show)
TIME SAVED – 128 HOURS (no training, no explaining)
FINAL SAVINGS – $3,200

15. **CANCEL YOUR CALLER ID** and extra phone line if you have one. I do not have caller ID or a business line (because it costs more). Here is how I get by without caller ID and with only one line for my home and business. Since I own several businesses, I simply answer the phone, "Hello?" I don't say a name of a business, because I would have to run through a long list and it might just be family or a friend calling. I do not let my children answer the phone. It would not be professional. I would really prefer for my answering machine to pick up all calls (then I could screen them). But I usually toughen up and answer the phone. Sometimes I don't want to speak to the person on the other end (telemarketers), and I just hang up or ask, "May I ask who's calling?" If I don't like the answer, I say, "She's not available right now. Can I take a message?" This isn't really lying, because I am a busy person and I never said that I wasn't Jamie. I am just too busy so I am *not available right now*. I value my time immensely. I spoke with my service provider to see what the additional cost would be to have a second line and caller ID. The savings calculation below does not include hidden fees or taxes that may be applicable. So the savings should actually be greater than shown. By answering my phone blindly (I don't mind), I am able to save up for a nice trip to the beach each year!

Believe it or not, I just got a call. I heard a recorded voice say, "Don't hang up, this is not a sales call." I ended the call right there and then with no hesitation.

SAVINGS – $560; TIME INVOLVED – 30 MINUTES (cancel caller ID and any extra phone lines)
1ST YEAR FINAL SAVINGS – $548; **FUTURE YEARS** – $560

16. **DO YOUR OWN TAXES.** I use *TurboTax Home & Business* to easily file my taxes every year rather than hiring a local tax professional. *TurboTax* walks me through every step so that I get my taxes done right. I feel secure knowing that they are on my side. I download the program right from the internet onto my computer, follow the steps, and then file when I am ready. When I first start-

ed doing my taxes, I bought the CD version of the program every year from a retail store or online. But then years later, I switched to the downloadable version because it saves a trip out (or shipping charges); and doesn't waste a CD and packaging material. You can even work online without downloading the program, but I simply prefer to work from my desktop.

"In 2009, the National Society of Accountants surveyed almost 8,000 tax preparers and found that the average fee for doing a Form 1040 with itemized deductions (Schedule A) and a state tax return was $229. . . . The average fee for a Schedule C (profit or loss from business) was $212 . . ." (SFGate).

I like to be in charge of my taxes and since I have to gather all of the records and paperwork myself (the hard part); I might as well save some bucks and do everything myself. I make sure to keep good records of my sales and expenses throughout the year so that tax time is easy and comfortable when it rolls around.

SAVINGS – $300; TIME INVOLVED – 1 HOUR (get TurboTax, follow the instructions)
FINAL SAVINGS – $275

17. DO NOT PURCHASE A ROLLING CHAIR FOR USE AT YOUR DESK. Did you ever wonder why they sell desk chair floor mats? Uh, it's because you could carve a whole in the floor or carpeting by rolling around so much. Yup. My office floor became ruined from my rolling chair. Luckily I had a few scraps of linoleum squares left in my attic from the previous home owner. I was able to repair the floor. Then I purchased really cheap carpet remnant squares from ***Ollie's Bargain Outlet*** to protect my floor from future damage. I could just get rid of the rolling chair and go with a standard chair. But I didn't feel like it.

Did you ever see a hole form beneath a dining room table? No? I didn't either. Did you ever see dining room chair floor guards for sale? Why not? Because dining room chairs do not have wheels that roll all over the place disfiguring and stretching things out until the flooring starts to tear and crumble due to constant friction. Wheels are bad, very bad! If you use a standard chair and don't slide it all around, you should be fine. Desk floor guards are expensive! Repairing a floor is too. Avoid these problems by using a chair with no wheels.

SAVINGS – $65; TIME SAVED – 1 ½ HOURS (no need to shop for a floor mat)
FINAL SAVINGS – $103

18. **EASILY RENT OUT YOUR SPACE.** Here is a wild idea. Sign up at *airbnb.com* and easily create a listing to rent a space on your property to travelers from around the world. I just went on the website and signed up. However, I chickened out at the last minute. I'll tell you why. First off, I don't want strangers in my home. So I was going to have them sleep on my trampoline for $5 a night and they have the option to use the restroom at the 24 hour gas station down the street. The system would not let me list a stay for $5, the minimum allowed was $10. The site was open to my trampoline idea though. They even allow igloos and tipis to be rented out. Well, if I was going to have people sleep on my trampoline, that could get tricky with insurance if the guests were to get hurt. I wouldn't mind them pitching a tent on my property instead, but still, they might jump on my trampoline and get injured. At this time, *airbnb.com* has insurance for damage that might occur to your property, but that is not going to help if someone gets injured. If you have great insurance, I say go for it! Rent a room or let someone sleep in a tent on your property. I would!

Another thing to keep in mind is tax time. According to **NOLO LAW for ALL**, "You can rent out all or part of your home or apartment for up to 14 days per year and all the rental income you receive is tax-free, no matter how much you earn. In fact you don't even have to report the income to the IRS." You also have to use your home yourself for more than 14 days out of the year or more than 10% of the time you rent it out for. If this doesn't apply to you, you'll have to pay income tax on the money you make from renting your property (Fishman).

Earnings – $240; TIME INVOLVED – 2 HOURS (create rental listing)
FINAL EARNINGS – $190

19. PAY WITH CASH IF THERE IS A SAVINGS OFFERED. When you make a purchase, be sure to ask if there is a discount for paying cash. If I am making a purchase at a large auction house, I always ask this question. I usually end up paying cash which saves me 2-3%. Not only will this save you money, it saves the auction company the fee they would have paid to process a credit card.

Always inspect the goods before you pay. One time I paid first with cash and the goods were not described accurately. I had bid online, looked carefully at the photos, and read the description provided. Then my husband and I travelled for pickup. The lot was worth hundreds less than I paid due to incorrect listing text. They would not give me the money back no matter what I did. I couldn't do a chargeback either because I didn't use a credit card. I felt like calling the cops. But instead I wrote a detailed online review and never purchased from the auction company again. I learned my lesson right then and there – inspect before you pay.

SAVINGS – $125 (use cash to pay if a discount is offered)

20. USE COPY, PASTE, AND OTHER SHORTCUTS ON YOUR COMPUTER. Quickly copy a search phrase, address, or other often used information by selecting the text with your mouse and then clicking CTRL and C simultaneously. When you want to paste you would click CTRL V. This is if you are using a personal computer (a PC, not a Mac). Okay, so you would simply select/highlight an item using your mouse and then click CTRL C, followed by CTRL V whenever you want to paste it. It beats doing things the drawn out way of highlighting, right-clicking, selecting copy, going to another document, right-clicking again, and clicking paste. There are also lots of other keyboard shortcuts that can save you time. Simply do a search online for keyboard shortcuts. This tip is bearing in mind that you use a computer throughout your daily tasks.

TIME SAVED – 7 ½ HOURS (saving seconds adds up during the course of a year)
FINAL SAVINGS – $188

1. **MAKE SOME INTEREST. START SAVING RIGHT NOW!** Money compounds daily. Every day matters. The more money you can stockpile, the more interest you can earn. You can earn interest in savings accounts, checking accounts, CD's, and more. Check online to find the bank offering the highest interest rates at this time. Shop around. At this particular time, interest rates are crap (too low). One of the highest savings accounts I can find available online only gives .85% in interest. A local bank is offering .05% which is even worse. Let's say you put $10,000 into savings. At the first bank (the online bank) you will make about $85 in interest for the year. At the other bank you will only make about $5. If there is no other way to invest right now, I would go with the online bank. It pays to shop around. It only takes a few minutes to **Google** up some comparisons.

EARNINGS – $85; TIME INVOLVED – 30 MINUTES (compare accounts, sign up, transfer funds)

2. **INVEST IN TANGIBLE ITEMS.** When interest rates are really low, I don't really like to put my money in bank accounts or CD's. If the stock market is high, I don't invest in that either. I want to make some money. At times like these, I often turn to tangible investments. I purchase art, property, collectibles, and antiques when I

can get them at low prices (hoping to sell them high when I can). So let's say I purchase $10,000 in goods and then sell them for double later. After seller fees and shipping, we'll figure on a 25% gain. That is really good money, but keep in mind that it takes more time than other investments because you have to sell the goods later. If you don't have many other investment options, this may be the way to go. Keep record of your purchases, fees, and sales. I use these records at tax time. The government will want their share of your earnings.

EARNINGS – $2,500; TIME INVOLVED – 48 HOURS (buy up some cool stuff at half price, then sell)

3. **GET FREE CHECKS.** If you need checks, get them for free when you sign up for a checking account. Beware of banks that offer too many gimmicks and prizes for signing up. Their fine print is usually lengthy and they could end up getting more money out of you in fees that more than makes up for the price that they spent on their gimmicks (trust me from my own experience and those of friends). However, there are some banks that don't have any tricks up their sleeves and you will probably find that I take advantage of their offers.

Yesterday, I signed up for a free checking account online receiving a $50 sign-up bonus. I receive free checks with my account and will even get paid 10 cents for every time I write a check, pay a bill online with my account, or use my debit card (up to 100 times per month). There is no minimum amount of money that I need to keep in the account. What a great offer! I have 2 other checking accounts. One makes .05% interest and the other makes no interest (but I get a lot of bonuses out of it such as credits for completing certain tasks). The account that makes .05% interest would only bring in $2.50 annually on a $5000 balance. With that account, I do not get free checks. It totally makes sense to get paid 10 cents per check I write, get free checks, and simply make zero interest on this new account that I signed up for. The $50 bonus for signing up is enough incentive. It's the equivalent of making .05% interest on $100,000 for a year. (I told you interest rates are crap right now).

If you need to pay for checks because you have no other option, you desire a fancy design, or want a customized Monogram; order the checks through mail order (the designs are usually really cool). It pays to order from *mail flyers* because the pricing is usually better than if you order directly online or straight from the bank.

SAVINGS – $15; TIME INVOLVED – 30 MINUTES (find a bank offering free checks, then sign up)

FINAL SAVINGS – $3

4. **AVOID LOANS IF YOU WISH TO SAVE.** A loan is a trap that sucks your money away. Avoid the black hole and *only spend what you have*. This is a huge tip. I know it is so tempting to want a house or a fancy new car right when you get out of college or to buy a motorhome when you retire. If you can afford those things, then go for it. But I would not recommend getting a loan to get the things you *want*. People don't *need* new cars. People can *rent* instead of *purchasing* a home.

Do you know how much money is being thrown away when you get a loan? Here is a simple illustration. I used Bankrate's Amortization Schedule Calculator to paint a not so pretty picture for you. On a $200,000, 30-year fixed-rate mortgage with an interest rate of 7 percent, you'd pay $279,016 in interest over the lifespan of your loan (Bankrate). This means that you would actually be paying $479,016 for your dream home plus your down payment amount. Yikes! Why would anyone want to pay more than double for a home just to get it now? Get a roommate and live in an apartment until you save enough for a house.

If you simply cannot wait to have the things you want, then get a loan. But for goodness sake, pay it off quick! Do not take 30 years, shoot for 5. You'll have to work hard at paying it off in just 5 years (pinching every penny, eating oatmeal instead of bacon and eggs, clipping coupons), but 5 sounds like a much better number than 30 in this case. Check out the details of your loan to see how much money in interest you will save by paying the loan off in 5 years compared to 30.

SAVINGS – $5,000/YEAR (share an apartment, save up for a home)

5. **BE YOUR OWN FINANCIAL ADVISOR.** I will never hire a financial advisor for their investment advice. I don't trust them and their fees are outrageous (in my opinion). When I first got involved in mutual funds (a mutual fund is a collection of stocks and/or bonds), I got ripped! I was told that if I invested my money, in 1 year I would have enough to put towards my future home. That was a falsehood. I actually ended up with less money than I started with.

At this point in my life, I only trust myself when it comes to investing. I used to get invited to fancy events by an investment company. Some of the events included baseball games with special dining, or hors d'oeuvres and wine at a private museum tour. At these events, the investment company would try to talk me into spending something like $600-$800 for their financial advice. I always turned the offer down stating that I am doing just fine on my own and letting them know that I took advice in the past and lost money. Since I have listened to myself, I have lost nothing (only gained). Eventually they stopped inviting me to the events. I'm still doing business with the company that I had a bad experience with (about 14 years ago), but I watch the mutual funds and record their progress every couple of months (keeping track of things myself). When I see my graph hit rock bottom, I buy-buy-buy! When I see the line on my chart getting close to hitting a high mark, I sell-sell-sell! The point is to buy when the shares are low and sell when they are high. This rise and fall that I follow can span a period of several years. When the stock market crashes, I rejoice as some others panic. It is easy rack up money fast when I invest in this way.

I predict what I think is going to happen with my investment by looking at the mutual fund's history. It is actually very easy for me. I concentrate on one mutual fund that I feel comfortable with. I track the progress in a spreadsheet program which can generate a graph for me whenever I prompt it to. The program that I use is **Microsoft Excel**. With this program, it is very efficient for me to track the ups and downs of a market. I actually copy the data directly from online and paste it right into the program. There is no chance for error as I am not manually entering price fluctuations; I am simply copying and pasting data right from the main source (the mutual fund company's website). **Microsoft Excel** can make the charts for me with complete accuracy. With the visual graphs that are generated, I can see the ups and downs of the market (plain as day). I feel very confident about this system (as it has never failed me).

Twice in my investing career, I got scared by big-wig gurus on television telling everyone to sell now. My graphs and research told me that I had months and months left to invest and stocks would continue to rise. But I listened to the so-called gurus. Though I still made $2,411.02 in profit in an extremely short amount of time, I would have made $12,537.64 profit by listening to my charts – instead of the opinion of the proclaimed experts. I still kick myself in the butt for that one. So now, it is certain, I only listen to myself when it comes to investing.

Another time I threw a very large chunk into a mutual fund and an advisor from the company called to make sure I knew what I was doing. He said, their research pointed at this being a bad decision. I said that my research says otherwise. The man tried to talk me out of it, but I did not listen and I walked away with thousands in my pocket only two months later. My yearly graph and transaction took roughly 30 minutes to complete. I'll take thousands of dollars for 30 minutes of work any day! By the way, when I invest, I am prepared to lose everything (though thankfully I have not). I am willing to throw half to two-thirds of my savings into so-called *risky investments* with no fear. I'd rather take the risk than to never risk at all. In summary, being your own investment coach can be a win-win. You do not have to pay for an advisor and you can build on your investment (trusting yourself only because you surely would not give yourself bad advice…at least I should hope not).

Keep in mind that the government will want a portion of your earnings and so will the company who will be processing your transaction. Factor this in when deciding when to sell and when to buy. I like to make things simple on myself, so I factor in that the mutual fund company will take 1% per year on my initial investment as a sales charge (check with your company). If I invested for more than a year (long-term), I factor in that the government will want 15% of my profit (gains). If I invested for less than a year (short-term), I factor in that the government will want 20% of my capital gains. The percentages I go with are just numbers that make me feel safe (according to my research). Do your own investigating to find out what your tax rates are estimated to be. The following information should help you out.

According to TurboTax, short-term capital gains (held less than a year) are taxed at the same rate as your ordinary income. Your ordinary income is taxed a certain amount based on your total taxable income. So the rate can range from 10 to 39.6 percent. On the other hand, long-term capital gains (held longer than a year) will be taxed less. "For 2013, the long-term capital gains tax rates are 0, 15, and 20 percent for most taxpayers. If your ordinary tax rate is already less than 15 percent, you could qualify for the zero percent long-term capital gains rate." (TurboTax).

SAVINGS – $700; TIME INVOLVED – 1 HOUR (be your own broker, track a stock or fund); TIME SAVED – 1 HOUR (no need to consult with an advisor)
FINAL SAVINGS – $700

6.   **SAVE TIME BY MULTI-TASKING.** If you double up on simple activities, you are saving time; and time is money. Don't shop multiple times each week. Take one trip out and make it a good one. Head out with a friend or your partner and open mail while they drive. Then let them do the same thing on the way home. Use your free coupons for the week while you travel about. Look for coins in the checkout area as you are waiting. Check your emails or make phone calls while you are standing in lines.

Here are some other ways to multi-task.

- If you tend to take a long time on the toilet, catch up on your reading at the same time (I think a lot of people do this because I know some).

- Brush your teeth while you wait for the shower to warm up.

- Clean the house while you are on the phone.

- Listen to an audiobook while you drive.

- Practice your singing skills while in the shower or doing dishes.

- Walk on a treadmill while you work on your computer.

- Read while you jog in place.

- Sketch while you are waiting for your meal to be served at a restaurant. *Actually, the first two books I ever published were a conglomeration of napkin sketches from restaurants. It was a bit of a joke.*

- Practice your dance moves in an elevator.

- Knit in waiting rooms.

- Write songs while driving. Memorize and practice the words, then write them down at red lights.

- Paint your nails while you wait for a bus or a ride.

Being double-productive is a great feeling! I'm sure many of you have great multi-tasking ideas just waiting to be released. Please share them with everyone online at *classycheapskate.wordpress.com*. If we all just multi-task for just 45 minutes per day, we can squeeze so much more out of life.

There are some people who claim that multi-tasking is bad. I've been multi-tasking for years and feel just fine. If multi-tasking is un-comfortable, by all means stop. I wouldn't enjoy trying to write a book and jog at the same time. It is just too much all at once and so I don't do it. I really need to concentrate when writing or painting. But when I'm stuck in a car on a long trip, I have no problem doing these things.

TIME SAVED – 274 HOURS
FINAL SAVINGS – $6,850

7.   **PUT THINGS IN THEIR PLACE.** Put things back where they be-long so you are not wasting your life looking for them all of the time. Not only that, put each item in a place where they are used most. If you mostly use hair-cutting scissors at the right side of the bath-room sink, place them in the right, bathroom sink drawer or cabi-net. If you mostly fill cups with drinking water at the kitchen sink, keep cups above the sink in a cupboard; not placed randomly in a cupboard all the way across the kitchen. School backpacks should be stored next to the exit door. If you think about everything in this way, you should save minutes per day which adds up to hours per year which should put a smile on your face. If you are like most peo-ple, at least once during the week you are struggling to find some-thing wasting 15 minutes or more looking for it. If you always keep things where you use them most, you will always remember where to find an item when it is needed.

TIME SAVED – 14 HOURS (keep things where you use them most)
FINAL SAVINGS – $350

8. **SAVE TIME – HANG UP THE PHONE.** Save as much time as you can because time is a precious, precious commodity. If a telemarketer calls, get straight to the point. Ask why they are calling. If you don't like the answer, hang up immediately. Don't worry about being rude. If you are on the phone with a friend, relative, or acquaintance then it is probably not a waste of time for you. It most likely brings you enjoyment. On the other hand, if a friend calls often and their conversations are real downers, then let them know. If they go on for an hour every day rehashing the same old stuff, politely tell them that you try not to have negativity in your life and that they should focus on the positive. If that doesn't work, stop answering the phone and let the answering machine pick up. By speaking 4 minutes less on the phone each day, you can save over 24 hours of your life each year. You can use that time to do something much more enjoyable. Think of the possibilities.

TIME SAVED – 18 HOURS (keep call time to a minimum)
FINAL SAVINGS – $450

NOTES

1. **GIVE YOUR TEN PERCENT,** or 2% or whatever you wish. Since I was a young child, I practiced giving 10% of my earnings to the church. This is called tithing. I believe that we are here on Earth to glorify God. I think God is glorified when we help to spread his word. I have never worried about money in my life and I don't think I ever will. I have never expected anything in return for my tithing. But, I have always been provided for. Things and opportunities tend to fall into my lap. I don't think this is a coincidence. It may be due to my hard work, skills, and pervasiveness. But who gives me those qualities? I feel that I am blessed. I love God, I work hard, and I help to share his word. If I lost everything I'd be ready to start all over again. Material things do not mean much to me (plus I don't like cleaning them). Experiences and relationships are much more precious.

"Every man according as he purposeth in his heart, so let him give; not grudgingly, or of necessity: for God loveth a cheerful giver." (2 Corinthians 9:7 *KJV*).

Instead of giving your money, you could opt to donate your time helping with things such as Vacation Bible School, Sunday school, or public events. Donate to a cause you believe in. I believe in helping to spread the word about God, the creator. If a person chooses to give 10% of their time each week instead of a percent of their earnings that would come to about 4 working hours since a typical work week comes to 40 hours. You can give more or less. 10% seems to be recognized as a standard.

"Lay not up for yourselves treasures upon earth, where moth and rust doth corrupt, and where thieves break through and steal: But lay up for yourselves treasures in heaven, where neither moth nor rust doth corrupt, and where thieves do not break through nor steal: For where your treasure is, there will your heart be also" (Matthew 6:19-21 *KJV*).

EARNINGS – ETERNAL RICHES; TIME INVOLVED – 208 HOURS (give your 10%)

2.   **SPLIT THE BILL OR RETURN THE FAVOR.** In my dating years, I didn't let my dates pay for a dinner or a night out unless they completely insisted which was very rare. I always offered to pay for my own share as I didn't want the date to feel I was using them. I think a person would be an *un-classy* cheapskate if they let a date pay for everything. Life is not all about taking. I'm here to make friends too! When someone (not just a date) buys me dinner, I usually invite them to dinner in return.

SAVINGS – FRIENDSHIP; TIME INVOLVED – 100 HOURS (repay favors)

3.   **CLEAN UP THE WORLD.** Give back by cleaning up the roadside or by helping to clean out people's houses. Friends will give us broken appliances just because they don't want to move the items (refrigerators, stoves, air conditioners, and even car batteries). Then we will take the items to be recycled for the metal. By doing this type of thing you can help others when they need it; you'll also build strong muscles and fatten up your wallet at the same time. But please don't hurt yourself lifting things or you'll be in the hole from medical bills.

Boxes marked "FREE" alongside the road often have metal in them (like shabby pots and pans). In my opinion, any garbage along the side of the road is fair game for the taking (such as empty soda cans, tin cans, metal shards). You can clean things up while finding new use for the discarded materials. Give (by cleaning up scrap metal) and you shall receive (a chunk of money in your pocket). Look for a local recycling center near you. Fill up your vehicle with all types of metal, take it there, and you will probably come back with over a hundred dollars in your pocket. When I say load up your vehicle, I mean really load it up. With the price of gas these days you'll want to make the trip to the recycling center worth the while.

You can also find metal at auctions. But often times there may be someone else who is doing the same thing as you. These people are called *scrappers*. If there is competition, you'll have to share the profits and that's not much fun. You'll have to be on the ball and not shy to yell out the lowest bid first. Be prepared to buy a whole truck load for a buck even if there is a bunch of junk in the pile. Sometimes I spray paint junk, add a bunch of rhinestones to it to jazz it up, and then resell it. Sparkles can help to sell anything.

EARNINGS – $200; TIME INVOLVED – 3 HOURS (collect metal, take 2 trips to recycling center)
FINAL SAVINGS – $125

I'll consider making art out of anything that I can find. I'm a junk artist – meaning I take discarded or unwanted items and turn them into something more. I don't like to just create art though; I like to make art that serves a purpose – something useful. Check out some of the items I have made which are shown on the next page . They are assembled using objects that were once considered junk or even garbage. One item is a shoe shine box titled *Dr. Shoe*. Another is a candlestick holder created from a broken glass, doll pieces, and a plastic milk bottle filled with rocks. The last one is a candle holder made of clay, titled *Crazy Town*. Maybe these will inspire you to create something too or simply open your mind to new possibilities.

　Living Big on a Small Income

4. **WRITE BLOGS** to help other people. Write about your experiences and let other people learn from them. When I want to look up information, I just visit one of my blogs instead of a file stored on my computer. You can actually make money off of blogs. Automatically generate earnings from valid clicks and impressions on ads that you allow to be placed on your blog. I use ***blogger.com*** to organize my thoughts and experiences for free, all the while generating income thanks to ***Google AdSense***. It is very easy to set up a blog with ***Blogger***. They even provide templates so that you can customize the look of your blog. I only write on my blogs when I want to record something important. It stands to reason that you will make more money if you write more. It also wouldn't hurt to have helpful, quality information available in your blog instead of a bunch of random, crazy thoughts. People will probably take your writing and the ads on your blog seriously if you are serious about your blog.

EARNINGS – $15; TIME INVOLVED – 1 HOUR (create blog page, record thoughts and info in an organized manner, allow advertising)

5. **MAKE YOUTUBE VIDEOS.** Teach people and/or entertain them through videos. You can monetize your YouTube videos allowing ads to be placed inside or near your video. You will need to associate an AdSense account with your YouTube account (it can be the same AdSense account that you use with Blogger). You can earn revenue that is generated from the ads! Obviously, you should be able to make more money if your video is entertaining and/or teaches people something they need to know. The more viewers you have the more money you stand to make. If you film your big toe for 2 minutes, I'm not sure you would generate as much money. Hmmm, maybe I should try this out and test the results. The amount you can make by monetizing your video is so varied. I'm going to pretend that the video in this example is good, but still pretty ordinary when I figure the earnings.

Here is a helpful note regarding YouTube ad earnings. At first I couldn't find my YouTube earnings when I logged into my AdSense account and viewed my *performance report*. In the end I found that I needed to look at my *payment history* instead. I went there and was able to see my YouTube earnings. If you try this tip out, you'll see what I mean.

EARNINGS – $15; TIME INVOLVED – 1 HOUR (create video, post video, enable ads)

6. **HELP THOSE IN NEED.** Not only is it the right thing to do, you might get a bonus out of it. One time my family was at the beach. Our hotel was far from the boardwalk, but we decided to walk to where the action was instead of driving to avoid the meter charges and to get some exercise. We had two very young children with us. One was riding normally in the stroller and the other was happily perched in the diaper bag area below. We didn't have a double stroller, so we made do. We were on our way to dinner and very hungry when we came across a man with a flat tire. He was Russian, only speaking broken English. He wanted to use our cell phone to call for help. I was leery about the situation because I had two young children and feared for their safety. He was on our phone for way too long trying to get through for help, about 30 minutes. My cell phone minutes were dwindling away and so was our vacation, so we offered to fix his tire for him instead. My husband removed the flat tire and replaced it with the man's spare one while I waited patiently with my fidgeting children. I fed them to pass the time. I was glad to help, but a little sad that some of our vacation was being wasted. We usually only stay two days at the beach because I have a business to run. Every minute is precious to us. After the work was done, about 45 minutes after running into the man, he was elated. He shook my husband's hand and slipped forty dollars into it. We thanked the man and were both surprised by the generous tip. We were also very happy because it paid for our dinner.

Though you may not always get monetary reimbursement for

your good deeds, you will be repaid in other ways. God will be certain to make that happen. A lot of things that take place in my life seem bad at first, but have a happy ending. Everything happens for a reason.

EARNINGS – $50 (good deeds will be repaid – eventually)

NOTES

1. **CREATE A PET CARRIER.** Make do with what you have. Instead of purchasing a pet carrier, you can opt to use a cardboard box like my family does. The great thing about using a cardboard box is that it folds completely flat! Space is valuable in this world, just like time. If the box does not have air holes, you will need to punch or cut some in the box so that your pet has sufficient fresh air.

SAVINGS – $25; TIME INVOLVED – 2 MINUTES (find a box around your house)
FINAL SAVINGS – $24

2. **ADOPT A PET.** Don't be picky. Instead of spending hundreds of dollars on a purebred pet, adopt one for free (even if it is a mutt). Isn't every pet special? Doesn't every pet deserve a home and loving care? Check in your local classified ads or online and you should find plenty of free pets being given away who would just love to be loved by you.

Some people want expensive purebred pets from high-end breeders rather than from an ordinary source. They hope not to have to deal with health and behavior problems as much (though the chance is still there). A good breeder checks the history of the pet's parents and more. What if we treated children who are up for adoption this way? Aren't we all special in some way and deserve a chance at a good life?

Here's a tidbit of pricing information on purebreds. Golden puppies range "in price from around $500 for a dog from a backyard breeder or a pet store to upwards of $3,000 for a show quality pup from a top breeder" (St. John).

SAVINGS – $1,750 (adopt locally, try the classifieds)

3. **MAKE PET TOYS.** Get Creative. You can make your own cat, dog, or pet toys. Some items that you can use include yarn, string, shelving, carpet scraps, fur, jingle bells, and feathers to name a few. Dogs love toilet paper rolls. Ferrets enjoy bottle caps. Our cat loves to climb our artificial Christmas tree, so we leave it up for the entire year decorating it differently as we please for each season and/or holiday. This is much cheaper than buying a climbing post. I looked at purchasing climbing posts and they were in the hundred dollar range! I bought my Christmas tree at 95% for a few dollars at the end of the holiday season (a much better option for me). Besides, I have bought my cat toys from the store which she has never touched. Her favorite toys were free items from around our house, like her rainbow string/cord that she chases all around the house as we drag it.

Dog owners spend about $55 on toys each year for their pet. Cat owners spend about $25 per year on their pet's toys (Weliver).

SAVINGS – $33.50; TIME INVOLVED – 1 HOUR (scrounge around, make some toys); TIME SAVED – 2 HOURS (no need to shop for pet toys)
FINAL SAVINGS – $59

4. **TOILET TRAIN YOUR CAT.** I would train my cat, but then I wouldn't have used litter at hand to create my famous kitty litter art sculptures. Sorry, no helpful hints on how to train your cat to use the toilet! You'll have to do an online search if you are interested.

Okay, okay. I actually think I might toilet train my cat. Visit ***www.wikihow.com/Toilet-Train-Your-Cat*** to see how you can do it. The whole length of the training process can span weeks to several months. It involves moving the litter box next to the toilet, slowly raising it to the level of the toilet (day by day), and then shifting it right onto the toilet. Eventually you remove the cat litter tray altogether. In the end, be sure not to teach your cat to flush! Your cat does not know how to conserve water like you do. Your cat is not the one paying the bills (wikiHow).

If you have an indoor/outdoor cat, you might as well just let your cat do its business outside since it costs nothing. If you have an indoor cat, the toilet training process might be worth trying since you won't have to purchase cat litter anymore. It seems like a good investment and use of time since you only have to train the cat once. Then each year after, you can reap the savings.

The total time involved in training your cat might be higher if you don't have 2 toilets because you'll have to move certain things during the training process when you or someone else has to use the toilet. My daughter came up with a great solution for this. You could actually train your cat to go in a plastic baby potty until they are ready to move onto the big people potty.

SAVINGS – $175; TIME INVOLVED – 3 HOURS (visit **wikiHow**, toilet train your cat)
TIME SAVED – 30 HOURS (no need to shop for litter or clean the litter box anymore)
1ST YEAR FINAL SAVINGS – $850; **ADDITIONAL YEARS** – $925

5. **TAKE ADVANTAGE WHEN PURCHASING FLEA TREATMENTS.** When I was to the local pet store purchasing monthly topical flea prevention and treatment for my cat. I noticed that the pricing for the treatment was the same for a small cat as it was for a large cat. The ingredients were exactly the same, but the large cat treatment had double the product in each tube. The outside of the box did not state this. You have to open the box to see the weight on each tube. Well, my cat is small, so I bought the large cat treatment and just used half of the tube. Since the ingredients are exactly the same, I saw no threat to my cat un-

less I would accidentally dump the whole tube onto her. To be safe, the treatment could be poured out onto a plastic spoon first or into a small measuring container. You obviously would not want to use the spoon or container for food purposes afterwards. There is no chance of over-treating if you measure things out properly. Now, please do your own research on this. Every brand is different. You need to be sure that you are not going to harm your pet. The ingredients and percentages must be exactly the same. Also, many flea treatments are locked up due to thieves; so you may have to look online to find the tube weight for the product you are looking to purchase to see if it is doubled in weight like mine was. I don't have a dog, but I'm sure it works in the same way. Heck, I probably could have bought a large dog treatment for my cat, but I didn't think of it until now. I will have to check the ingredients and percentages to see if I can pull this one off next time.

A week or so later . . .

Here is an update – I've checked at the pet store and found that I could purchase treatment for an extra-large dog instead of for a small cat to save money. The ingredients are exactly the same and the percentages are exactly the same for the brand I researched. My small cat needs a .4 ml dose. The extra-large dog dose comes in a 4 ml tube. That means I can get 10 doses out of one tube for the same cost.

I've also found other people online who are doing the same thing. Check out what one person shared, ". . . I asked my vet about it. He got out a box of Advantage for large dogs and a box of Advantage for cats. He compared the ingredients. He was surprised to find out they were the same. Now, they tell their clients about this, saving them money" (lisaviolet).

SAVINGS – $168 (if you have a small pet, take advantage of it)

6. **GET A CHICKEN AS A PET.** If you are set on having a pet, get one with benefits. Chickens are loveable and even have their own personalities. Plus, they give you eggs! Our chickens each lay one egg a day. You don't have to live in the country to have a chicken. I have friends and relatives who have chickens living in their back-yards. I know people who watch TV with their pet chickens. You can even have chickens in the city. Just check to see if it is allowed where you live. There are many sites online that will show you how to build a coop. My parents who live next door converted their dog house and pen into a coop. The chickens roam free in a fenceless yard at certain times of the day. When we want the chickens to re-turn to the pen, we shake a bucket of meal worms and they come running like little Velociraptors. Actually, Velociraptors are said to have been very similar to chickens and not much bigger. How cool is that? Didn't you always want a pet dinosaur?

SAVINGS – $91/CHICKEN (choose a chicken as your pet, get eggs as a bonus)

7. **SHOP AROUND FOR VET SERVICES.** When it was time for my cat to be spayed. I found out that my veterinarian's office charges $220-$245 for this service depending on factors such as the weight of a cat. However, another nearby vet only charged $115. The less expensive vet would not perform the operation without first seeing my cat on a separate day for $35. The vet wanted to perform a physical even though I told her that my cat had just had one. She simply would not combine the appointments. I told her I would call back after I check to see if 2 trips would be worthwhile just for the savings. I ended up going with the cheaper vet because it was worth the savings.

So here is how the story goes. I looked up the vet's address on the internet and got directions. It was nice because they even showed a picture of the building on the webpage. It kind of looked unprofes-sional though, especially since there was no sign. It was almost as if someone was working out of their home, but I heard good things about the company, so I still went. I took my cat in to see the new vet at the scheduled time, but nobody was there. It also looked like a home. The waiting room looked like a living room with TV and all; and the long receptionist counter sort of looked like a kitchen. It was nice, but it was weird because there was a sink on the other side of the counter. I yelled for service over and over, but nobody ever came. I saw a door that was open a few inches and a light was on. I almost ventured in to see if there was an office I should go into, but I didn't. I went back outside and happened to see a guy I graduated with and asked him about this place. He seemed confused. He said it was not the vet's office. I was on the wrong street. However, I was at the address that was listed on the internet. Okay, so I walked into someone's house and they probably feared for their life having someone yelling for service. So I was late for my first appointment and told the vet that someone had the wrong address and photo listed on the internet and they should do something about it. So, the vet looked over my cat and It took about one minute since my cat was fine. I paid the vet $35 for about one minute of service and scheduled the operation. That really bugged me that someone could make $35 in one minute. But, I guess it is standard procedure.

The day of the operation came and it happened to be the worst possible day of the year. It was a blizzard, school was closed, and I had to drive at about 5 miles per hour the whole way. I didn't enjoy it especially since my cat gets anxiety in the car. By the time we got there, her heart was beating out of her chest. I thought she was going to have a heart attack; I was really worried for her. The moral of my story is that you can hit some bumpy roads when trying new things. But in the very end, things worked out and I saved a few dollars. It was an experience to say the least.

SAVINGS – $83; TIME INVOLVED – 10 MINUTES (make calls to find the best price)
FINAL SAVINGS – $79

$

1. **CANCEL YOUR CABLE TV SERVICE.** What?! That's right. I cancelled my cable service a few years back and don't regret it at all. I never had satellite service so I won't comment on that. But I know that the price of my cable television service went up drastically over the years. The price went up so significantly, that I looked around for another option. I found **Netflix** and subscribed to it as soon as I cancelled my cable service. I received my first month of Netflix service free; and from then until now I have only paid $7.99 per month for the service. If the price went up a few more dollars, I would still pay it. **Netflix** is a service that allows you to watch shows at any time using your Wii, Xbox, PS3, Personal Computer, Mac, Tablet, Mobile device, and more! In my house, we even have people watching different shows, from various devices, all at the same time.

I enjoy watching my favorite shows on our big screen television using our Wii gaming console to stream the content. It is so easy! Plus, what I really love is that I don't have to watch commercials anymore! Sometimes about a third of a television show's air time is actually commercial advertisements. Besides that, we had cable television when my kids were younger and they were constantly begging for toys that they saw in commercials – not so anymore. I don't miss commercials one bit. During the Super Bowl, I could just visit a friend if I want to see the renowned commercials. However, I usually just take a peek online. That's enough to satisfy me.

Another great thing about **Netflix** is that you can stop a show if you get sleepy or if something comes up. You can easily resume it later on. **Netflix** remembers where you left off. They even suggest shows that suit your style and each family member can have their own *viewing area* with their own show suggestions. I can actually log in to my child's section to see what they have been watching (the system keeps track automatically).

My husband and I really like that you can watch past seasons and episodes all in a row. I never worry about missing a show or having to watch it at a certain hour. There is no waiting until the next week to find out what happens next. If I can't wait, I could literally watch 2 episodes or more in a row! Without the extra time added of having to watch commercials, you might as well watch 2 episodes! Not only that, I have the service billed directly to my credit card each month helping to rack up credit card rewards in the process. I also save time by not having to manually pay the bill every month.

SAVINGS – $1,100; TIME INVOLVED – 20 MINUTES (cancel current service, sign up for **Netflix**)

1ST YEAR FINAL SAVINGS – $1,092; **FUTURE YEARS** – $1,100

2.   **HUNT FOR TREASURE.** I go geocaching (real-live treasure hunting) with my family. I became a free member at **geocaching.com**. There are treasures hidden all over the world that you can find using GPS coordinates. My family and I geocache for exercise and for the treasure. At the time of writing this, there were 2,480,918 active geocaches (treasures) hidden worldwide (Groundspeak). I typically use my cell phone to lead the way to the treasure. If I don't want to go over my phone usage limit, I write down the coordinates, and use a GPS navigation device (the **TomTom** from my vehicle) to find the treasures instead.

When you take a treasure, you are supposed to leave a treasure of equal or greater value in its place. Most of the treasures I find are low cost trinkets that are worth a few cents. I usually leave gift certificates

behind for one of my businesses valued at $10 or more. It makes a good outlet for advertising. However, from what I've read in a few blogs, some geocache members seem to frown upon this sort of thing. Why wouldn't someone want a gift card, coupon, or certificate? One blogger stated, "…it's another opportunistic ploy that hijacks our game for commercial gain" (Geonarcissa). Personally, I would be thrilled to find a gift certificate, so I will surely continue to leave them for people until a rule becomes enforced that says I can't. When I leave a gift certificate, I take any trinkets that might be in the container. I use the trinkets that I find to make my *junk art* sculptures. In conclusion, the biggest benefits of geocaching are free entertainment, exercise, and possibly advertising for your business by leaving freebies behind. I wouldn't just leave a business card in the treasure box. When I find a business card, I am turned off by it. I sarcastically think, "Wow! Thanks for the treasure." It seems as though the person who left it behind is only interested in benefiting themselves.

Check out the *cost of entertainment* statistics shown below. Here is the approximate price per hour for various forms of entertainment the way Tom Barlow rolls (Barlow).

Dining out - $10/hour
Reading - $0.42/hour
Watching TV - $1.14/hour
Trip to the Movies - $6.50/hour
Flatwater kayaking - $19.67/hour
Bike riding - $0.60/hour
Golfing - $14.25/hour

Okay. So I'm going to average out the cost of entertainment, accounting for inflation since it has been several years since Tom Barlow published his findings. Average entertainment comes to about $8.67 per hour. For the sake of simplicity, the calculation for this tip is including entertainment savings only (not exercise or advertising savings).

SAVINGS – $225/PERSON (go treasure hunting once per week)

3. **UTILIZE PLAYGROUNDS.** There are so many fun playgrounds in my city that provide hours of free entertainment for my children. There is a sprinkler playground with lots of water fun, a large wooden playground called "Fort Discovery" that looks like a big winding castle with forts and obstacles, a skate park, and more! If I take my kids to the playground, I usually sit under the shade creating art while I watch them play (but I will sometimes join in on the fun). Explore your area to see what is available. It helps to check out your local area's website (if they have one).

SAVINGS – $195/PERSON (go to the playground once per week)

4. **GET YOUR OWN GEAR.** Renting roller skates and bowling shoes is not cheap. My family does not rent this type of equipment. We each have our own pair that I obtained as hand-me-downs, online through eBay, at secondhand stores, or through amazon.com. The items more than pay for themselves. We use coupons from pizza boxes to earn free bowling and we are often invited to skating parties, so it makes sense for us to own gear instead of renting it.

For this savings calculation, I'm going to estimate that you will use your gear once per month and that the gear will last you 15 years. I'm sure you can get your gear to last longer than that though. I still wear my great-grandmother's bowling shoes that she wore during her bowling league and they look like new! By the way, she was still bowling in her 80's. This past year, my son wore his great-great-grandmother's bowling shoes in his league. Luckily, we all have the same size feet (though not for long). My son is growing fast. It's not preferable to buy equipment for growing children. But, as they outgrow it, you can resell it on eBay or at a yard sale. Otherwise, you can make the equipment stretch farther by shoving toilet paper in the tips of the shoe. Just purchase the gear at one or two sizes up and it should get you by for several years. I prefer the reselling option better though. You don't want your kid to look like Bigfoot.

I've actually used sneakers for bowling and have never been yelled at by the staff. But they were new sneakers only used for bowling. You could use your old sneakers as bowling shoes and just slap some leather from an old jacket on the bottom for that special glide if you care about sliding. I personally play for fun, so I don't care about all of the technical mumbo jumbo. All I care about is keeping the lane clean. The alleys don't want people tracking dirt and chewing gum up onto the lanes with their street shoes.

For this calculation, I'm also going to hope that you get your equipment for $10. You can do it (bargain shopper)! From what I've seen, the average rental is about $3 (give or take). Skate rentals are usually less than the bowling shoe rentals, but I averaged things out.

SAVINGS – $530/PERSON; TIME INVOLVED – 1 HOUR (shop around for 1 set of gear)
1ST YEAR FINAL SAVINGS – $505; **ADDITIONAL YEARS** – $530

5. **SWIM AT OFF HOURS** and cut your spending drastically. Many swimming pools offer discounted rates at certain times. My family doesn't like to swim all day anyway, so getting a summer pool pass does not make sense for us (I did the math). It also doesn't make sense for us to have our own pool. It is too much care. We do not have the time and we really don't have the space. The regular cost of admission at our local pool is $4. At the discount time, it is only $2. So our family of 4 can swim for just $8 total for 2 hours straight. A summer pass for a family of 4 is $150. We would have to make something like 18 trips to make a summer membership pass worth the while. We would have to go more than once per week. However, we like to do other things each week than just swim.

SAVINGS – $20/PERSON (swim 10 times at half price)

6. **GET A GROUPON.** I was getting ready to take my kids to *Bounce Fun Plex* in Shamokin Dam, PA. It's an amazing, fun place for kids

(ages 4 and up; and even adults) to bounce on trampolines and more. Kids are literally bouncing off of the walls at that place! My son loves to play dodgeball there while jumping on trampolines. My daughter's favorite things to do there are bounce into the big foam pit and go down the large inflatable slide. Anyway, we were getting ready to leave from home and I decided to check for coupons online first. I found a great deal at **groupon.com**. **Groupon** offers lots of great money saving offers and you can even search by area. So, even when you are on vacation, you can look up the local offers. Normal admission to **Bounce Fun Plex** for 2 is $18.00. I purchased a **Groupon** for just $10. I saved $8 and all I had to do was pay online with my credit card and click "print". It was so easy! I saved over 44%. Some people work a whole hour for $8 take home pay so this is a pretty big deal.

SAVINGS – $40; TIME INVOLVED – 25 MINUTES (purchase 5 **Groupons** a year)
FINAL SAVINGS – $30

7.   **GAMBLE FOR FREE.** When I gamble at casinos, I like to do it for free. One time my family and I went snow tubing at a ski resort and I noticed that our lift passes had coupons for free credits at a local casino. So, after we were done tubing, we headed to the casino. My husband dropped me off at the door because we didn't want to pay for parking (and we had kids with us). I went inside to the guest welcome center. It turns out I also got some free credits for being a first time guest! Next time you are passing by a casino, ask if first time members get any benefits. I found out later (on their website) that I could have received even more credits by giving them my email address (wish I would have known). So I found a machine and spent all of my credits as fast as I could. I called my husband on my cell phone and told him to pull up and get me. I joyfully cashed in my winnings and walked out the door minutes later with about $65 in my pocket. Then my husband took his turn and did the same thing. He also walked away with money (I forget the amount, but our combined winnings paid for our tubing). By

the way, we didn't even pay full price for our snow tubing. We went during the discounted session which just happened to be going on when we arrived at the ski resort. What luck!

SAVINGS – $65; TIME INVOLVED – 15 MINUTES (if passing by a casino, check for offers, play free)
FINAL SAVINGS – $59

8. **AVOID SPENDING MONEY ON LOTTERIES** and games of chance unless your chances are good. I know we are talking about entertainment here, but if you feel like you have to play the lottery for entertainment (or to get rich), why not try BINGO instead. Your chances of winning are much better. Plus, with BINGO, you get to play with friends and the entertainment lasts much longer. On top of that, charity BINGO's raise money for a good cause.

A really good chance at winning would be if you place a ticket in the entry cup of an item at a Chinese auction that has no tickets in it (except for your ticket of course). If you place your ticket in at the last second, your chance of winning is 100%.

According to the Powerball website, your chances of winning the Powerball Grand Prize are 1 in 175,223,510. The chance of winning a million dollars is 1 in 5,153,632.65. These chances are based on a $2 play (Powerball).

Did you know the chances of dating a millionaire are wonderfully 1 in 215 (Josef)? I'm not sure I believe this statistic though as Josef cites Funny2.com as the source of this information. Funny2.com does not cite a source (that I can find). It could be a big fib floating around the internet. But either way, it doesn't hurt to start dating!

I can't let this go. I'd like to know if this number could actually be true. Let's see, "The number of U.S. *households* with a net worth of $1 million or more, excluding primary residence [the value of their main home], rose to 9.63 million in 2013, according to a new report from Spectrem Group, a consulting and research firm" (Fox).

According to the United States Census Bureau, the estimated U.S. population in 2013 was 316,128,839. Okay, so let's say that you are a man or a woman looking to date. You can choose from a pool of about 158,064,419 people (50.8% are female). If you are willing to date a man or a woman (you're not picky), then you can choose from 316,128,838 people. Add one more to that number if you are willing to date yourself. Now, mind you, you can't be picky with hair color, weight, race, personality, age, and such. I'm getting close to wrapping things up here. Some of the millionaires in the pool might already be married. So you might have to date a married person. Okay, it looks like 3% of people could be millionaires. That's roughly 1 in 33 people. I completely believe the odds now! The United States Census Bureau also reports that there are 2.61 people per *household* (2008-2012), which probably helps contribute to the final odds of 215 to 1 as your chances of dating a millionaire. Awesome! I feel like a real sleuth.

In closing of this tip, "the average American loses almost $400 per year to gambling" (Muniz). By the way, if you are a gambling addict, the numbers shown below will be way off.

SAVINGS – $400 (gamble for free or don't gamble at all); TIME SAVED – 15 HOURS (no traveling associated with gambling, no time spent gambling)
FINAL SAVINGS – $775

9. **BRING YOUR OWN DRINKS TO FAIRS**, carnivals, and similar events. My family only drinks water when we go out, so we are surely not going to pay for bottled water at fairs or events when we can easily bring our own. Even if we drank soda, we would much rather stick several cans in my purse instead of buying drinks while we are out. Fair food is good though. I'm willing to shell out a few bucks for something special like a hot sausage sandwich or a funnel cake.

SAVINGS – $3/PERSON (bring your own drinks to events)

10. **DO NOT PAY TO WATCH MOVIES.** A lot of people I know just can't wait for the newest release. If a person doesn't hit the theater right away to see the movie; they will wait a little bit and opt to order the movie on demand, purchase it outright, or rent it. Listen, I rarely pay for movies. You can watch free movies on **Netflix** if you have the service. If the movie is not available on **Netflix**, you can try renting it for free from **RedBox**. My family watches for **RedBox** coupons on our favorite food products in the grocery store. Sometimes pizza boxes will have a coupon for a free **Redbox** rental. Everyone has to eat and who doesn't love pizza – right? We have even received free coupons that print out along with our receipt at checkout. Once I got my first rental I started receiving free movie rental offers through email. I can rent free movies from my local library as well. If you just want to see a favorite clip from a movie, check out **youtube.com**.

SAVINGS – $60 (be patient and watch the movies for free)

11. **SKIP IN-APP PURCHASES.** If you don't know what I am talking about, let me explain. If you have games on your phone and a screen pops up asking if you would like to make a purchase, don't do it. For example, if you are playing **Candy Crush** and you can't beat a level, for goodness sake, do not pay to beat the level. If you can't beat it on your own, then you need to face reality – you suck at the game or the level is just too hard to beat easily. Keep trying to increase your skills or get lucky. Better yet, quit playing. You might be wasting your real life hanging out in *Virtual Land* too much. I have an inkling that the whole system is set up knowing that you will become addicted and frustrated and eventually pay to beat a level. Is it worth it? Would you pay to win a 5k race in real life? No! There is no joy or pride in that.

SAVINGS – $15

12. **VISIT FAIRS AND COLLECT FREEBIES.** Fairs can be fun and

free. There are many types of local fairs – fun fairs, health fairs, community fairs, fireman's fairs, and the list goes on. While you are at a fair, be sure to collect up as many freebies as you can. Actually, you can do this at events too. Collect things such as free hot dogs, popcorn, drinks, potato chips, bottled water, candy, hand sanitizer samples, pens, notepads, insect repellent samples, balloons, stickers, temporary tattoos, and more. If there is too much free food and you are full, still accept the sample, and stick it in your backpack or purse. You can always eat it for your next meal. Don't drink the bottled water at a local event. You can drink tap water when you get home. Save it for your children's field trips because everything has to be disposable while on the trip. Then you don't have to purchase bottled water when a field trip rolls around. If you don't have kids, save the water for a time when you will need a disposable water bottle. Or, serve it to guests at your house who don't like tap water.

SAVINGS – $50 (visit fairs and events for fun, collect free samples, save extras)

13. **TAKE PRACTICE SHOTS IN MINI GOLF.** If nobody is behind you during mini golf, squeeze in some practice shots. You'll get a bigger bang for your buck.

SAVINGS – $9

14. **DO NOT PAY FOR MUSIC.** You can listen to music on the internet at **pandora.com** or **spotify.com**. Take the music on the go by listening to it from your smartphone. You can also opt to listen to good old-fashioned radio. Expect to hear commercials with any of these listening options.

People in the United States spend about $43 on recorded music each year (Statista).

SAVINGS – $43; TIME SAVED – 2 HOURS (no need to shop for music)
FINAL SAVINGS – $93

NOTES

1. **MAKE YOUR VACATION PAY FOR ITSELF.** People usually travel in groups for vacation (going alone doesn't sound like too much fun). So when one adult is driving, the other can be working. Instead of wasting hours on the road just sitting in a vehicle, you could be doing work you enjoy (for me it is painting or writing). You can even chit-chat at the same time. It helps to have the right tools with you. For example, I could bring my laptop and write a story, design a customer logo, or record business receipts. I am an artist, so I usually bring my art bag and paint during road trips. In fact, I sketched all of the illustrations in this book on a road trip to the beach. You could bring a stack of coupons, clip them, and organize them. You can go through your mail. Think about the possibilities for a little bit. Maybe you want to record some of your thoughts on one of the "NOTE" pages in this book so that you don't forget your great ideas when your next vacation rolls around. I spend about 36 hours on long road trips each year and I make good use of that time. By the way, I work on short road trips too, but have not calculated that into the savings. When my husband is driving to our consignment booth, I am tagging the items that will be for sale.

The average American makes $24.53 per hour (YCharts). So if you are in your vehicle for long stretches of time, it probably pays to get some stuff done along the way.

EARNINGS – $880; TIME INVOLVED – 36 HOURS (work during road trips)

2. **TAKE ADVANTAGE OF BARGAIN NIGHTS!** There is an awesome amusement park situated near to where I live. It's called "***Knoebels Amusement Resort***" in Elysburg, PA. **Knoebels** has fun, food, and fantasy for everyone! It is the world's largest free admission amusement park (free parking as well). The cotton candy and snow cones are very reasonably priced, so I don't feel guilty indulging the children. You can even bring your own food if you like and you won't be hassled about it. They practically encourage it sporting huge pavilions at the entrance of the park where you can sit comfortably under shade and eat. But we usually just buy a yummy pizza to share. My family visits on bargain night where we can ride for 4 hours straight for only $10 each (2014)! I kept track one time and if we had paid for each ride individually, we would have spent $130 for the four of us. We were literally running from ride to ride to see how many we could squeeze in. We saved the "Skloosh" ride for last and went home soaking wet. It was our favorite ride of the day!

We take advantage of bargain or value times at least two times a year. So the savings calculation will account for two trips.

SAVINGS – $45/PERSON (look for bargain or value times)

3. **GET FREE HOTEL STAYS.** Tomorrow my family is going on vacation. We will be staying for free at a hotel thanks to a credit card incentive that I had signed up for a while back. We even get free continental breakfast. I love that! After I was done booking our stay online, a pop-up gave me the option to sign up for a credit card. The offer stated that I would receive enough points for another free hotel stay after making my first purchase with the card. Then after I book one hotel stay, I can earn enough points for another 3 stays. Well, I signed up right away and was approved. Looks like I have next year's vacation covered too!

SAVINGS – $140; TIME INVOLVED – 15 MINUTES (sign up for credit card offer)
FINAL SAVINGS – $140

BONUS TIP: We are going to visit an amusement park during our trip. Since we don't like to spend all day at a park (we like to do other things too), we are going to take advantage of an offer that is only available at the gate. The offer states that we can have unlimited fun and rides for three hours straight at a reduced price. I'm all for that! I can't wait until tomorrow!

4. **DO NOT INCUR ADDITIONAL HOTEL FEES.** Keep your hands out of the mini snack bar in the hotel fridge. Pack your own snacks. Bring a jug of water on your trip or stock up on free tap water at local fast food chains. The water in hotel rooms is usually jacked up in price.

Here are some other things that you should be careful of. Do not order room service unless you are royalty. Don't use the phone in your room. If you have small children, remove the phone cord and hide it because kids love to play with the buttons on the phone. Don't play on demand video games or rent movies. Bring your own handheld video game and watch regular TV. Since I don't have cable, basic cable gets me excited enough, so I'm happy with the free services that are included with my stay. I don't purchase shows on demand or rent video games in the room. Oh, and don't allow the cleaning staff to enter your room or you'll be expected to leave a tip. I always place the privacy sign on my door and then I ask the staff for my daily supplies when I see them in the hall – that way I'm not missing out on the freebies that I deserve.

Get this, if I am planning on staying more than one day at a hotel and I want my room cleaned without having to leave a tip; I have actually booked the first day under my name and the next day under my husbands' name. That way we just grab our bags and go down the hall to our new room. If you are staying longer, you can just alternate names every other day. You can get more room freebies this way too. We really prefer to just hotel hop to switch up the view and have done this as well. It makes the trip more fun when you get to stay at a new place each day. We pack very light anyway, so it doesn't bother us at all. We keep our items in our bags the whole time because we think hotel dresser drawers are gross. It's just a grab and go situation.

SAVINGS – $112

5.   **STAY FOR FREE OR STAY FOR CHEAP.** There are many free or low cost options out there. You just have to know where to look. Check out **airbnb.com** to find really cheap stays. You may have to stay in some strange places, but it could be a pretty cool experience. There are free options available as well and they are all over the globe. Check out **couchsurfing.org** or **globalfreeloaders.com** to find a bunch of places offering free stays. You might have to sleep on a couch in some cases, but many people will even feed you or let you use their fridge. I don't know why someone would want you to stay at their location for free. Maybe they want to eat you for dinner. Just kidding. There are some very nice and caring people out there looking to share good times with visitors and/or learn about other cultures. I wish I was as friendly, warm, and welcoming. I have to work on that. Finally, you could opt to swap houses with someone by visiting **homeexchange.com**, **knok.com**, or **lovehomeswap.com**.

If you don't feel like crashing at someone's house whether they are home or not home. Then use your smarts when booking hotel rooms. Choose the parking lot view and you'll save lots. You usually only sleep in the hotel anyway. Who's going to hang out on their balcony? At least I know I don't.

SAVINGS – $900

6.   **USE A SLED AS BOOGIE BOARD.** My family picked up some brand new winter sleds at a Goodwill store a few years back. They were a great bargain and made of a foam material similar to that of

a boogie board. So instead of purchasing boogie boards for use at the beach, my family uses the sleds. What's great is that there are even handles. They are fancier than the boogie boards I see people bringing to the beach and they are a good size. Finding two uses for one item saves money and takes up less space in storage.

Find yet another use for your sled. Use it as a raft in a pool. Slide down the stairs in your home if you dare. I'm sure some other great uses for a sled will pop into someone's head soon! Share your idea with us online at **classycheapskate.wordpress.com**.

SAVINGS – $25 (use a sled as a boogie board)
TIME SAVED – 1 HOUR (no need to shop for a boogie board)
FINAL SAVINGS – $50

7.   **USE A GoPro CAMERA.** You shouldn't need an expensive camera for use in your personal life (if you are a photographer for a living, it might be a different story – but maybe not). When I take vacation photos I use my *GoPro HERO* underwater camera and get rave reviews when people see my photos. This camera is affordable, but does not sacrifice quality. It can be used in dry situations; or it can be placed in its housing for use near or under the water. My *GoPro* camera is tiny. I can easily stick it in my pocket and it is designed to take abuse. I have taken it down waterslides, in the ocean, through theme parks, in swimming pools, and have even dangled it on a string over a bridge to see what was in the water below. What's great is that it can function as a camera or as a video camera. It also has a timer. Professionals even use the *GoPro* camera – attaching it to windshields to shoot driving scenes. I've seen it firsthand. So it seems that professionals even respect this sweet little device. I picked my camera up for about a hundred dollars a few years back. You can get a new camera nowadays for about $200. But I would highly suggest buying a used camera or an older model for less. You don't need the newest model especially if the old version has so much to offer and does an awesome job! Check eBay to find a bargain. I just checked out eBay and you guys are missing out on some great deals!

Living Big on a Small Income

Did you ever see people walking around while on vacation with fancy thousand dollar cameras and lenses? Of course you have! I see it all of the time. First of all, they have to lug the thing around. Second of all, they have to worry about damaging that expensive piece of equipment. How can you have fun on vacation if you have to worry about your camera the whole trip? I saw a guy drop his camera recently. When I drop mine, I just say, "Oops." When they drop theirs, you might hear a *not so pleasant* word or two. So the moral of this story is – get a good, cheap camera, enjoy your vacation more, and come home with amazing photos to boot! My most recent vacation photos are shown over there on the left.

SAVINGS – $900 (if you need a camera, get a **GoPro**)
TIME SAVED – 30 MINUTES (keep your camera in your pocket, no more digging through a camera bag; or packing a camera away when you need to go on a ride or for a swim)
1ST YEAR FINAL SAVINGS – $913; **FUTURE YEARS** – $13

8. **SAVE BY BOOKING IN ADVANCE.** Often times you can save a few dollars here and there by booking things in advance. This includes hotel stays, theme park tickets, train tickets, airfare, shows, and more. You can even save by pre-registering and paying for other things in your life including clubs, memberships, programs, and events.

SAVINGS – $130 (book tickets in advance)

9. **VACATION WITHIN YOUR OWN CITY.** Who says that your city isn't extraordinary? Many of us don't take notice of how great our own areas really are. By not having to travel far, you will save a lot on gas and/or airfare. Consider this an adventure into the land of make believe. Pretend you and your family are travelers from afar. Bring cameras with you and start exploring the area. Oh, you haven't eaten at the bar on the corner? Really? Bars aren't your thing? Well they are now. Ride the fake bull you never had the nerve to

ride. Make your vacation exciting by doing things you haven't tried before! Do some karaoke and make sure someone is snapping pictures to record your awesome times. Are you rough and tough? Try dining at a formal gourmet restaurant. You might like it. I tried it and it was an awesome experience. You're saving so much on travel expenses during this trip that you can almost do anything you want without having to worry about money. Remember, you don't have to drive far because you are vacationing in your own city. And think of the amount of time you are saving. You might be saving 12 hours or more of traveling time. You just saved yourself a vacation day! Woo-hoo! And the best part about all of this – you get to sleep in your own bed at night! Ahhh. Hey, you don't even have to pack your bags!

If you don't know how to find things to do, you can start by looking in the yellow pages. You can also visit *groupon.com*, *livingsocial.com*, or simply start walking and let no building go unnoticed.

Here are some more activities that you could try out:

Go swimming, roller skating, ice skating, bowling, **miniature golfing**, hiking, biking, sledding, tubing, rafting, skiing, treasure hunting, fishing, geocaching, kayaking, **canoeing**, **horseback riding**, or gambling. Visit a park, museum, art gallery, library, country club, cemetery, **comedy club**, **drive-in theater**, fair, carnival, zoo, farmer's market, flea market, auction, spa, coffee shop, yard sale, pet store, aquarium, consignment store, pawn shop

Play cards, poker, board games, video games, **laser tag**, BINGO, **tennis**, badminton, **dodge ball**, **croquet**, or horseshoes. Take a class such as **gymnastics**, karate, **Zumba**, fitness, yoga, Pilates, **cooking**, **painting**, **pottery**, or **dancing**. Get a machine that makes ice cream, bread, snow cones, fondue, or cotton candy and test it out. Purchase a cheap disco light and have a dance party at home. Buy a mini chainsaw and practice carving logs with it. Pick strawberries, pumpkins, or berries. Forage for edible food.

Have a picnic, breakfast in bed, squirt gun battle, or water balloon fight. Watch a movie, **play**, or demonstration. Go **camping in your backyard** – roast some marshmallows, hot dogs, and S'mores. Watch a movie at home complete with popcorn. Get some snacks like chips and dip; or crackers, cheese, and wine.

Get ice cream, a banana split, a massage, or a unicycle. Attend a Chinese auction, **concert**, **art show**, **trivia night**, book signing, or **swap meet**. Go on a **factory tour**, boat ride, or wine tasting tour. Make some mixed drinks, smoothies, cookies, fudge, or anything your heart desires. Learn the **Happy Dance**, *Electric Slide*, or *Cupid Shuffle* by watching **YouTube** videos. Learn to juggle, rollerblade, or play guitar.

Cook a fancy dinner, paint, run a 5K, **fly kites**, dance at a club, try **skateboarding**, maybe try some stunts, walk in a stream barefoot, take a bubble bath, wear a mud mask, try to capture a ghost on camera, build a huge snowman, scrapbook your adventure, **make a movie**, play with makeup, dye your hair, learn to crochet, take piano lessons, get a **Slip 'N Slide**, run through sprinklers, learn a magic trick, decorate a room, paint a room a new color, **enter a contest**, buy a **trampoline** and set it up, record a song and make a music video, play at a playground, shoot pool even if you suck, roll down a hill, carve the best pumpkin ever, or **use a metal detector**.

SAVINGS – $1,100; TIME SAVED – 13 HOURS (no need to drive far, no need to book a hotel stay)
FINAL SAVINGS – $1,425

10. **TAKE THE MOST COST EFFICIENT METHOD OF TRAVEL.** Visit *costtodrive.com* to see if driving or airfare is cheaper for your trip. Don't forget to factor in how much more time one method will use than another. Be sure to figure in driving time to an airport and waiting time which can be lengthy. Also, you may have to factor in a car rental, taxi, or public transportation since you won't have a vehicle at your destination if traveling by plane. Below, you will see

how much I save each year by driving to our typical vacation getaway rather than flying.

By the way, if you have more than one vehicle, you can compare the cost of driving each one. You might be surprised to see that you've been driving the wrong one all along.

SAVINGS – $228; TIME INVOLVED – 9 HOURS (drive rather than fly)
TIME SAVED – 9 HOURS (no need to book flight, check in, arrive early, or get transportation to final destination)
FINAL SAVINGS – $228

11. **PACK LIGHT TO AVOID BAGGAGE FEES.** If you are going to travel by plane, just bring the maximum amount of free bags allowed on the flight. Make one of those an empty bag for goodies that you plan to bring back with you. The less you have to deal with the better you will feel anyway.

SAVINGS – $50; TIME SAVED – 15 MINUTES (no need to pack or unpack as much)
FINAL SAVINGS – $56

12. **CARRY YOUR OWN BAGS.** If you carry your own stuff, you can avoid tipping staff members at hotels. I took a trip to Washington, DC one time and checked in at a hotel. I had all of my bags in hand and was headed to the elevator. A bellhop started to take my luggage. I told the bellhop that I was fine and that I would carry the items myself. He insisted and I countered back that I would take care of it. Well then he just took my rolling suitcase and bag and put it on a cart. I followed him in awkwardness to my room. I thanked the man and started to unpack. Then he had the nerve to boldly ask for a tip. I told the guy that I don't carry cash. Then my husband started sweating drops of embarrassment. He didn't have any cash either. I said to the bellhop, "I told you I would carry my own stuff. Sorry." I hope the guy learned his lesson. He made everyone uncomfortable, the opposite of what the situation is supposed to be.

SAVINGS – $4 (carry your own bags)

13. GET A CHEAP ROOM ON A CRUISE SHIP. When you book a cruise, look for the cheapest room available. The lower decks are almost certainly cheaper, plus if you get motion sick, the boat will rock less if you are on a lower level. That's one reason I like to stay on the lower level. Also, you don't really need a window view or a balcony. The interior staterooms are cheaper so go for that option. I don't know about you, but I'm not going to be staring out my room window much anyway.

Booking late can have its benefits too. Cruises like a full ship. So they often times lower the rates to fill it up. Book your room 1 to 3 months before the sailing date. If you wait any longer, they may be full.

SAVINGS – $1,247 (get the cheapest room)

14. AVOID THE TOLL ROUTES. When you are traveling, avoid the toll routes. My husband and I have noticed that toll charges have increased drastically over the past several years. It is no longer worth the price to us. By avoiding toll routes when we go on a simple four hour road trip to the beach we save about $25 all around. As a bonus, you will find more *FREE boxes* (unwanted items that people set out on the roadside) along the back roads than you will on a major freeway. You're chances of finding a FREE box on a toll road are probably zilch.

SAVINGS – $25; TIME INVOLVED – 30 MINUTES (don't take toll roads)
FINAL SAVINGS – $13

15. BRING YOUR OWN FOOD. Pack as much food as you can when vacationing. For example, food at tourist locations is usually expensive. Eating out in general is costly. Bring a large Styrofoam container (maybe two) to keep food cold during the trip. If you are staying at a hotel, you can use free ice from the ice machine to keep your cooler and contents chilled throughout your stay. Or, if you are not staying at a hotel, use ice packs from home. If your hotel room has a mini fridge, you can keep items cold in there. You can live it up on vacation by bringing wine, cheese, and crackers. Stock up on your favorite cracker when they are buy one get one free. Same thing with cheese. Buy the cheapest bottle of wine at your local spirits store and then hit the road Jack.

SAVINGS – $125; TIME INVOLVED – 15 MINUTES (pack a cooler full of your favorite food items); TIME SAVED – 10 HOURS (no need to eat out at a restaurants for most of your trip)
FINAL SAVINGS – $369

16. **GET FREE RIDE TICKETS.** My family has discovered something very interesting while visiting the amusement park at the beach each year. If you stand in line at the booth to buy the ride tickets, people who are leaving the park will hand their tickets to you because they know they will not be coming back again since they don't live in the area. It happens to us often. When they hand the tickets to you, you can leave the line and go ride some rides. When you run out of tickets, have everyone go stand in line again for a just a few minutes. It seems like they hand the tickets to people at the back of the line. The more people you have the greater chance of being handed tickets. We might just be lucky people, but I don't think so. Anyway, you could literally get by with a free night at the park. It's worth a try if you were planning on standing in line anyway because if it doesn't work out you have not wasted any time by trying. You can just buy tickets when you get to the front of the line like you were going to do anyway. Hey, don't forget to look for tickets on the ground. You're family can make a game of this you know. Don't forget to save half tickets. You can find another half ticket later on and combine them.

SAVINGS – $8 (you don't have to stand in line the whole time)

1. **DO NOT BUY ICE CREAM AT FULL PRICE.** I do not prefer to buy ice cream from stands or parlors (sorry if you happen to own one). I don't even like to pay full price for ice cream at grocery stores. When my family goes on our yearly beach trip, we do not pay $6 per person for an ice cream cone. My family walks a few blocks down to the local grocer where we can "each" buy a whole gallon of ice cream for less *if we wanted to*. But we just get one to share or purchase a box of pre-made ice cream cones. In the process of walking a little farther to get to a store, we burn a few calories (a good thing when you are getting ready to pig out). We usually have a vote to decide which kind we will get. On top of that, we usually only buy ice cream when it is buy one get one free or on super sale. At home, we get to enjoy the flavors we love even when they are not on sale because we stock up when the price is right. Planning ahead is a sweet idea.

"Did you know the U.S. enjoys about 48 pints of ice cream per person, per year? That's more than any other country! On average, that means each of us consume 48,000 calories and spend $144 a year ($3/pint), just on ice cream" (apardue).

SAVINGS – $72/PERSON (buy ice cream at half price)

2. **DO NOT CONSUME LIQUID SUGAR.** I do not feel that soda is worth the calories or the money. I feel the same way about juice. Why? Do some research online and you'll probably find fairly quickly that these drinks pack on the pounds and drain energy at the same time. You might have a different view (my husband thinks it is worth the enjoyment). Don't you want to stay fit so that you don't run into health problems in the future? Okay, I might seem over the top with this one, but I feel so strongly about this that I call soda *evil*. My friends and family think I am weird. I would much rather eat calories than drink them down in one big gulp.

In our house, we drink water and milk. Except for my husband who has a secret refrigerator in the basement due to his *addiction*. Soda becomes a special treat when the rest of us attend birthday parties and other events that supply these sugary beverages. So by not purchasing soda and juice you can save money and probably some medical bills down the road. Plus you might look pretty awesome if you strive to keep fit! So the minimum you will save in this scenario is the amount you would have spent on soda, juice, or similar sugary beverages.

When I go to a restaurant, I never purchase a drink (what a rip). However, I will take the drink if it comes with my meal. Otherwise, I order a tap water with lemon. I've never met a slice of lemon that wasn't complimentary!

"Sugar-sweetened beverages are linked to more than 180,000 obesity-related deaths worldwide each year" (Wade).

SAVINGS – $850 (drink tap water rather than sugary drinks)

3. **BREW YOUR OWN COFFEE.** I find it a waste to buy coffee at a fancy coffee shop. Actually, I find it a waste to purchase coffee anywhere. You can make good stuff at home! Get yourself a coffee brewer (if you are a coffee person). Pick one up at an auction for a buck or less. I don't drink coffee. Reason one being that when I

worked at the local police station, they had caffeine listed as a drug on a wall poster. It can't be good for your health. Reason number two is that it stains teeth terribly (so do most colored drinks). Oh wait; there is a reason number three. I think it tastes like crap. It must be why they say it is an acquired taste. I value a white smile and if I need a pick-me-up, I'll opt to get more rest.

By brewing your own coffee, you save about $1.85 per cup. You also don't have to go through a drive-through or stand in line. Let's say you brew just one cup a day for yourself instead of purchasing it at coffee shop. Look at how much you can save per year.

SAVINGS – $675 (brew your own coffee instead of buying it already brewed)

4. **REUSE TEA BAGS.** This will cut your tea spending in half. When you are done drinking a tea, save the tea bag. You can either use it right away to make a second cup for you or a friend; or place it in your fridge for later.

SAVINGS - $18

5. **DRINK TAP WATER** or opt to use a water filter if you must. You can use a *pitcher* that filters the water for you; or you can install a *filter* on your *kitchen tap*. These are not expensive items and not hard to find for sale. Another cheap option would be to purchase local spring water. We used to use filters in our house, but now we prefer this option. I'm sorry – did I say, "we"? I meant my husband prefers spring water. I have always preferred to drink tap water. Our local water report says that it is safe to drink the tap water, but my husband insists on the spring water. In our area you can fill a gallon container with spring water for just thirty cents. You can also fill up for free at a natural spring if you know it is safe. If you are going to use a jug, do not use an old milk jug. Bacteria can form inside even if you rinse it out thoroughly. Use a glass wine bottle or purchase a gallon jug of water to get you started.

Okay, let's get statistical! If a family of four switches from drinking bottled water to using a water filter, they could save $2,878.57 each year. If that family skips using bottled water and filters altogether (drinking tap water), they can bring their yearly drinking water costs down to $1.10 (Cancio).

On a side note, did anybody else ever notice that the price of water is sometimes more expensive than soda? What gives? Soda has sugar and stuff in it. It even has calories and needs to be carbonated. I still don't get how you can take water, add stuff to it, and alter it creating an item that sells for less.

SAVINGS – $775/PERSON (drink tap water, stop buying bottled water)

6. **START A GARDEN** to save money on groceries. It is very easy to plant a garden in your yard. If you don't have a yard, you could have a hanging garden or simply place your plants in pots. Having the plants off of the ground also makes it harder for animals to eat your crops. You could place your plants on balconies, the rooftop, or any other available space. Just go to your local greenhouse to get started. Be careful though. I see neighbors who plant way too many plants each year and have trouble even giving all of the food away. Some of it ends up rotting on the ground. 1 of each type of veggie plant should suffice. Except for things like onion plants which only produce 1 onion per plant. If you are into canning, then by all means, plant more! Cucumbers make great pickles. Tomatoes can give you tomato sauce for the winter. Stuffed peppers are delicious. Put the tomatoes, onions, and peppers together for some delicious salsa. I guess you could be a *non-classy* cheapskate and just ask the neighbors for their extra crops (since they probably planted too many anyway).

I did some calculations by examining my own garden. It looks like tomato plants get a real bang for your buck yielding lots of poundage. Pepper plants are my second choice followed by cucumber plants. Onions come last in my book because you only get one onion per plant unless it is some multiplying variety. I averaged everything together for the savings calculation below. By the way, I like to plant lettuce too…but it seems like it doesn't last that long.

Check out the photo of the popping corn I just harvested!

SAVINGS – $100; TIME INVOLVED – 2.5 HOURS (shop for 5 veggie plants, plant, water regularly); TIME SAVED – 4 HOURS (no need to shop for veggies)
FINAL SAVINGS – $138

7. **SAVE LEFTOVERS AND EAT WHAT YOU BUY.** I always save leftovers from restaurants and from at home. If there are leftover buns in a bun basket at a restaurant, I save those as well. They make great snacks for our chickens. If you save leftovers, be sure to eat them all before they go bad. Also be sure to eat what you purchase from the grocery store. My husband has the habit of buying too much food. If I lived alone, there would probably be zero waste (except for stems, rinds, and inedible things).

According to the National Resources Defense Council report,

"Americans discard 40 percent of the food supply every year, and the average American family of four ends up throwing away an equivalent of up to $2,275 annually in food" (Gillam). By eating everything you buy or grow, you would see a huge savings in your grocery and dining bills. If you spend $100 per week on groceries, then you could save $40 per week if your waste currently averages 40% and you are able to reduce your waste to 0%.

SAVINGS – $570/PERSON (don't waste food, buy less, eat it all)
TIME SAVED – 100 HOURS (eating leftovers means cooking less!)
FINAL SAVINGS – $3070

8.   **DITCH THE OVEN.** Sometimes it doesn't make sense to heat up a full sized oven. At our house, we cook what we can in the toaster oven, toaster, or microwave. The microwave is really fast and efficient at boiling water.

My husband got creative while in his work truck. In the winter, he got in the habit of heating his soup can in front of the heating vents on his dash. Though it didn't make the soup hot, it was nice and warm (much more inviting than eating cold soup while on the road). He only had to pull back the can lid and slurp it down, no utensils necessary. He has even done this with a co-worker sitting right next to him. This could get some people talking, but I guess my husband didn't care. Good for him. Some people might say that he lacks pride.

I've heard of people claiming that if you are cheap, you have no pride. Is pride a good thing? Here is a passage that I found in the Bible. Proverbs 29:23 states, " A man's pride shall bring him low: but honour shall uphold the humble in spirit" (*King James Version* [KJV]). So what does it mean to be *humble in spirit*? I think that means that you shouldn't be embarrassed to heat up your soup can in front of a heater in your truck! Ha, sounds good to me. Check this passage out. It is from 1 Peter 5:5, "... for God resisteth the proud, and giveth grace to the humble" (*King James Version* [KJV]). Yes, why yes he does. God loves his little, classy cheapskates.

Back on topic, I'm not going to bore you with calculations; but you are probably only saving 5 cents per hot meal by heating things up in the microwave. Over the course of a year though, I think it is worth it. It is faster and saves energy. You have to say it does make sense.

SAVINGS – $40 (use small devices to cook food)

9. **USE LEFTOVER CRUMB REMAINS.** That sounds kind of gross, but I didn't know how to word it. What I really mean is that you can use leftover seasonings and such. For example, I just finished off a jar of smoked almonds that I got at an amazing price – buy 1 get 2 free – and there was a bunch of seasoning left in the bottom of the container. I was actually going to throw it out, but thought it would be a complete waste. In addition, it would be disgusting to just eat it straight. I'm going to save that smoked seasoning to use on burgers and steaks. If I had to buy a jar of seasoning, it would cost about five dollars. I would say that the seasoning I just saved would fill 1/8th of a jar. If I do this with all of my products from now on, I won't have to by seasoning ever again.

Did you know that there are a bunch of people who use the bar-b-q seasoning crumbs leftover from their *Middleswarth* potato chip bags to coat chicken and chicken wings? *Middleswarth* chips are arguably the best potato chip in the world, but are only sold in brick and mortar stores throughout central Pennsylvania. The good thing is that you can purchase them online by the case at *pasnacks.com* (best online price) or by the bag at *middleswarthchips.com*. Check them out for yourself. I never have any seasoning left in my *Middleswarth* chip bags though because I eat every last crumb! The seasoning is just too good.

I wonder what could be done with leftover cereal powder. If anyone has any clever ideas, leave a comment for me online at *classycheapskate.wordpress.com* or message me through Face-

Book at *facebook.com/classy.cheapskate.jamie.jay*.

Okay, I just got done fixing myself a burger and noticed that my pickle jar had a lot of juice left in it. It was about half full. I was just dying to know what I could do with it. I know my daughter usually drinks it and I'm not kidding. It is pretty good. Anyway, I visited *bonappetit.com* finding some pretty cool ideas! My favorite was that you can sprinkle or spray pickle juice on weeds to kill them. You can also clean copper or simply substitute vinegar in recipes with pickle juice (Bon Appétit).

SAVINGS – $15 (save your seasonings, powders, and crumbs, then use them)

10. **DO NOT PURCHASE ALCOHOL IN RESTAURANTS.** It's a rip off folks! I don't know why anyone would want to spend as much money on a glass of wine at a restaurant as they can spend for a whole bottle of it at a liquor store. I guess people do this for socializing purposes and maybe to show off that they can afford. But, can you really afford it? is this what you want to waste money one? Well, you could just start a new gang that drinks from flasks before they enter a restaurant. That would be a good idea except that it is illegal in most states. So it looks like you'd have to do your drinking at home.

The average spent per household on wine at full service restaurants in the United States in 2012 was $32.33 (Bureau of Labor Statistics). This figure doesn't include other types of alcoholic beverages. I'm sure other types of alcohol such as fancy mixed drinks are even more popular using up a huge chunk of precious cashola.

SAVINGS – $100 (drink in the parking lot or don't drink at all)

11. **PACK A LUNCH.** It saves money and is usually the healthiest option. Rather than eating out on your lunch break or ordering take out, you can bring your own bagged lunch. Same thing goes for school lunches. My kids don't like all items in every school lunch and are not allowed to take leftovers home. So anything they don't

like is just thrown in the garbage as wasted money. But if my kids bring a packed lunch, nobody can stop them from taking leftovers home if they can't eat all of their food.

SAVINGS – $1,050; TIME INVOLVED – 30 HOURS (pack your lunches)
TIME SAVED – 85 HOURS (no need to drive or stand in line for your lunch)
FINAL SAVINGS – $2,425

12. **EAT WELL AND SKIP THE VITAMINS.** People were meant to consume food. I don't think God planned for us to take vitamins to supplement our food intake. I think that if people eat a balanced diet to begin with, they should not need to take vitamins.

Americans spend $30 billion every year on supplements. "Despite the popularity of supplements, many individuals are capable of obtaining all of the required vitamins and minerals through a healthy diet alone" (Bellows, Moore, Gross).

SAVINGS – $140; TIME SAVED – 24 HOURS (no need to shop for vitamins or to take them daily)
FINAL SAVINGS – $740

13. **SAVE FOOD CONTAINERS.** My husband and I save plastic containers like the ones that whipped cream comes in. We clean them and use them as food storage containers for in the fridge instead of buying containers at the store. I have even used the saved containers to hide geocache treasures. If you don't know what a geocache is, check out tip number 2 in chapter 11.

SAVINGS – $6

14. **DO NOT PURCHASE PLASTIC WRAP.** I just use food containers with lids. Why would I need plastic wrap?

On the other hand, zip baggies are worth the expense. It saves you the time of having to wash dishes. If I have a zip bag that didn't get dirty from use, I usually save it. They are good for organizing household items such as crayons, markers, pens, and more. I recently cut bags apart to cover plant seedlings. Normally people use plastic wrap to cover newly planted seeds, but I cut the zip bags apart and used them instead since I never buy plastic wrap.

SAVINGS – $8; TIME SAVED – 30 MINUTES (no need to shop for plastic wrap)
FINAL SAVINGS – $20

15. **ATTEND SEMINARS JUST FOR THE FREE MEAL.** My husband and I attend seminars in return for free meals. We call it *date night*. Anytime that we get an offer in the mail, we take them up on it. Usually we learn something new such as how to save energy, but we never give in to the solicitations. We've been to enough seminars that we've learned a few tricks. If they ask someone to say a prayer, do it. You might get a free water saving showerhead out of it. If they ask for a volunteer, raise your hand fast, you might get a ten dollar bill as a thank you.

SAVINGS – $50 (go to 2 seminars a year that offer free, fancy meals)

16. **AVOID LEAVING TIPS.** You can avoid leaving tips in many ways. One way is to not eat out at all. Another way is to get takeout. You can also eat at restaurants that don't require tipping such as fast food restaurants or restaurants that only have a tip jar set out. One of my favorite restaurants is *Panera Bread* where no tipping is necessary. Their food seems healthy and of high quality, but the prices also reflect that. They do have a rewards program that you can sign up for. If you sign up, you can expect special discounts every now and then; and also a reward such as a free pastry on your birthday. Things change all of the time in this crazy world, so check the current offer out online at your convenience.

SAVINGS – $100

17. **GET DISCOUNTS AT RESTAURANTS.** Use *restaurant.com* to get dining certificates at huge discounts. But don't shop direct through the site if other options are available. Wait for an awesome offer on the radio or on another website such as a drugstore site. You can really make out and even get certificates for free. I've done this and the great thing is that the certificates do not expire!

Another website where you can find discounts on local dining is *groupon.com*. This is also a great way to try out restaurants that you have never been to before without taking much of a risk.

SAVINGS – $240; TIME INVOLVED – 1 HOUR (purchase discount certificates throughout year)
FINAL SAVINGS – $215

18. **SAVE FOOD PACKAGING.** Get paid for your garbage. Save any-thing made of metal including tin foil and cans. Recycle them once a year at a recycling center. Also save cool looking cardboard food boxes to sell someday at auction. I'm careful to buy undented mer-chandise when grocery shopping and I get a tad sad when a family member rips a cereal box that I was intending to sell someday. I've already sold cardboard boxes for $150. Packaging becomes sought after when it is discontinued. I have been saving for most of my life, so I have a constant supply to sell. My newer boxes go to storage, while my older boxes come out of storage.

EARNINGS – $250; TIME INVOLVED – 3 HOURS (save packaging, sell online or at auction, you might have to wait until the items become valuable)

19. **TAKE TURNS COOKING WITH NEIGHBORS**. It doesn't take much longer at all to cook a meal for 2 as it does for 4 or more. Talk with a friendly neighbor that you like and see if they would like to take turns cooking dinners. One night they would eat at your house, the next night you would eat at their house. I'm lucky because I like my neighbors since they are family. You know, you don't have to eat at their house. You could simply have them fill

a container for you. That's totally cool. You could call it a meal exchange when you first propose the idea. It might make everyone more comfortable. But if you enjoy the company, then go for the option of eating in each other's homes. My parents and I enjoy exchanging soups, stuffed peppers, and more. It really saves time over the course of a year.

TIME SAVED – 91 HOURS (you only have to cook every other night)
FINAL SAVINGS – $2,275

20. **USE LEFTOVER BOILED WATER.** There is no need letting it go to waste pouring it straight down the drain. If you have leftover boiled water, let it sit on your stove to add humidity to your house in the cold months. In the summer you can pour it over weeds to kill them off quickly.

Hey, want to make your house smell awesome without the use of chemicals? Take some orange peels saved from a previous snack and place them in the leftover boiled water. Then you can humidify your house and create a lovely, natural, citrus aroma at the same time.

SAVINGS – $30 (use hot water, not a humidifier, use as weed killer)

21. **CLEAN WITH FOOD SCRAPS.** Orange peels can be run through your garbage disposal to make it smell better. Shine leather shoes with a banana peel; then wipe with a damp cloth. Place coffee grinds and water in a spray bottle; then use it to clean glass surfaces. Do you have a piece of potato that was no good for eating? Take the chunk of potato and use it with a little bit of baking soda to diminish rust spots. If you've ever made pickled eggs, you'll know that there is a lot of juice left over. Since it is acidic, you can rub some over rusty metal to help remove the rust spots as well. You can also do this with pickle juice leftover from a jar of pickles. Lighten stains on wood and piano keys with outdated mayonnaise. Did you leave

some ketchup on your plate – poured out too much? Use the left-over amount to clean tarnished brass, copper, or silver items. You never know what other uses you can find for items that are usually taken for granted. Off the subject a bit, if you have an oily face, you can use your precious resource to polish things. Doesn't that sound gross? Just don't tell anyone.

SAVINGS – $25; TIME SAVED – 1 HOUR (no need to purchase cleaning supplies)
FINAL SAVINGS – $50

NOTES

1. **STAY FIT** through exercise. Exercising is a smart choice. It plays a big part in staying healthy which can help you to avoid many types of diseases and ailments. In turn, this should help to keep your medical bills down. Besides staying fit through exercise, you'll want to eat right, be aware of germs (don't touch your mouth, wash your hands, stay away from sick people), and avoid unhealthy habits such as smoking. I also want to add that you'll want to avoid dangerous stunts. For example, my family does not climb high trees, jump off of tall buildings, get in fist fights, or drive recklessly. Summing it up, you should be able to save a lot on medical bills, medicine, and remedies by exercising, as well as eating right, steering clear of germs, keeping healthy habits, and avoiding dangerous stunts.

Nobody in my family has been to the doctor for years, besides my children's yearly physicals. This is a huge savings for us as we avoid the out-of-pocket expenses associated with visiting the doctor.

Back in 2012, the Health Care Cost Institute reported that out-of-pocket spending on co-payments and deductibles averaged out to $768 per person that year (Lowrey). In comparison, my family has spent zero dollars in extra costs at the doctor and hospital for many years straight equating to thousands of dollars in savings. Just in the last 4 years alone, we have saved over $10,000 on out-of-pocket copayments and deductibles because we have taken care to stay fit and in good health.

SAVINGS – $768/PERSON (keep active, stay safe, eat healthy)
TIME SAVED – 3 HOURS (fewer trips to the doctor)
FINAL SAVINGS – $843

2. **DO NOT PAY TO EXERCISE.** You don't need to pay for exercise classes or gym memberships. You can stay active just in your everyday activities. For example, don't worry about finding good parking spots, just walk farther. You waste time driving around looking for a good spot anyway. Doing your own physical labor rather than hiring someone else to do it for you also plays a big part in staying fit and saves a bundle of money at the same time. Take care of your own lawn. Do your own house cleaning. Shovel your own snow.

On top of having to spend money when you take an exercise class or gym membership, traveling to a gym or other facility takes time (and gas). Remember, *time is money*. Besides, it doesn't seem that people utilize their gym memberships.

It is reported that when gyms sell their memberships, they expect that only 18% of the members will actually use their membership regularly according to The International Health, Racquet, & Sports-club Association (Muniz).

Let's say a typical gym membership costs about $525 per year. Or that, for almost precisely the same price, you can take two, $5 exercise classes per week. So you can save $525, plus gas, plus traveling time just by finding alternate ways of exercising. Take the time you would have spent driving, taking a class, and working to pay for the class; and use that time to work for yourself (all the while getting free exercise). You'll get work done around your house without having to shell out the money to hire someone to do it for you. Having a cleaning person clean your house once per week can easily cost $2,000-6,000 per year. $2,000 is a real bargain, $8,000 would be about the most you would pay for a once a week house cleaning visit. You can work up a real sweat cleaning your house at full speed ahead for an hour. Depending on where you live, getting your lawn mowed could range from $650-1,000 or more. When you don't need grass to be mowed, you might need snow to be shoveled. We'll factor in the same amount of savings if you do your own shoveling – an average of $825.

SAVINGS – $7,175 (skip the memberships, do your own work)
TIME SAVED – 155 HOURS (no drive to class or gym, no class time)
FINAL SAVINGS – $11,050

3. **TRY NOT TO SIT TOO MUCH.** It exerts more energy to stand than to sit. So you are actually getting exercise (burning more calories) just by standing. By standing, you could also avoid expensive chiropractor bills that result from sitting too long; not to mention money that would have been spent on over-the-counter pain medication. Sitting too much can cause back problems. A lot of my regular work requires me to use the computer, so I stand to do it. I do not have a chair at my laptop computer. I used to sit while I worked and I felt an overall sense of un-wellness (it was not a good feeling). When I started the habit of standing while I worked, I felt healthy again. I now work at a taller desk (my buffet table) that allows the proper height for me to type and use the mouse to create websites, answer emails, and more. I also stand to paint and sculpt my art creations. Recently, I started sitting to write this book (using a different computer that was not set up for me to be able to stand and work at the same time). I regretted it. The feeling of un-wellness set in and I started to get back pain. I'm happy to say that I adjusted my situation. I am now standing and writing the remainder of this book (and feeling great). If you work a lot at a desk job, arrange things so that you can stand instead. Raise your surface somehow, even if you have to build a riser or buy a new desk.

Evidence shows that when we are inactive, our bodies go downhill. It's called the "physiology of inactivity". Let's say there is a group of people who sit and watch television for more than 3 hours each day. The people who exercise regularly are still as fat as the people who don't exercise at all due to the effects of sitting for extensive stretches of time. Sitting for long periods of time also puts you at "increased risk of obesity, diabetes, heart disease, a variety of cancers and an early death" (Judson).

Let's talk a little more about standing. You can stand in the back of a room to listen when you are at lectures or speeches. Try to stand at events, at children's activities, while riding metros, and more. It all adds up to better health saving you money that would have been spent on chiropractor bills and popping pills to mask pain. As an added bonus, you are getting free exercise without even knowing it. The biggest benefit is that you'll feel better overall.

If you can't control yourself and find yourself sitting, then get rid of every chair you own! I really like that idea. I have over 25 proper places for people to sit in my house. If I got rid of my 3 couches, 2 futtons, loveseat, and various chairs, think of all of the space I would have! Wow! I'm getting really excited by this idea. I may never buy a chair again. When I have playing card parties, my guests will have to stand while they play. They will be naturally compelled to mingle and stay active, or be forced to go lay down on a bed. Maybe I'll keep one or two chairs for the comfort of the elderly or the injured.

SAVINGS – $350 (stand as much as you can)

4. **USE A TREADMILL AT YOUR DESK JOB.** Instead of sitting eight hours a day at your job, you could be walking on a treadmill getting fit. Keeping your body in shape will make for a more enjoyable life and cut health costs. By walking while you work, you are saving time that might have been spent exercising during non-working hours. Multitasking means savings. If you work out five hours per

week, now you can use that time to work or do something much more exciting.

I know treadmills sound like they would be an expensive item. Not true. Sure, you can get a new electrified model that is already rigged as a desk for anywhere from $1,299 to $2,999 (PCE Fitness). However, I went a different route. This summer I went to a local auction where a treadmill didn't even sell for a buck. By the way, finding a treadmill at an estate auction is not rare. Okay, so I asked the auctioneer if he would take fifty cents for it. I knew if it didn't work well for use while I work, I could always scrap it for the metal and make a few bucks. Well, the auctioneer budged and I went home with a treadmill. It was manageable for my husband and me to carry; and the best part about it – it didn't require electricity! That's a double win. The treadmill is my new best friend. It even came with batteries so that I can track my mileage if I desire. Hey, the batteries were probably worth fifty cents. I got a real bargain – once again.

My treadmill is adjustable as far as the workout is concerned. Since I am powering it with my body, I set it on easy. When working, I don't want to exert myself too much ending up all sweaty. I want to be able to walk most of my work time at an easy, steady pace that does not interfere with my train of thought; or make my muscles ache so much that I can't walk the next day.

So, how do you convert a treadmill auction treasure into a desk? For me it was easy. I could have easily removed the whole front portion if I wanted to and keep just the bottom walking track – adding a high desk or table to work off of. Instead, I strapped my laptop onto the top portion and set up a table below for paperwork and my mouse. Just try to get creative and maybe a little inventive. You should be able to work through things just fine. If you don't have a high desk around your office or house, you could make one. Check out secondhand stores or store clearance sections. Maybe an outdoor bar would work for you and you could pick one up at the end of season on clearance. You can do it! This is such a great tip. I hope if you are a desk job worker that you do not pass up trying this out. I know it sounds like work, but it is so good for you.

For this savings calculation, I am going to assume that you do not currently pay for exercise and that you only work out five hours per week. I am going to include the cost savings of purchasing a used treadmill at a deep discount such as I did (the savings will only apply to the first year since you will not have to purchase a new treadmill every year). Who knows – maybe you will do better than me and find yourself a free treadmill! I am not including any savings that are related to a good state of health (fewer trips to the doctor) as that was factored into a previous tip in this chapter.

SAVINGS – $2,149; TIME INVOLVED – 4 HOURS (get a treadmill, set it up, walk while you work)
TIME SAVED – 260 HOURS (no need to exercise before or after work)
1ST YEAR FINAL SAVINGS – $8,549; **FUTURE YEARS** – $6,500

1. **SAY GOODBYE TO MOST CLEANING SUPPLIES.** "Cleaning is essential to protecting our health in our homes, schools and workplaces. However, household and cleaning products – including soaps, polishes and grooming supplies – often include harmful chemicals. Even products advertised as 'green' or 'natural' may contain ingredients that can cause health problems" (American Lung Association).

Cleanliness is important, but I feel that most people (at least in North America) go overboard (way overboard). I do not use store bought cleaning supplies and I do not clean often. If a mess is made, I usually just wipe it up with a damp rag. I would like to state that my family is rarely sick (feel free to check our school attendance records and medical records). My husband and I are barely fazed when our children bring home another perfect attendance award from school. It is commonplace to us. I know families who use store bought cleaners and are constantly paying for visits to the doctor's office, are in debt, and live paycheck to paycheck (just sayin').

Instead of using pricey, chemical laden, household cleaning supplies; use other inexpensive, common items such as water and vinegar. I throw a little vinegar and water together into a spray bottle if I want to help sterilize a surface such as countertops. Through online research I found that vinegar (the acid in vinegar) will even kill off the flu virus. Most vinegar (white, malt, or other) is about 5% acetic acid which kills bacteria and viruses (Collignon). Now, not every strain of bacteria can be killed by vinegar under every situation. So washing dishes is one thing I do not mess around with. Our family uses hot water to kill bacteria and dish detergent to fight grime and oil. I want to make sure my family is eating off of safe surfaces.

You can clean your toilet using water. I do not buy toilet cleaner. I use a toilet brush to swish the water around and then I flush. In fact, I think I inherited the toilet brush from a relative who passed away. What good does toilet cleaner do? Does it sanitize your toilet for a few minutes? Someone is going to go to the bathroom soon anyway and mess things up all over again. It's not worth it to me to sanitize the inside of the toilet.

I don't use dusting spray in my house. I use a dusting wand. But I don't use the faux, fluffy, plastic kind where the handles are always breaking off. I got a natural duster with a thick wooden stick and wool that collects the dust. It has held up for years and cost me the same price as the imitation dusters that were always breaking. I used a coupon at **Bed Bath and Beyond** to get my handy device at a very reasonable price. So, get yourself a good duster. You need something strong that you can whack off of your back porch railing to rid it of dust. Anyway . . . you don't need fancy cleaning supplies. I use my wool duster for dusting everything. I even dust our wood floor with it because it reaches nicely under couches and chairs without having to move anything.

Here are some other helpful cleaning tips. In the bathroom, clean your mirrors when everything is humid from a hot shower. Use a dry washcloth to wipe the mirrors down and they will look fab. If you have a really fussy surface like stainless steel on a refrigerator to clean, try vinegar and water. Spray it on and wipe it off with a clean cloth. Bathtubs and old toys can get stubborn dirt spots. Try cleaning with baking soda. Add a tinge of vinegar to form a bubbling effect. Baking soda has a bit of texture that can help remove thick grime. When I buy items at estate auctions they are sometimes filthy and need this extra scrubbing power to remove the built up filth. And finally, did you ever hear of spit-cleaning? Spit is awesome! Did you know it will dissolve sticker residue? Try it out for yourself. It also makes great hairspray! If you are on the road and have one hair sticking straight up on the top of your head, just wet it down with a little saliva and you'll be good to go.

In 2009, the average person spent $659 yearly on cleaning products alone (Cetawayo). Factor typical inflation into the mix and we're looking at $762 for the year 2015 ($860 for the year 2020). If I had to go the rest of my life with only eight cleaning supplies, I would choose water, vinegar, baking soda, Dawn dishwashing liquid, a wool duster, a rag, dust pan, and broom. Oh, I also really like old toothbrushes. They are very handy for scrubbing caulking and tight places like behind faucets.

SAVINGS – $750 (clean using water, vinegar, and detergent)

2. **REUSE VACUUM SWEEPER BAGS.** Don't throw them out. You are able to use them many times by cutting open the end, dumping the dirt out, and then taping the end shut with duct tape. I don't know if this is good for your health, but I'm still trucking along. Half of the time, I prefer to simply clean up with a broom and dustpan anyway and I'm sure more allergens are put into the air using this old fashioned method than sucking dirt up into an old vacuum bag.

SAVINGS – $12 (instead of changing the bag, dump it)
TIME SAVED – 1 HOUR (no need to shop for more bags)
FINAL SAVINGS – $37

3. **DON'T WASH DISHES BY HAND** – time is valuable. Since we are on the topic of health, it makes sense to talk about washing

dishes. If you don't eat off of clean dishes, you are probably going to get sick. In our house, we simply do not own a dishwashing machine (our house didn't come with one). My husband is the machine (usually). We save about $135 per year by hand washing dishes, but we lose 30 hours of time. Still, we continue to wash by hand for several reasons. Kitchen space is saved and we do not have to worry about purchasing, servicing, or replacing a dishwasher. On top of that, dishwashers seem to be harsh on dishes. Your dinnerware will last longer and look nicer if you wash by hand. For example, if there is a design on a glass cup, it fades over time after so many cycles through the dishwasher (I've noticed this with friend's dishes).

Using a dishwashing machine makes more sense, but here are some tips for anyone interested in hand washing dishes. To make things easier on yourself when hand-washing, always be sure to rinse your dishes immediately after eating so that the grime doesn't get caked on. Here is another tip – do not launder your dish rag. Since it is wet with soap and hot water anyway, just zap it in the microwave to kill any germs that might decide to live on the rag. It doesn't save much money, but this keeps the dishcloth smelling fresh. And, here is one more related tip for you. My husband covers baking sheets and pans with tin foil so that he does not have to scrub them. He then recycles the metal. What a time saver!

Since it takes time to wash dishes by hand, it actually makes sense to have a dishwashing machine. On average, I estimate that an extra 73 hours would be spent hand washing dishes as opposed to letting the dishwasher do the job each year. If you have nothing better to do with your time, then hand wash the dishes 'til your hearts content. If you can make more money some other way, I say use a dishwashing machine to do the job for you. But again, you also are saving precious kitchen space and helping your dishes to last longer if you don't have a dishwashing machine. I'll also add that the dishwashing machine isn't always safe for all dishware; so you will probably be hand-washing dishes at some point anyway.

Typically, a dishwashing machine will last 10 years and costs $500. If you equate things out, this comes to 63 cents more to do a load of dishes using the dishwashing machine rather than washing a load of dishes by hand. On average, a dishwashing machine runs 215 loads per year (Trent). The savings calculation below factors in the purchase price of the dishwashing machine spread out over 10 years. The cost of repairs is not factored in.

SAVINGS – NEGATIVE $135 (put dishes in dishwashing machine)
TIME SAVED – 73 HOURS (no need to hand wash dishes)
FINAL SAVINGS – $1,690

4. **SHOULD YOU GO THE DISPOSABLE ROUTE?** I've contemplated skipping using dishes altogether and just using paper plates, but have not gotten to that point in my life. I know other people who do this. I feel like it would be wasting paper, but if they are recycled paper plates, I would feel better about it. Think how much valuable time it would save to eat off of paper plates. It would also save a bit of dish soap. You could also use paper cups, bowls, and plastic utensils. You would not have to wash those items, but you would still have to wash pots and pans. Economically, it is cheaper to wash dishes than to use paper plates. But using paper plates saves time if you don't own a dishwashing machine. So if you can use the time you would have spent washing dishes and work and make money instead; it would make sense to use paper or plastic dinnerware. Still, you also have to shop for these items which takes a little bit of time. You might also have to pay for garbage removal and walk the used dishes out to the curb. Though where I live, you can have a huge garbage can emptied for only about $2.50.

I just placed a fake order online for paper plates, bowls, cups, and plastic utensils so that I could get an idea of the cost of disposable dinnerware if someone were to order in bulk. It took me 15 minutes to check out. However, I did not complete payment. I added a year's worth of dinnerware to my cart (paper plates, cups, bowls, and plastic utensils). With ground shipping, the estimated total came to $388.72. If you decide to purchase disposable dinnerware, you can order in bulk at **globalindustrial.com**.

In the end, it seems to only make sense to use disposable dishware if you do not own a dishwashing machine and your savings would only be your time. I think I will stick to ceramic dishes for now. I would rather save the Earth's resources. Plus, my plates are so attractive and sturdy. I don't really want to eat off of cheap, flimsy paper plates. I also don't want to create more trash than necessary.

SAVINGS – NEGATIVE $394; TIME INVOLVED – 15 MINUTES (order disposable dishware); TIME SAVED – 73 HOURS (no need to wash dishes)
FINAL SAVINGS – $1,425

5. **DITCH THE PILLOW.** Who said we have to use pillows? They are a breeding ground for bacteria which can lead to health issues. The health issues can lead to medical expenses and a decreased quality of life. Plus, pillows cost money to purchase and clean. People who use pillows spend about a third of their lives smacked right up against one. It's like cuddling with a cesspool. So, do we really need to use pillows? I do just fine without using a pillow. I sleep on my back because it seems to be the best choice for the body's alignment. If you were to sleep on your side instead of your back, you would probably require a pillow to keep your head in the proper position. It would not be good for alignment to have your head hanging downward over your shoulder when sleeping on your side. Going a little off subject, if you sleep on the same side a lot, your face can become deformed over time because of gravity and the pressure of sleeping on one side of your face (I notice this when I look at people and can usually pinpoint which side they sleep on). But sometimes a face looks a bit deformed because the person chews food and/or gum on one side all of the time causing one jaw muscle to wither while the other is built up strong. The whole process of sleeping on one side is similar to how pressure was applied to the heads of ancient cone head babies to achieve

deformation. I believe that not only your face, but your body can become deformed by sleeping on your side with everything being pulled down to one side for long stretches of time (most people sleep for 7 to 8 hours each session). Over time, one shoulder could rise up more than the other when you are standing normally. Also, think about the pressure it puts on your internal organs. On top of all of that, if you sleep on your side or stomach, wrinkles can develop on your face because it is mushed up against a surface.

Sleeping on your back allows for your weight to be evenly distributed throughout your body. This allows for proper alignment and creates less points of pressure (Caldwell).

Over time, a person's head can be trained to push forward. Older people often have this look. Sleeping on your back using a fat pillow could be the culprit. If you are used to using a pillow, I would suggest gradually reducing the thickness of what you sleep on or you might have pain as you move to being pillow free. Your body is probably trained to have the head forward. It is best to take things slow just like most things in life. You could even use folded towels to achieve the correct height as you transition to being pillow free. If you think that a pillow is better for you, by all means, keep using it. Think about this though. Do we give pillows to babies? Why not? Is it because we don't feel like making tiny baby pillows? I think not. We don't give them pillows because they probably don't need pillows (and they could suffocate as well).

Did you know that pillows can harvest fungi? If you go to bed with a wet head, you might even find black mold growing under your pillow case (I've seen it in my lifetime). Pillows can collect body moisture, drool, blood, dead skin cells, snot, and more! This is irresistible to fungi and dust mites. Did you know that dust mites eat fungi? A research study completed by the University of Manchester, led by Professor Ashley Woodcock in 2005, found up to 16 species of fungi in a single pillow (with synthetic pillows bringing in even higher numbers). Fungus can affect our health causing problems with the lungs, sinuses, and even the brain. Aspergillus fungus can invade the body and is very difficult to treat. It can even lead to death. Did you ever notice hospital pillows with plastic covers on them? There is a good reason for this (University of Manchester).

Let's pretend that you already have a pillow and it is still good. It would be a waste to just throw it out. In my house, I used old pillows to stuff a bean bag chair. My children wanted bean bag chairs really bad for a play space. The bean bag chairs that they wanted at the store were $99 each on sale for $75. I thought this was outrageous. I was in a thrift store that same week, and my daughter found an empty bean bag for 99 cents. It looked brand new. The tag said to have it filled at a special store. Instead, I filled it with old pillows. My daughter is happy because she has a bean bag chair. I'm happy to have saved so much money and find a good use for my old pillows. Before I stuffed the bean bag, I washed the pillows and thoroughly dried them using the high heat setting on my dryer to kill any fungi that might have existed. If you can't wash an item, placing the item in your freezer for 24 hours should kill off any dust mites. However, it won't get rid of allergens. You could use a dry steam cleaner to finish the job. By the way, if you are going to have a bean bag, make sure it is not a porous material like pillow fabric or you'll have the same problem that you were trying to avoid in the first place with fungus and dust mites finding a home in the cushioning.

Here is some advice if you still plan to use a pillow - "Experts say you should replace your pillows every two years, but that can be costly. Instead, buy pillow protectors that usually cost between $10 and $20" (Johnson). Or you can just opt to go pillow free (like me). If you need some support under the hollow of your neck, you can do what the ancients did! Use a stone pillow! Better yet, do what the ancient Chinese did and use porcelain as your material of choice for your pillow. I'm sure mites, mold, and fungi would have a hard time burying into a shiny, glazed porcelain surface. It would be very easy to wipe down as well. I'm definitely going to make myself a porcelain pillow when I get the time! Luckily I'm an artist who owns a kiln.

In ancient Chinese culture, a soft pillow was thought to zap the body of energy. A hard pillow was thought to revitalize a person. It was even believed that Jade pillows could increase intelligence! In the Bible, there is even mention of sleeping on stone pillows (SlumberWise).

SAVINGS – $12.50 (sleep without a pillow from now on)
TIME SAVED – 1 HOUR (no need to shop for a new pillow every 2 years)
FINAL SAVINGS – $37.50

6.   **ONLY BRUSH YOUR TEETH ONCE PER DAY.** Take this advice from someone who used to brush 3 times a day until my gums started receding. I was told that if my gums continued to recede, I would need an operation. I stopped immediately and have been brushing only before bed for about 13 years now. My gums no longer cause sensitivity and are not receding. In addition, I have never had a cavity in my life. So either I am lucky, blessed, or brushing thoroughly once per day is as good as brushing 3 times per day. The most important thing you can do is to brush before bed because you don't want bacteria to grow overnight. It is also very important to clean every surface of your teeth as well as the roof of your mouth and your tongue. Take the time to hit every surface, don't rush it. Follow this tip and you will benefit from saving at least 50% on toothpaste; and probably spend less on dental bills related to receding gums. By the way, I only use a pea-sized amount each time I brush which helps to conserve toothpaste. Consult your dentist to see if brushing once per day (before bed) will work for you.

SAVINGS – $30 (brush only before bed, pea-sized amount)
TIME SAVED – 6 HOURS (less time spent brushing)
FINAL SAVINGS - $180

7. **DRINK TAP WATER TO PROTECT YOUR TEETH.** Personally, I grew up on tap water. Here are some really cool statistics. The amount of tooth decay has been reduced by 55% since WWII due to fluoridation of community tap water. But the amount of people reached by community water containing fluoride is only 62%. So it looks like fluoride plays a major part in staying cavity free (Focused Care Dental, Valley Dental Group).

When fluoride is consumed (taken into the body), it is incorporated into the actual structure of *developing* teeth. So it seems important for a child to actually drink the fluoridated water. Fluoride also protects the teeth when it comes in contact with the actual surface. "Scientific research continues to support the benefits of fluoride when it comes to prevention of tooth decay and its safety at current recommended levels of 0.7 to 1.2 ppm" (KidsHealth). If you are leery about ingesting fluoride, you could choose to simply swish tap water around in your mouth instead of swallowing it. That is cheaper than having a fluoride treatment done at the dentist – for sure!

SAVINGS – $50 (drink or swish tap water, help to avoid cavities)

8. **QUIT USING TOBACCO.** Tobacco use is extremely expensive and bad for your health. It can control your life and waste your precious time. Get this – low-income New York smokers spend about 1/4th of their income on cigarettes. As a whole, U.S. smokers are spending about 1/7th of their income on cigarettes (Maranjian). Ugh. I can't even imagine having to spend that much on a habit. It is a nasty situation.

Think of it this way – if you spend as much time and energy quitting as you do smoking, then you should be able to kick the habit. If you can't kick the habit, then at least roll your own cigarettes. You might not be saving your health, but you'll at least be saving some money.

SAVINGS – $4,400 (quit smoking cigarettes)
TIME SAVED – 48 HOURS (less time purchasing and using tobacco)
FINAL SAVINGS - $5,600

9. **BE YOUR OWN DOCTOR.** Though I am able to fight off ailments on my own and nurse injuries without visiting a doctor, I'm not saying that this technique is for everyone. This is a touchy subject. Obviously, if someone in my family did not appear to be getting better after trying a remedy, we would look for outside help. But, my family does not go to the doctor for ailments unless forced to do so. We work at getting back to health on our own whether it involves the cold, flu, bronchitis, sprains, strains, pink eye, and more. I watch to make sure things do not get out of hand. For example, I make sure a fever does not get too high or that dehydration does not occur. I knew a normal child that had a high fever at about age 5 and stayed at that mental capacity into adulthood. The fever rendered the child abnormal. I keep a close eye out to see if someone really needs medical care as opposed to my care. So far, my children have never *required* the care of a medical doctor except for vaccinations required by the state for children to attend public school. By treating things on your own, you can potentially avoid co-pays and deductibles associated with your health insurance.

Average medical out-of-pocket expenses for a family of four in *quarter one* of 2012 came to $670. Take note that is only for quarter one. This does not include pharmacy, vision, or dental expenses (Simplee). That means a *single* person spends about $670 *per year* on out-of-pocket medical expenses. If you can treat things on your own, you could see a nice yearly savings here. Instead of traveling to the doctor, you or someone else can take a trip to the store for whatever supplies that you may need in order to get yourself or a family member back into shape.

As a family unit, we don't go to the doctor or hospital unless it is life or death. My husband cut his head open when he was getting in my parents' van which resulted in a 2" gash. I've had this happen to myself before, but maybe a 1" gash in my head and in a different situation. We've also had cuts to our fingers, but didn't get stitches. You don't need stitches folks. Simply stop the bleeding by applying pressure. Then spray the area with antiseptic. By the way, I bought our antiseptic online and when I went to use it I noticed that the label read "Antiseptic for Dogs." I don't have a dog, but I figured if it won't kill a dog, it won't kill us. Guess I missed the "dog" part when I got the antiseptic for free on Amazon using my credit card rewards. Oh well, we have all used the product at least once by now and are doing just fine. It really has great results. After the antiseptic is sprayed on, simply apply some ointment. If it is a finger wound, you'll want to wrap the wound and be sure not to move your finger for a day or two so that the skin can fuse back together. When you wrap the wound, be sure that the skin is together nicely so that you have minimal scarring. Back to the head wound scenario – At night, wrap the area in gauze and hope it stays on until morning so that your bedding doesn't get blood or ointment on it. Then don't wash your head for three days and apply new antiseptic and ointment every night. You don't have to wear a bandage during the day because the skin on your skull doesn't move much or touch things like other areas of the body. Then on the fourth day you can wash and it should be looking nice. We have never had infection – the skin is always nice and white . . . no pink except for the cut area. If you look gross during the process with ointment and a scab on your head, get over it. You could wear a paper, Burger King crown to try to hide it. I'm just making a joke, don't worry, I'm not that looney. You don't want to wear a hat that might rub the wound; a crown would let your head breath at least.

My daughter cut her chin open pretty badly by falling one time. It looked horrible and we were on vacation. I went to a CVS Pharmacy, bought some supplies such as butterfly bandages, and worked my magic. Actually, my father worked his magic because I couldn't bear to see the wound on my baby girl. I've gotten a little stronger since then. She was careful not to move the area much for a few days. A year later, her scar was almost invisible. Our bodies do not need painful stitches (to an extent). If you get a shark bite, go the freakin' hospital. Yikes!

We do not go to the hospital for a sprain, broken toe, or finger. I have not been to the doctor in many years. I just take care of myself. If I get cancer . . . I could be screwed. But I think my body would give me a sign of it somehow and then I would go to the doctor promptly.

SAVINGS – $650 (take care of your own ailments and injuries)
TIME SAVED – 18 HOURS (less trips to the doctor)
FINAL SAVINGS – $1,100

10. **LET A FEVER DO ITS JOB.** If one of my children gets a fever, I let the fever fight off whatever it needs to fight off. I carefully monitor the fever to be sure it does not go too high. I get nervous if it approaches 101 degrees (which is rare for us). I will not put my child to bed for the night without fever reducer if it gets that high. It's not worth the risk. In the day, I may use a cold washcloth or bath to help soothe a fever if it gets a little too elevated for comfort. By dealing with fevers naturally, you can avoid spending money on fever reducing medications.

SAVINGS – $10 (let a fever do its job, monitor it)

11. **SOOTHE BRONCHITIS AND COUGHS;** and avoid buying cough medication. In the 1970's, my mother lived in Tetonia, Idaho at the foothills of the Teton Mountains; in a remote area far from help. Her nearest neighbor with electricity was three miles away (besides that, there were the "boys" who lived one mile away in a windmill farmhouse). Well, my mother came down with a bad case of Bronchitis and had trouble sleeping due to it. A neighbor came to the rescue with a "Hot Toddy". I do not know the neighbor's name, but

am thankful that they were so willing to help. My mother experienced great results from the Hot Toddy (an age-old remedy) which was a hot drink composed of herbal tea, a one ounce shot of whiskey, and a teaspoon of honey. My mother says that they also added a pat of butter (maybe to soothe and coat the throat).

SAVINGS – $10; TIME INVOLVED – 10 MINUTES (fix yourself a "Hot Toddy" when needed); TIME SAVED – 5 MINUTES (no need to take time to get other medicine)
FINAL SAVINGS - $8

While we are on the subject of living remotely in Idaho, I'd like to share that my mother also lived with my father, grandmother, and grandfather at the time. When it came time for a bath, they all shared the same bathwater because the water was hauled in and heated up just for that purpose (no running water). It was out of necessity that they had to share. My mother was always first because she was the "cleanest" (or was she just super *classy* like me). This whole idea sounds repulsive to me, but there are people who *have* to share bathwater. There are even some modern people who *choose* to share bathwater to save some dough. In ancient days, bathhouses were way more common. I'm so glad I don't live back then.

12. **GET RID OF PINK EYE.** Like I said, we fight everything ourselves. Pink eye was going around our elementary school and my daughter picked it up. Luckily I got to fight it over a weekend. I made a cup of Chamomile tea using distilled water (from my mother's distiller) and squeezed a bit of fresh lemon juice into it as well. I kept this mixture in the fridge. I had my daughter lie down on her back and close her eyes. Then I took two cotton balls and soaked them in the mixture, squeezed them a bit so that they were not dripping wet, and then placed the cotton balls over her eyes for several minutes. You do not want to drip the mixture directly into the eye or it might burn. I repeated this with fresh cotton balls two to three times per day. When she went to bed, I just left them on

her eyes. It didn't take long before the eye discharge was completely gone. No more infection! However, when it was time to go back to school, my daughter's teacher insisted that Nicole go home because her eyes were a bit pink (remember, pink eye was going around). I told the teacher that Nicole was over it. The school insisted on Nicole seeing a doctor or she could not come back to school. I knew Nicole was better, but took her to the doctor immediately. The doctor tested Nicole and said that the infection was gone (that my remedy worked). I got a note from the doctor that Nicole was allowed to go back to school. I was a little upset though (Nicole's perfect attendance was ruined and our doctor is located in another town). It wasted my time and money. By the way, I had treated my son in the same way when he was in nursery school when he had gooey eyes one morning (I never really saw pink in his eyes, so it might not have been pink eye). Maybe I caught it before it turned into something worse. I think gooey eyes are a sign of infection. So if I ever see this sign again, out will come the cotton balls, lemon, and chamomile tea bag.

SAVINGS – $20; TIME INVOLVED – 10 MINUTES (boil tea, add lemon juice, cool, apply); TIME SAVED – 1 ½ HOURS (no need to visit the doctor or get a prescription filled)

FINAL SAVINGS - $53

Here are some bonus tips (they may or may not save you money, but are worth passing along):

Soothe a sting. When a Cicada Killer (huge ground wasp) stung me this past month, my mother came to the rescue with a special concoction. It was **Aztec Secret Indian Healing Clay** mixed with a bit of vinegar. We added a dollop to my skin where the sting occurred and within minutes I was feeling peachy. The clay drew the venom right out of my body as it dried.

Avoid flying if you have congestion. I took an airplane ride one time with sinuses that were acting up. The pressure in my ears (even while chewing gum) was so intense that it felt like a knife was stabbing my eardrums. In another instance my aunt was on a plane ride that resulted in bleeding ears (maybe from a rapid descent combined with nasal problems). Can you imagine the excruciating pain? Stay away from planes if you have sinus problems. You could get injured requiring medical care.

13. **WEAR GLASSES** and make them last a long time. If you have eyes that need a little assistance, then opt for glasses instead of contacts. The expense of glasses is less than that of contacts. I can't even remember the last time I was to the eye doctor. I do not have eye insurance and since I can see just fine with what I have, I don't go. I know, the eye doctor says it is important to go, but I'll take the risk. You make your own decision on this. I got my glasses for free when I used to work for a design firm. I used my yearly health budget to buy an awesome pair. That was about 14 years ago and I'm still wearing them to this day. I seriously think I can make them last another 46 years if my eyes do not change drastically.

The annual cost of glasses is $370 (Wanda Northam).

SAVINGS – $370 (don't buy more glasses)
TIME SAVED – 2 HOURS (skip a visit to the eye doctor)
FINAL SAVINGS – $420

14. **MAKE CONTACTS LAST LONG** and re-use lens solution (at your own risk). For days when I want to look natural, feel prettier, or when I am going to be more active than usual, I wear contacts. 5 years ago I bought a bulk supply of contacts for $216. I only dispose of a pair when they start to feel a little dryer or uncomfortable. Though I do have special, intense cleaner that will usually clean them up good enough to last a bit longer as it helps to remove natural deposits such as calcium and protein. I also re-use lens solution for about a week before changing it out. I leave it in the contact case without dumping it. A bottle of solution lasts me what seems to be 2 years. I don't keep track. I have 10 pairs of contacts left. I go through 1 to

2 pairs of contacts per year. So, I probably have another 5 years' worth of contacts left. They do have an expiration date. I don't care. I put them in disinfecting solution before I wear them, so if there is any chance of contamination, I nail it. There should be no contamination unless there is a pinhole in the packaging. I also store my contacts in a cool, dry place.

"Though soft lenses are sealed in an airtight container, it's possible that over time the seal of the container can become compromised, possibly leading to contamination of the saline solution and lens inside." The lenses should be free from contamination up until the expiration date shown. Four years is the typical amount of time allowed for expiration from the date of manufacture (Gary Heiting). The way I see it, if you disinfect the lenses, I don't see why you can't use them past the point of expiration. Again, use your own judgment. I'm responsible for myself and I feel confident in what I am doing. If you do not feel confident or safe, then only purchase 4 years of contacts at a time or whatever the expiration date is for the contacts you are going to purchase.

Someone I know buys disposable lenses and wears them just as if they were regular contact lenses because disposable lenses are cheaper. Their eye doctor told them that they were exactly the same as the regular contacts. I found some important information that I should share with you:

"Some of today's disposable lenses are made of the same materials as traditional lenses; other disposables are made from new materials developed especially for disposability" (Liz Segre). So check with your eye doctor or the manufacturer to find out if they are of the same material. If so, you can make disposable contact sets last for years and years at a low cost.

The annual cost of contacts is $795 (Wanda Northam). The savings calculation shown is for typical contact lenses, not daily disposable lenses. So you can save even more money if you can find a daily disposable that is made of quality material.

SAVINGS – $773 (buy contacts in bulk, make them last)
TIME SAVED – 2 HOURS (skip a visit to the eye doctor)
FINAL SAVINGS – $823

15. **SKIP THE FLU SHOT.** I worked for a company at one point in my life where the workers who opted to get the flu shot got sick and the workers who didn't get the shot stayed healthy. Now, I'm not certain they got the actual flu, but they became ill with vomiting and all. I have never had the flu shot and when I saw the results of it firsthand, I plan to never get the flu shot in my life. As I've stated over and over again, my family is very healthy overall and none of us have had the flu shot (that we know of). Maybe a sinister nurse shot us with some, unbeknownst to us. I highly doubt it though.

According to Kelly Brogan, MD, referencing an article posted on the International Medical Council on Vaccination's website, "I have several pediatricians as patients. Unprovoked, all of these women have confessed to me that they have observed increased virulence [disease/sickness] in their vaccinated populations." Kelly goes on to explain that there are studies showing the increase in infection associated with the vaccinated population. In one study, 115 children were tested. Some were given a placebo and others were given a real vaccine. Those that received the real vaccine had a 4.4 times increased rate of non-flu infection (Brogan). So it appears that the body works hard at fighting the vaccination, so much that it can't fight other things off as effectively.

SAVINGS – $30; TIME SAVED – 1 ½ HOURS (no need to travel and get a flu shot)
FINAL SAVINGS – $68

1. **USE ROCK SALT AS DEODORANT.** My deodorant has lasted over 13 years now and it cost me nothing. I use natural salt rock as deodorant. It can also be called crystal deodorant rock. You can find this in health and wellness stores, vitamin shops, or online. I heard bad reviews about regular deodorant and the chemicals in the ingredients not being good for the body. I switched to salt rock deodorant when someone I knew passed their rock salt deodorant on to me because it wasn't working for them. It smelled like onions when they gave it to me, but I washed it off. The reason it was stinky was probably because they used it after armpit stink had already set in. Bacteria already started to grow under the arms when the person attempted to use the deodorant. You need to rub the rock across your armpits right after a shower when you are still wet. The salt will stick to your clean body and prevent the stinky bacteria from growing in the first place. I only apply this once per day and I smell great all night and all the next day. Sometimes I skip a shower and I go another 24 hours smelling like a person who uses regular deodorant (minus the scents). By the way, if you try rock salt deodorant, and it comes in a plastic holder, feel free to chisel it out of the holder to double the life of it. There is another half a stick hidden in the bottom of some brands. If a regular person goes through a $5 stick of deodorant every month, then I just saved over $780 on my deodorant (not

including tax). I imagine I will get another 7 years or more out of it (we'll see). In that case I will have saved $1,200 over the course of 20 years just by switching to rock salt deodorant. Be sure not to stick your rock deodorant under hot water, this will slowly wear away the rock (wasting it). Just rub it over your slightly wet underarms and it will last much longer.

SAVINGS – $60 (use salt rock deodorant); TIME SAVED – 30 MINUTES (no need to buy more deodorant throughout the year)
FINAL SAVINGS – $73

2.   **TURN CRAYONS INTO MAKEUP.** I just can't stand seeing crayons go to waste. Every time we eat out at a restaurant with our children and crayons are provided, I shove them in my purse at the end of the meal. Not only do I make lipstick and eyeliner out of crayons, I also make Halloween makeup and candles.

INGREDIENT AND SUPPLY LIST:
crayon(s) with wrappers removed
coconut oil
pot or pan
small metal or glass bowl
small lidded container
spoon
pliers

Here is what you do. Put your pot or pan on a heat source. Fill it with about a half inch of water and bring it to a boil. Reduce the heat. Place your small metal or glass bowl in the middle of the water. Use a spoon to throw a dab of coconut oil into the small bowl. Add a piece of crayon in any color you desire. Mix the two ingredients until they are melted and combined. Add another color to create your own shade if you desire. For a more translucent shade, add more coconut oil. The reason why you do not just throw the ingredients right into a pan is because they might burn. I use the double-boiling technique. It is the same technique that is used to melt chocolate.

At this point, I use pliers to remove the container and pour the hot liquid into a small container to store the makeup. I use a contact lens case, but you can simply use an eye cream jar or any other jar that you have saved up. When I apply the makeup, I use a paintbrush. It does the job very well.

The best part about this process is that crayons are non-toxic because they have to be safe for children. There is nothing odd about using crayons for this purpose. In fact, it may even gain more popularity since it is safer than many makeups on the market. By the way, make sure the crayons are labeled as being non-toxic just to play it safe.

If you think it is a waste to buy a whole jar of coconut oil for this project, think again. I have had a jar around for over 10 years. When I was pregnant with my children, I rubbed it over my stomach to prevent stretch marks and I'm happy to say that I do not have any. You can use coconut oil for massage purposes, dry skin, dry lips, wrinkle cream, chemical free makeup remover, and I've even eaten it on Triscuit crackers. I store my jar in a cool, dry pantry. By the way, since the jar I have is old, I no longer eat the product. I only use it for non-consumable purposes at this point.

If you are interested in making candles, see chapter 1, tip number 14.

SAVINGS – $75; TIME INVOLVED – 1 HOUR (gather supplies, make a years' worth of makeup); TIME SAVED – 2 HOURS (no need to shop for makeup throughout the year)
FINAL SAVINGS – $100

3. **BUY MEDIUM-THICK TOILET PAPER.** Whoever says that you should buy thin toilet paper is talking a load of crap. No pun intended. When I go to a restaurant, store, or other facility and they have thin toilet paper provided, I make a huge ball with it. I'm sure I waste twice as much of the thin paper than if they had normal to thick style paper on hand. Just look for a deal or use coupons for the good stuff and stock up on it when the price is low. By getting the sale price and using only a few sheets of medium-grade toilet paper per sitting, you should be able to save a good amount of cash over the course of one year.

SAVINGS – $30/PERSON (do not buy thin toilet paper)

4. **MY HUSBAND HAS AN ANNOUNCEMENT.** My husband, Nate, wanted to share a tip with you. In college, he had a professor that would not take a job in Iran because the professor would have had to clean his butt with a hose instead of using toilet paper. Nate said, "It would be a good idea to do this to save money instead of buying toilet paper." I said, "This book concerns classy cheapskates, not gross cheapskates." By the way, Iranians apparently think our toilet custom is gross according to blogs that I have read. So Nate started telling me how you could have a hose coming in through the window of your bathroom and it could be situated next to the toilet. The idea of this just disgusted me. I exclaimed that I think this idea was already invented and it is called a bidet (a French toilet device that sprays water on your bottom). He exclaimed, "Now, there's your high class!" I said, "I don't think you can crap in a bidet though." I think they are two separate devices. I think you have to have a toilet too. I said, "I can invent a double-duty device called the 'Crap-o-Matic'." He just rolled his eyes. Besides, it's probably been invented already. So the moral of this announcement is that you may want to keep an open mind and try using a bidet in your home (or some other similar device). In my home we spend about $50 per year on toilet paper per person (always purchased at a discount). It might make sense to try a bidet.

Update: I just found out that you can purchase an add-on bidet for about $100. You just add it on to your current toilet. With a bidet, you still have to pat dry. It cuts down on toilet paper use though. Let's assume you will use half as much toilet paper since you are basically just patting dry. Keep in mind, if you have a family of four, you will not see a savings the first year of use. If you live alone, you will not see a savings for about 6 years. This is one tip I've never tried and I think I'll pass on it. I can just imagine feces being sprayed everywhere in a very unsanitary way. I also picture dirty water spraying out under the toilet seat onto the floor. I'm sorry, I can't recommend doing this.

SAVINGS – $25/PERSON; TIME INVOLVED – 2 HOURS (purchase and hook up an add-on bidet)
FINAL SAVINGS STARTING ON THE 7TH YEAR – $25

5. **WATER THINGS DOWN.** You can lengthen the usage of bathroom products by adding water to them. I take liquid soap and water it down very well until the consistency can be pumped through a foaming soap container. When you pump out a puff of foamy soap, it is mostly air and water with a little bit of soap mixed in. You don't use much product, but it does the job. One time, Bath and Body Works was giving away free foaming soap. I saved the container after we used all of the soap up and added my own concoction to it. Guests feel special using my fancy faux *Bath and Body Works* soap. By watering things down, I make the product last four times as long. It would be best to use distilled water for this trick. Some products might spoil if you don't. However, I use regular tap water for our hand soap and have seen no problem with it.

Here is another related tip. When your conditioner, shampoo, or cream is almost all, add some water to it, and shake it up. This will help you to use every last drop of the product that was stuck to the container walls.

SAVINGS – $100/PERSON; TIME INVOLVED – 1 HOUR (water down products throughout year)
FINAL SAVINGS - $75

6. **BUY SHAMPOO IN BULK.** I buy a huge (and I mean huge) container of shampoo and conditioner in one at *Sally Beauty Supply* for only a couple of dollars and pour it into a smaller container for use in the shower. This product is intended for beauty salon usage. However, the container states that it is also intended for daily use (so the quality must not be lacking). It also smells very nice. My family has still not used the entire container (in fact we have barely grazed it). I'm thinking it could take several more years to use it up.

SAVINGS – $30/PERSON (purchase bulk shampoo/conditioner)
TIME SAVED – 2 HOURS (less time shopping for shampoo and conditioner)
FINAL SAVINGS – $80

7. **SKIP A SHOWER.** Showers use up time and money. They can also dry out your skin causing skin problems. It is okay to skip taking a shower especially in the winter. If you work like a dog in the summer, sweating buckets, I would not recommend skipping a shower.

Instead of showering every other day, you could opt to take a *quick* shower. Usually I prefer a long shower, but if I need a quick rinse, then a speedy shower it shall be. I don't wash my hair if I am just jumping in for two minutes to wash the sweat off of my body.

Another savings option would be to replace your showerhead with one that uses less water. I don't like this method. I like a good stream of water. It feels like I am able to wash away suds better with a stronger stream of water. It is also more luxurious. This is one area of my life where I don't choose to skimp.

So how much will you save by skipping showers? Well, that answer varies. Keep in mind that I'm averaging figures for this book. I don't take my high or low numbers for the savings shown. I go with the middle of the road statistic. Your savings could be higher or lower depending on your cost of water, your shower head, what you pay for energy, the type of water heater you have, the length of your shower, and what temperature you have it set at.

SAVINGS – $50/PERSON (take a shower every other day)
TIME SAVED – 24 HOURS (less time spent in the shower)
FINAL SAVINGS – $650

8. **USE YOUR HANDS** – instead of a washcloth when you bathe. I don't buy washcloths for washing my face or for in the shower. These cloths are breading grounds for bacteria. I've used other people's showers who had washcloths hanging that just wreaked of mildew. By washing naturally, you don't have to purchase washcloths or wash them (a waste of time and water). I thought about this and it seems like some people would be disgusted by this. After careful research, I found that many people ponder the idea of whether to use a washcloth or not. One person stopped using a washcloth when their dermatologist told them it was causing skin problems. The people who are disgusted shouldn't be. If you use a washcloth, it touches your butt and you have to wring it out afterwards using your bare hands. For people who use a shower pouf, that is even more disgusting. Do you wash it? I've heard nasty things about poufs. In any case, I hope everyone starts by washing their face and ends with the rear (instead of vice versa).

Check out these 2014 poll results from Glamour magazine showing what people suds up with:

 51.79% of people use a *pouf*

 27.68% of people use just the soap (their *hands*)

 17.29% of people use a *washcloth*

 3.24% of people use *something else* such as a sponge (Shapouri)

This poll started in 2008 and is still active, accepting new answers to add to the poll results.

By the way, I just placed my vote and the results now read:

 51.74% of people use a *pouf*

27.74% of people use just the soap (their *hands*)

17.28% of people use a *washcloth*

3.24% of people use *something else* such as a sponge (Shapouri)

The World could change forever if you follow this tip! History is in our sudsy hands! A new movement has just begun. I hope you make the switch today! But no matter how you bathe, you can take the Glamour poll online by visiting:

http://www.glamour.com/lipstick/blogs/girls-in-the-beauty-department/2008/10/poll-do-you-use-a-shower-pouf

SAVINGS – $10 (wash with your hands, don't purchase washcloths)
TIME SAVED – 1 HOUR (no need to launder washcloths)
FINAL SAVINGS – $35

9. **DON'T WASH YOUR HAIR EVERY DAY.** Washing hair can dry it out. The natural oils in your hair are good for it. If you skip washing your hair for a day or two, you can save shampoo, and cut the length of your shower down which saves time and money. You save even more time by not having to style your hair all over again each day. If you think your hair will look too greasy, keep a can of **Oscar Blandi** dry shampoo in your cabinet. A spritz of dry shampoo at your roots or oily areas will get you by another day without having to wash your hair. I use this product if I happen to go more than 2 days without shampooing. I have fairly long hair, so washing it takes a few minutes; then I allow it to air dry, and finally I have to style it. It's a process that I don't enjoy. I have never actually gone longer than 3 days without washing my hair (that I know of), but there are actually people who do not shampoo their hair at all. Do a Google search and you'll find people who never use shampoo.

SAVINGS – $50 (wash hair every other day)
TIME SAVED – 12 HOURS (less time spent on washing hair)
FINAL SAVINGS – $350

10. **LET YOUR HAIR AIR DRY.** I don't use a hairdryer. First of all, it damages hair; and second of all, it wastes a bit of electricity. Be sure to towel-dry your hair by blotting and/or wrapping (don't rub the towel over your head or you could damage your hair). Then let your hair air dry before going to bed. You wouldn't want your bedding to get damp and grow disgusting things like mold which could actually make you very sick. The biggest savings with air drying your hair is your time saved.

If you are ever interested in knowing how much electricity you will save by not using a device, simply plug it into another handy device called the **Kill-A-Watt**. It can tell you how much electricity is being used. Do a search online if you are interested. It is a low-cost item.

SAVINGS – $5 (let your hair dry naturally)
TIME SAVED – 22 HOURS (no more using the hairdryer)
FINAL SAVINGS – $555

11. **CUT YOUR OWN HAIR.** I cut everyone's hair in my family. I have a pair of scissors and a **Wahl** men's hair trimmer. The reason I do not go with generic brands for the trimmer is because they don't last me very long. When I used to buy generic, I had to buy trimmers fairly often. The **Wahl** trimmer was still affordable, has lasted a good amount of time now, and I expect it to last many years to come. All in all, it is cheaper to buy better quality in this situation.

I am a woman with longer hair. When I cut my hair, I merely put it in a ponytail holder. I pull the band down almost to the end of my hair, and then cut right below the band. I then split my hair into low pigtails and pull each to the front. I pull the bands down near the ends of my hair and trim. This keeps the sides of my hair from being longer than the back. Finally, I put my hair in a high ponytail and pull it straight back to trim it if I want to create a layered effect.

For the men in my family, I use an electric trimmer. I choose the

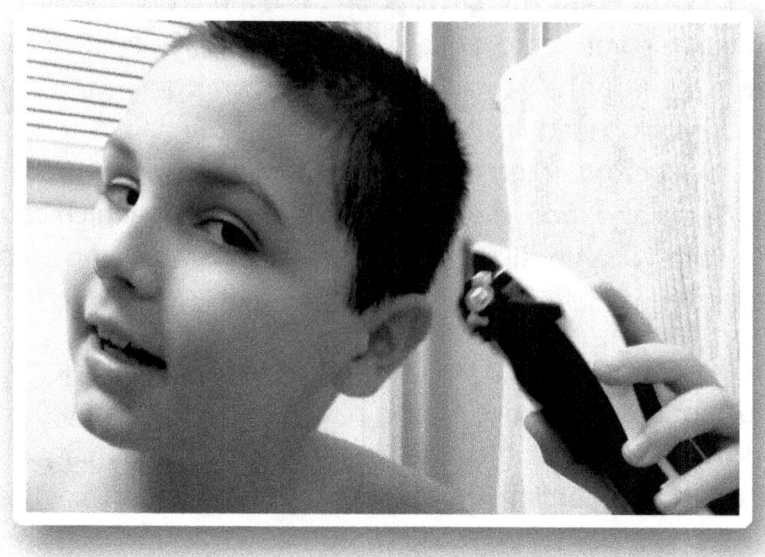

proper *length* attachment and then run it over their entire head. Sometimes I use a shorter attachment for the sides of their heads. To finish things nicely, I remove the attachment and shave their neck and sideburns. I then take the scissors and trim any longer hairs that I may have missed around their ears. That's it. They just shower while I clean the hair off of the floor.

By cutting everyone's hair in my family, I am saving money, time, and gas. I can also cut their hair whenever I want without having to make an appointment. We get exactly the look we are shooting for without having to explain it to a hairdresser over and over each month. I am also faster at cutting hair than a salon is. Stylists try to get all fancy, have to wash your hair, and seem to like to dry your hair for you. Besides that, I am an introvert, so the chit-chat at a salon tends to annoy me as well. Bringing this tip to a close, the cherry on top is – I don't have to leave a tip!

SAVINGS – $240 (cut your own hair or get a pal to do it)
TIME SAVED – 9 HOURS (no trips to the salon)
FINAL SAVINGS – $465

12. DYE OR LIGHTEN YOUR OWN HAIR. When I dye or lighten my own hair, I purchase a box of product and get several uses out of it. Let's say you only have roots to deal with. There is no use buying a root touch up kit. Get a full sized box. Let's say there are two parts to mix. If one is 8 oz. and the other is 4 oz.; simply take 2 oz. of one, 1 oz. of the other, and mix them together. Use this smaller amount to touch up just your root area. You will get four uses out of just one box. This is a nice savings and you might feel like a chemist when you are done. Oh, and you are also saving by not having to visit a salon. You don't have to sit in a chair reading a magazine waiting for your hair to get done. Since you are at home, you can do whatever your heart desires. You don't even have to tip yourself and you can do your hair in the middle of the night if you feel like it.

SAVINGS – $800; TIME INVOLVED – 4 HOURS (purchase hair product for the year, do your hair); TIME SAVED – 24 HOURS (no appointments to schedule or go to) **FINAL SAVINGS** – $1,300

13. FIND USES FOR OLD MAYONNAISE. I don't know about you, but in our house the mayonnaise in our fridge seems to go out of code before we can finish it off. Rather than risking getting food poisoning or throwing the product out, try conditioning your hair with it. Simply get in the shower with your jar of mayo. Then wet your hair, rub in a couple dollops of mayonnaise, and let it get to work while you wash the rest of your body. The longer you let it in your hair, the more it will have time to penetrate. So enjoy the steamy shower, shave to pass some time, and then rinse the mayo out of your hair. You'll want to shampoo once or twice to get it thoroughly clean. I think you'll be pleased with the results. Save the rest of the mayo for another time. You might want to write "conditioner" on the jar before you put it back in the fridge.

For any guys or gals reading this book who have short hair, there are other options for your mayo usage. You could do a deep body conditioning to battle dry skin. Pretend you are having a fancy facial and smear it all over your face. Add some dabs to your fingernails.

I just did a search online and found that some people use mayonnaise to battle head lice. "Many dermatologists now recommend using mayonnaise to kill and remove head lice from kids instead of toxic prescription drugs and over-the-counter preparations." You are supposed to massage the mayo into the hair and onto the scalp. Then place a shower cap over the head before bed and let it work some magic while the patient sleeps. Just shampoo and use a lice comb in the morning, then repeat in about a week. You can even use mayonnaise to polish plant leaves and piano keys; remove crayon marks, bumper stickers, and tar; and also relieve sunburn pain (Reader's Digest).

SAVINGS – $20; TIME SAVED – 1 HOUR (skip shopping for certain products throughout the year)
FINAL SAVINGS – $45

14. **NEVER BUY A TOOTHBRUSH.** I think it is important to visit the dentist every 6 months for a cleaning. At the dentist, you should get a free toothbrush, floss, and a sample of toothpaste if you are lucky or ask for one. I use the sample toothpastes for trips and sleepovers that my kids go to. There is no need to buy a toothbrush in between cleanings. That is just wasteful.

SAVINGS – $20 (don't purchase toothbrushes); TIME SAVED – 30 MINUTES (no need to purchase toothbrushes throughout the year)
FINAL SAVINGS – $33

15. **SKIP WEARING JEWELRY.** I'll admit – I have my ears pierced. However, I wear the same pair of earrings every day. They are simple faux diamond earrings. Just enough bling to set things off, but not so flashy that people will notice I wear the same earrings every day. I save a lot of time by not having to pick out jewelry every day and I only clean my earrings a couple of times a year.

In the United States, each person spends an average of $94 per year on jewelry (Bureau of Labor Statistics).

If you feel that you have to wear jewelry, you can always get it for less at local estate auctions or at secondhand stores.

SAVINGS – $94 (don't purchase jewelry); TIME SAVED – 20 HOURS (no need to shop for jewelry, put it on, take it off, or clean it)
FINAL SAVINGS – $594

16. **CLEAN EYEGLASSES WITH YOUR BREATH.** This includes all types of eyewear – eyeglasses, reading glasses, sunglasses, and goggles. Do not purchase cleaner specifically for the job of cleaning your eyewear. Just breathe some hot air onto the surface of the lens and rub clean with a soft shirt that you will probably be wearing – so that is very convenient.

SAVINGS – $6 (use your breath to clean lenses)
TIME SAVED – 15 MINUTES (no need to shop for lens cleaner)
FINAL SAVINGS – $12

17. **PAMPER YOURSELF**, don't pay to be pampered. Why go to a salon to have a manicure, pedicure, or waxing done. If those things are important to you, you can save a bundle by doing them yourself. I personally don't want to pay someone to do personal things such as that to me. However, I do know people who feel special when they have someone else pamper them. It all depends on what is important to you and what you feel is worth spending your money on. I personally would not work for one or two hours just for a half hour of pampering at a salon.

SAVINGS – $600 (do your pampering at home)
TIME SAVED – 12 HOURS (no need to travel to be pampered)
FINAL SAVINGS – $900

18. **SHARPEN YOUR DULL RAZORS.** Instead of throwing your old razors out, sharpen them on an old pair of jeans. You can cut a section of your jeans out and keep it in a bathroom drawer so that it is handy when you need it. Simply take your razor and run it over the

jean material over and over until you feel it is sharpened nicely. You do not want to run the razor towards you as if you were shaving. You want to run the razor away from you in the opposite direction, in a non-cutting motion.

SAVINGS – $40

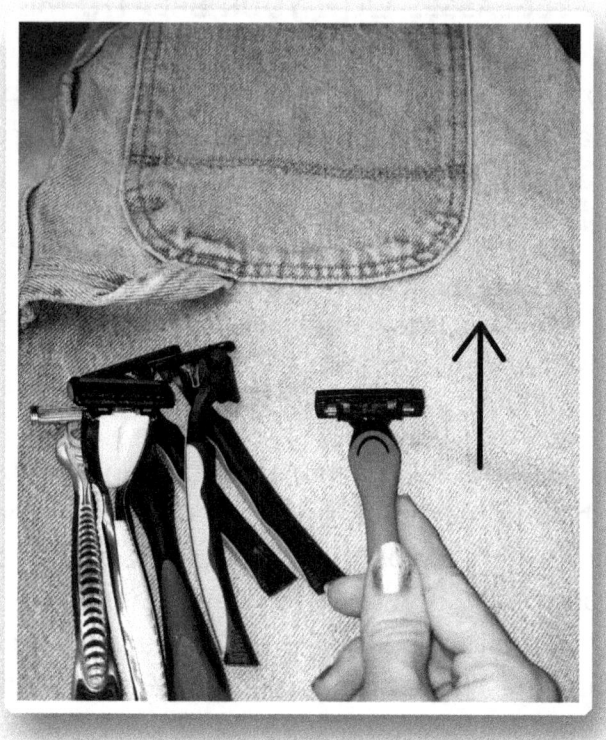

19. **DON'T SHAVE IN THE FALL OR WINTER.** If you are a woman, don't shave your legs in the cold months when you wear pants. It is annoying to have to shave anyway and it saves money of course. This technique probably will only work if you are married or a nun. If you are dating, please don't follow this rule unless the guys that you date don't care about hairy legs. My leg hair is blonde and sparse so I really don't care what my husband thinks, not that he even cares.

I've seen women who have black leg hair and don't shave in the summer. I didn't enjoy looking at it and won't recommend that you go the whole year without shaving. Going half of the year is more acceptable since you can hide it. It's obviously not a classy thing in this day and age to walk around in the summer sporting hair on your legs if you are a woman. Females could get away with this type of thing much better in the beginning ages. Today, we think of ourselves as being more civilized having shaved bodies. How strange is that? I guess you can relate it to doing your hair. Brushing your hair shows that you care about yourself and what others think of you. Shaving your body shows that you are well groomed and meticulous.

For you fellows out there, stop shaving your face in the cold months of the year. Call it your hunting look. You'll look burly and garnish some attention as well. Think of it as a free, winter face mask – an attractive and convenient one at that.

SAVINGS – $35; TIME SAVED – 15 HOURS (no need to shave)
FINAL SAVINGS – $410

20. **AN OILY FACE IS A PRECIOUS RESOURCE.** If you have an oily face, take advantage of it. A lot of women purchase expensive face blotters to get rid of their face oil. Don't waste your oil. Use the back of your hand to blot your face. Then you are at least conditioning your hands which will help produce fewer wrinkles over the years. Do this with the top of your wrist as well – another area that is prone to wrinkle. This will keep your hands looking as youthful as your face. You can rub the back of your fingernails over your face as well. Never touch your face with your fingertips or palms because they are areas that tend to carry germs and bacteria. You don't want a breakout. Having an oily face is not a curse, it is a blessing. You will have fewer wrinkles than your dry-skinned peers because your body produces a natural moisturizer. You can also use your oil as lip balm.

SAVINGS – $25; TIME SAVED – 1 HOUR (no need to purchase paper blotters, creams, or balms)
FINAL SAVINGS – $50

1. **WEAR A UNIFORM.** By wearing a uniform, you can save several minutes a day by not having to pair up a matching outfit. You also don't need to go clothes shopping unless one of your uniform pieces gets damaged. You can save money on your entire yearly wardrobe because you will only need about 5 uniforms in your closet which you can just wash when needed.

It doesn't matter if you don't own a business or even work for anyone. You can make up your own uniform. I don't think I'd dress like an officer on duty though (you might get into a little bit of trouble). You could simply just wear solid colored pants and a professional shirt with no logo (or a made up logo). Just let people assume you are a business person. If your friends inquire as to why you are always dressed the same, just tell them the truth. You wear a uniform so that you never have to think about what to wear and it saves a load of cash which you can then spend doing awesome stuff with them! Yes, this is eccentric, but awesome at the same time! I designed a t-shirt which I wear. On cooler days I just throw a zippered sweatshirt over it. I had a bunch of these t-shirts printed up and even sell them online to make some cash on the side.

SAVINGS – $1,500 (pick out a uniform, purchase it); TIME SAVED – 50 HOURS (no need to shop for clothing, no need to match up outfits)
FINAL SAVINGS – $2,750

2. **RE-WEAR CLOTHES SEVERAL TIMES.** It will save you money and time associated with doing the laundry. If you have not sweated buckets during the day or rolled in mud, by all means re-wear your clothing over and over again before washing them. You will not be disgusting. If you are worried that people will be disgusted by this, don't tell them. If you wear a uniform, nobody will notice anyway. If you have a stylish, well-varied wardrobe, simply switch out pieces by hanging used clothing on the back of your bedroom door. You can just swap to another unwashed outfit so that you don't wear the same look in front of the same person two times in a row during the same week.

Here is how to tell if you can wear a piece of clothing again or if it will need laundered: Does it have any type of odor (besides good fragrance)? Is it stained? If it has a stain, can you do a quick spot clean with a cloth? Obviously, if it stinks or has several stains, wash it.

SAVINGS – $20 (re-wear your clothing several times)
TIME SAVED – 30 HOURS (less laundry, less picking out outfits)
FINAL SAVINGS – $770

3. **SAVE SOCKS FOR SPECIAL OCCASSIONS.** There's nothing I look forward to more than matching socks. Yeah right. So whenever I can, I wear sandals. That way I don't have to worry about washing and matching the little critters. By doing this I save time. I also save money because I don't have to buy socks as often.

By the way, you know how socks seem to go missing? In our house, we have a spare sock drawer. Every now and then we go through the drawer to see if a match showed up and end up saving a few little lives in the process. This is another money savings. There is no use throwing a sock out prematurely. They are usually just stuck inside the sleeve of a shirt somewhere.

SAVINGS – $30 (wear socks only half of the year)
TIME SAVED – 1 ½ HOURS (less laundry, less matching)
FINAL SAVINGS – $63

4. **SAVE OLD SOCKS TO USE AS RAGS**. Save your socks when they get a hole in them. Never buy a cleaning cloth again. Just slip a sock over your hand when you need to polish something. Use socks to apply stain to furniture. I keep a sock slipped right over my furniture stain bottle so that it is always handy when I need it. Wash your car with a sock, dry your car with a sock, or let your kid make a sock puppet. In the olden days, people used to make stuffed animals out of old socks – take sock monkeys for instance. If you scrub something disgusting with an old sock you won't feel guilty throwing it right out because you were going to dispose of it anyway.

SAVINGS – $10; TIME SAVED – 15 MINUTES (no need to buy cleaning cloths)
FINAL SAVINGS – $16

5. **WEAR SHOES UNTIL THEY FALL APART.** My family wears shoes until the soles fall off. We don't need to donate them because there is nothing left of them by the time we are done. I have even glued my soles back on to get another month's use out of a pair.

SAVINGS – $80 (wear shoes until they fall apart)
TIME SAVED – 2 HOURS (no need to shop for new shoes during the year)
FINAL SAVINGS – $130

6. **DON'T BUY NEW PANTS.** If you find your pants getting snug around the waste, do not buy new (unless you are still growing taller of course). It will just give you a reason to get fatter and fatter which could lead to poor health and that could lead to more doctor bills. Plus, buying new clothing because you are gaining weight is money that does not have to be spent. Instead, use the "Troutman Dining Clip" until you can get your pants to fit correctly again by exercising and monitoring your food consumption. The "Troutman Dining Clip" is a device that comes from my childhood (over 25 years ago). My parents have the last name Troutman – they

thought they came up with a great invention when they placed a rubber band through the buttonhole on their pants and looped it around the button to create roomy expansion to add comfort after a large meal while dining out. I'm sure many other people through history have done this as well because several years ago, my parents saw a commercial on television featuring a device that would allow you to expand the waistline of your pants. But a rubber band will do the job. I used one during pregnancy and post pregnancy to expand my pants so that I could wear what I already had instead of purchasing maternity clothing.

SAVINGS – $600 (temporarily expand your pants with a rubber band)
TIME SAVED – 6 HOURS (no need to shop for a new wardrobe if you gain weight, just make sure you lose the weight to fit back into your pants normally)
FINAL SAVINGS – $750

7.   **NEVER BUY LAUNDRY DETERGENT AGAIN,** use a laundry ball. Just pop the *Miracle II Laundry Ball* in your washing machine and let it go to work gently scrubbing your clothing using its 209 spikes. Currently, the ball is only $35 at *miracle2angels.com* (Miracle 2 Angels). You do not have to refill the ball or anything and it can even be used as a body massager (the product claims so). The Miracle II Laundry Ball can last many years – mine is still going strong after many years of use.

SAVINGS – $32 (skip detergent, use a laundry ball)
TIME SAVED – 1 HOUR (no more measuring or shopping for laundry detergent)
FINAL SAVINGS – $57

8.   **USE CHEAP HOTEL SOAP ON CLOTHING STAINS.** It works wonders. So if I stay at a hotel, I save the soap for use at home. Before I place clothing in the washing machine to be washed, I check for stains. If there is a stain, I grab a chunk of the cheap, hotel bar soap, add a little warm water to the stain, and work it all around. I discovered how well hotel bar soap worked while on a vacation twelve

years ago. I got some kind of purple berry stain on my light-colored shirt and thought I was doomed. I resorted to a bar of hotel soap and it worked wonders! Now I always have a glorious piece of hotel bar soap sitting on my washing machine. I use it to get out all kinds of stains – blood, grass, chocolate, and more.

SAVINGS – $10 (don't buy stain removers, use bar soap)

9. **WASH SMART.** According to dailyfinance.com, a load of laundry costs an average of 60 cents to wash if you use the hot wash cycle in combination with the warm rinse cycle. You can get the cost of the cycle down to just 4 cents if you use the cold wash cycle along with the cold rinse cycle (Cheung). I personally like to wash with warm water and then rinse with cold water. I think that warm water gets clothes cleaner, but that hot water can damage and weaken fabrics. When I wash whites, I let the basin fill up a quarter of the way with hot water and then switch to warm for the remainder of the fill, ending everything with a cold rinse. If you completely switch to cold cycle, you can save a good amount per year. The savings shown are assuming that you do about 90 loads of laundry per year.

SAVINGS – $50 (switch to cold/cold cycle)

10. **KISS DRYER SHEETS GOODBYE.** Dryer sheets seem like a dumb idea. Apparently they are used to combat static. I don't care about static. They do not seem worth the expense to me. I do not buy this product. It just seems frivolous. Also, dryer sheets seem to be packed full of chemicals due to the different "fresh" scents available these days.

SAVINGS – $5 (don't use dryer sheets)
TIME SAVED – 1 HOUR (no need to shop for dryer sheets throughout the year)
FINAL SAVINGS – $30

11. **DON'T IRON.** Don't iron clothing, tablecloths, or even curtains. I never iron. I just remove the laundry from the dryer promptly. Drying clothing in the clothes dryer doesn't create wrinkles. You get the wrinkles if you leave them in the dryer for too long once it finishes because the clothing is all bunched up.

I don't bother with line drying. I think it makes clothing stiff. I also think it takes up too much time to hang them. If you dry things outside, they can collect pollen and dust, and the sunshine could harm or lighten the material. A bird could poop on the clothing – and in the winter the clothing might freeze.

TIME SAVED – 52 HOURS (no need to iron)
FINAL SAVINGS – $1,300

1. **SHOP SECONDHAND.** You can stock up on necessities at a fraction of the price if you shop secondhand instead of buying new. Actually, sometimes you can get brand new stuff while shopping secondhand. Acquire things such as clothing at yard sales, thrift stores, consignment shops, and auctions. One of my favorite places to stock up on household supplies is at local auctions. I usually buy up the box lots for a buck. In the past, I have filled my van to the brim with boxes full of goods all for under $5. In those boxes are treasures such as household cleaners, gift wrap, gift boxes, batteries, and more! The fun part is rummaging through the boxes with my family. Anything that we do not need or will not need can be sold or donated. When bidding on items, you must stand close to the auctioneer. Always be alert and be sure to be the first to go a buck. I never like being the one who has to pay two bucks! Sometimes there are box lots that look like complete junk. But take a look at the box. Is it a storage bin made of plastic? Does it have a lid? Storage bins are expensive if you buy them new. Sometimes it pays to bid a dollar on those junk boxes just to get the plastic storage bin. The so-called *junk* inside of the bin can be recycled if it is metal or it can be donated to someone who can use it.

Another place I like to visit is the ***Goodwill Outlet Center***. The one I visit is a hidden treasure in Lancaster, Pennsylvania. My family visits once or twice a year during our vacation travels. There are also other stores scattered across the United States (search for Goodwill outlets easily online at **goodwill.org**). Here is how the store works – you dig through bins that are piled high with donated items (it was overwhelming the first time I entered the store), you fill your cart, you proceed to the register, then they weigh your items. In the end, you pay per pound. The floor even has a scale so that you do not have to take the items out of your cart to have them weighed! It is awesome.

This past trip to the outlet paid for our vacation. I hit the *mother lode*! Did you know that *mother lode* actually refers to where the most amount of gold or precious material can be found in a certain area? It was almost like the mother lode was carted right to me! Okay, it was literally carted to me. I was standing in the store when all of a sudden a huge bin of fresh product was being pushed my way. It was filled with brand new, tagged and untagged artificial flowers! I am known for having a yard full of artificial flowers, so this was right up my alley. Now, I had to practically wrestle some very large ladies just to snatch the mother lode up. I am a waif at just 90 pounds and 4'10" tall. I was there first, but they came swarming in like oversized locusts forcing me to budge out of the way (each one of them being almost 3 times my weight, maybe more). One of the women even strategically blocked my way with a cart. I moved it with a gentle hand and a kind word, even though she did not care for that maneuver. I knew I had to take action fast if I was going to take the mother lode home with me. Every second mattered. I was grabbing everything I could because I could always put it back later. The other women were being picky and that cost them big time.

In the end, I was one happy gal and didn't put one item back. The entire, heaping cart load of product cost me less than $25. I really made out because flowers are light weight. If your cart weighs over 20 pounds, you get each pound for less money. My order came to a little over 19 pounds, so I threw a heavier artificial plant on top of the cart to reach the 20 pound mark saving several extra dollars. Each flower grouping was marked anywhere from $3 to $18.20 and I walked away with 102 artificial flower groupings. I purchased 70 tagged products, the combined priced value totaling $466.34. I also loaded my car with an additional 32 unmarked plants with an estimated value of $213.18. My daughter placed a few toys in the cart including a Barbie and my husband had some trinkets thrown in as well. I put an auto sun shield in the cart because it weighed barely anything and we needed one. It was practically free. The total value of the flowers alone came to $679.52. What a bargain! Remember, I paid less than $25 for the entire cart. By the way, the stores' carts are HUGE! You cannot pass another shopper coming the other way in an isle. That's how big the carts are. So it is hard to maneuver through the isles when treasure hunting. I abandoned my cart several times just to grab a deal since traffic jams tend to occur. So don't ever feel like you have to be tied to your cart, but keep a watchful eye on it. You don't want a vulture to swoop in and take a precious gem while your back is turned. In the end, I sold most of the merchandise even though I LOVE artificial flowers and it ended up paying for our trip!

Hey, I just wanted to let you know that you can find all kinds of clothing sizes at secondhand stores. Real people of all sizes donate the clothes, so if you are looking for an odd size, you might just find it. I am petite and usually have trouble finding just the right clothing in regular stores. When I visit the secondhand stores, I can find my size easily. Clothing has already been tailored and hemmed. I like that I don't have to hem my pants because some other short person already had it done for me. Another great thing is that if I don't like the style of the season, the secondhand stores will have styles from past seasons which had styles that I did like. The whole situation rocks!

Many years ago I purchased a great quality, hip looking winter coat in my favorite color at the Goodwill for $6. I have worn it for over 10 years now. Just think if I had purchased a new coat every year at full price. I probably saved $500 to $1000 dollars by purchasing used and sticking with what I've got until it wears out.

SAVINGS – $1,300 (shop secondhand for clothing and supplies); EARNINGS – $400 (sell unwanted items from auction dollar boxes and bargain bins)
FINAL SAVINGS – $1,700

2. **BARTERING IS COOL.** – *Listia* is a great site where you can give and get free stuff. On this site, you give away what you don't want and pick up some great things that you need. You can list something, people can bid on your auction using their points, you supply the item (ship it, allow pickup, or deliver electronically), and then you get points to spend. For example, you could give away some unwanted clothing in return for some toys for your children. Check out *listia.com*. I have found them to be a great community of people.

Keep in mind that bartering is typically reported to the IRS using form 1040, Schedule C if it is considered business income. This probably will not pertain to you, but I am not a tax expert. You are to report the fair market value of the items that you receive if it is of a commercial basis. According to the IRS, the term barter exchange "does not include arrangements that provide solely for the informal exchange of similar services on a noncommercial basis" (IRS). I would assume that most people using Listia are not doing so for commercial purposes. It is more like a huge yard sale. This is information that I have learned. For more detailed information, you may visit *irs.gov*.

SAVINGS – $100 (barter instead of shop)

3. **SHOP AT WALMART.** I always thought it was best to shop at secondhand stores, consignment stores, yard sales, flea markets, and similar places. However, yesterday when I was shopping for

shoes and lunch boxes I made a discovery. I went to the thrift store and found a pair of shoes that were new and would fit my son. However, they were not a name brand that I knew of and were priced at $15.99 (also, they were my son's least favorite color). Additionally, I found a used lunch box for $5.99, but it was not large enough and was a solid color (just boring). **WalMart** was right next door, so I thought I would give it a shot. I don't usually shop there. I found a pair of sneakers in my son's favorite color for only $5.00 on clearance. They were Avia brand. I'm not sure I've heard of that brand before either, but they were a good quality for my ten year old. Then I found a lunch box for my son in his favorite colors! It was brand new, not used, less than the price at the thrift store, and had a cool, retro design to it. WalMart saved the day and beat out the secondhand store!

SAVINGS – $400 (shop WalMart instead of high-priced stores)

4. **SHOP THE CLEARANCE SECTIONS.** You can find extreme bargains in the clearance section at stores like the Gap, Crazy 8, Gymboree, Boscov's, and more. Just this past weekend I visited *Toys "R" Us* and picked up items for 95% off in their clearance bins. The deals were just out of this world! From memory, cell phone cases were just ten cents after the discount. I bought my daughter fancy packs of Novi Star doll clothes for just 40 cents each. When I checked out, I used a $5 birthday coupon. My total came to 65 cents and the receipt declared, "YOU SAVED $32.51". Included on that receipt were also a *Klondike Choco Taco* ice cream treat and a *Giant Ice Cream Sandwich*. You can't get much better than free ice cream. Yum!

SAVINGS – $500 (shop clearance sections)

5. **SHOP AT THE END OF EACH SEASON.** You can save 75% or more if you stock up at the end of each season on things like bathing suits, Christmas trees, winter coats, clothing, swimming pools,

and more. In this case, you would most likely be buying ahead of time for the next year. I do this for my children's clothing purchasing it one size larger than currently needed. We purchased a fancy, flocked, Christmas tree at 95% off at an end of season sale. It was a $260 tree that we got for $13 (it even came set up and lit with lights and was hauled out of the store for us by an employee). We will never need to buy a tree again. Think of the savings! Artificial trees purchased on clearance are a great choice because of the savings. You also won't be bringing pests or allergens associated with real evergreen trees into your home; and you don't have to kill a tree.

Here is a list of items that I shop for in specific months because they appear to be at the best bargain price at that time. I shop a year in advance for many items:

January – Christmas items, holiday decorations, toys, bedding, flooring, movies, exercise equipment, video games
February – winter clothing, coats, indoor furniture, home renovations, chocolates (after Valentine's Day)
March – humidifiers, small electronics, televisions, winter sports gear
April – computers, digital cameras, snow blowers, cruises, sneakers
May – spring clothing, cordless phones, mattresses, athletic apparel, camping gear
June – dishware, pots, pans, summer sports gear, tools, gym memberships
July – swimsuits, video cameras
August – summer clothing, air conditioners, backpacks, outdoor furniture, office items
September – dehumidifiers, outdoor plants, bushes, trees
October – bicycles, gas grills, lawn mowers, school supplies
November – fall clothing, costumes, baby items, GPS navigation devices, toys, wedding dresses, frozen turkeys
December – home appliances, houses, champagne

SAVINGS – $750 (shop ahead at the end of each season)

6. **STOCK UP WHEN THE PRICE IS RIGHT.** When you see an item at an unbelievable price, load up your cart. Stock up on things like toilet paper and cereal. Cereal has a very long code most of the time. If you see a name brand cereal that you really like and it is priced for $2 or less in the 2nd decade of the 21st century, snatch up a bunch of boxes! You will always have it on hand and will save time having to buy it again in the future. To you people of the future, I'm sure you know what a good deal is when you see one. So, use your own judgment when deciding if something is worthy of stockpiling or not.

SAVINGS – $104; TIME SAVED – 3 HOURS (you stocked up, no need to shop)
FINAL SAVINGS – $179

7. **FIX THINGS OR LEARN TO ADAPT** – instead of shopping for new. For example, my camera latch won't stay latched anymore as of about two years ago. I could buy a new camera, but instead I opt to live with it. I just let it flap open when it wants. I could tape the latch down or just rip it off completely and leave the battery and SD card exposed for easy access. There are so many options.

You can repair many items instead of buying new. Repair clothing with a needle and thread. I am loaded with supplies such as this thanks to yard sale free boxes and dollar boxes at auction. Make sure to save buttons off of old clothes in case you lose a button off of a newer piece that you really like.

I recently fixed my couch. My kids jumped on it too much and broke a board. I used spare parts that came with a childproof gate to fix the broken board. It saved the couch and took only a few minutes of time. I fixed my heirloom dining room chair with some *Gorilla Glue*. A section of wood had broken. I glued it back together, tied some rubber bands real tight around the area that was glued, and then used a bit of brown paint to blend the repaired area. It only takes a few minutes for these types of fixes. I think the chair took me about 15 minutes to repair (if that). It beats buying a whole new set of matching chairs for my dining room suite. The hard part is deciding to start the job. At least that is the difficult part for me. What you could do right now is throw yourself a fix-it party and bask in the savings!

Keep glues of all kinds in your house. Two part epoxy, fabric glue, wood glue, hot glue, and more. I even have parachute glue on hand. That's good for lots of different projects. If you have the sole of a shoe fall off which seems to happen with shoes these days, just glue it back on instead of buying a new pair. You can squeeze a lot more life out of them with the help of a little glue.

If a zipper pull breaks off of a bag, coat, or pants; simply add a paperclip so that you have something to grab when zippering things up. There is no need to discard of an item due to a broken off zipper pull.

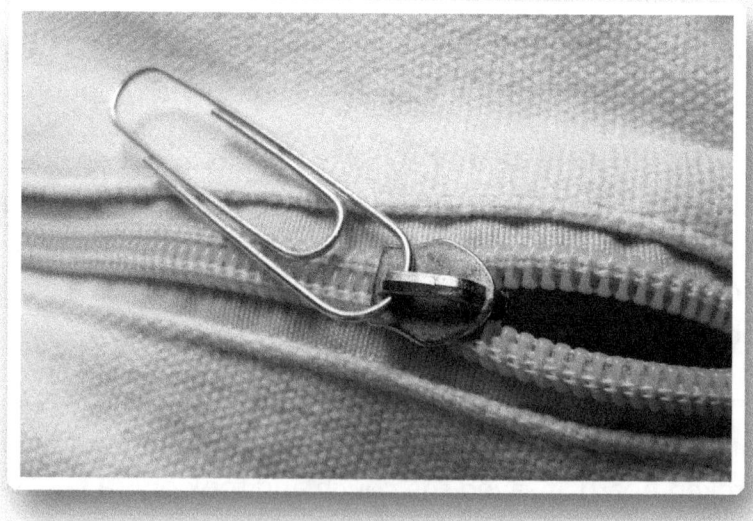

If all else fails, learn to adapt (this is covered in the next tip). For example, the scrolling wheel on my mouse stopped working about a year ago. I didn't purchase a new mouse; I just stopped using the wheel on mine and opted to use the scrolling bars on my screen instead. It took a little getting used to, but adds to my improvising skill set. I adapted for a few days, now it is second nature.

SAVINGS – $1,500; TIME INVOLVED – 1 HOUR (repair at least 4 damaged items)
TIME SAVED – 2 HOURS (no need to shop for new items)
FINAL SAVINGS – $1,525

8. **DEAL WITH DAMAGE IN CREATIVE WAYS.** If an object gets damaged and you don't know how to repair it, then work with what you've got. For instance, my husband and I received a carpet cleaner as a wedding gift eleven years ago. Not too long after, it stopped spraying water and soap mixture out. That function simply would no longer work. I continue to use the carpet cleaner, but simply spray the cleaning solution by hand using a squirt bottle. In fact, I don't even purchase the expensive cleaning mixture anymore. I simply use dishwashing liquid mixed with hot water. The suction function works magically, so I can't see throwing away a device simply because one function does not work. My arms get a good workout from squeezing the bottle so much – free exercise. If there is a stubborn stain such as chocolate on carpeting, I wet it with the hot mixture, then rub cheap white bar soap over the spot. Then I let the machine do its job.

Other items that I have continued to use in a state of repair over the years include things such as my refrigerator, microwave, and toilet. My old refrigerator lights burnt out and I couldn't remove them because they corroded into place for some reason. I just left them and used the fridge with no lights. You could purposely place burnt out bulbs in your fridge to save electricity leaving just one for light if needed. When I shopped for a new refrigerator, I purposely bought one that had the least amount of lights. It was much cheaper than the upgraded model that had many lights and I love saving time not having to replace a bunch of bulbs. On our households' microwave, the digital display stopped working many years ago. We press clear and enter the numbers blindly. It's not a big deal. Finally, our toilet doesn't flush well. We barely flush it anyway, so it doesn't pose much of a problem.

Here is another way to make due. Let's say your water bed bursts. Simply move into your child's bottom bunk or start sleeping on the floor. Now that's a technique for the die-hard cheapskates out there. Hey man, back in the olden days whole families used to share a bed. Actually, in many parts of the world they still do. I've slept in my kids' bunk beds, on the floor, on the couch, on a cot – you name it. And I didn't just sleep in these places for a day; it was prolonged lengths of time. I don't always sleep in odd places to save money; I have also done it out of convenience. For example, one time I wanted to take my time remodeling my bedroom, so I simply slept elsewhere in the house.

SAVINGS – $130 (think of other ways of doing things); TIME SAVED – 1 ½ HOURS (no need to shop for replacement item or dispose of broken item)
FINAL SAVINGS – $168

9. **DON'T BUY A TOMBSTONE** – make one. Tombstones are expensive. You can make a tombstone for yourself or another family member by first constructing the shape out of wood and nails. Some home improvement stores such as Lowe's will even cut the wood for you if you purchase the wood at their store. If available, I prefer to use scrap materials that I already have. Cover your shape with metal lath (wire mesh). Secure with some cable staples. Cover the surface with mortar. Before the mortar sets, use craft stamps to stamp your inscription! You could even just use a pencil to poke in the shape of the letters that you desire. Get as fancy as you want. It's not like you are paying per letter. The supplies are cheap enough, so you can make your tombstone any size and shape that you want (just be sure you are able to move it when you are done). Check out the tombstone that I started to construct for myself. It's about 7 feet high and looks similar to an Easter Island head symbolizing adventure and mystery! A tombstone this large and elaborate would have cost me well over $2000. I actually think

I am going to be cremated, so I'll probably convert this tombstone into a miniature golf course obstacle where you have to get the ball through a pipe in the base of the head. Right now I have it sitting along a trail in the woods as a visitor attraction.

SAVINGS – $900; TIME INVOLVED – 4 HOURS (sketch/plan, get supplies, construct tombstone); TIME SAVED – 2 HOURS (no need to shop for a tombstone)
FINAL SAVINGS – $850

10. **BURY LOVED ONES ONLINE.** I was sitting in a restaurant one Sunday with my family when the subject came up about my deceased grandmother. My grandmother had been cremated, but never buried in our family plot. The conversation quickly turned to laughter when I mentioned that I create a "virtual cemetery" online. I exclaimed, "We don't have to bury Grandma – I'll make a virtual graveyard!" Well, I made sure that the idea didn't get swept under the carpet. I just recently completed the website and now anyone can create a personalized resting place, a place of homage for a loved one at a very low cost online. A plot can be visited and updated anytime, anywhere – without the need to travel. You can even bury a beloved pet on the website. At *EasyPlots.com* you can pick out a stone, have it placed in a cemetery of your choice, decorate the plot with flowers, pinwheels, and more (you can even see who added the decorations and on what date). I even added the option to add photographs to the personal plot page. It's literally a virtual burial site and memory book in one. I found the idea to be quite unique and from my research, the first of its kind. Who knows, maybe it will catch on! This is the first that I am advertising my business to the masses (right here nestled within the pages of this book).

NBC News reports that "Cremation is cheaper than burial. The average cost of a funeral today is about $6,500, including the typical $2,000-or-more cost of a casket. Add a burial vault, and the average jumps to around $7,700. A cremation, by contrast, typically costs a third of those amounts, or less" (Mathisen). If you opt to go with cremation and go with a virtual service online instead of a live service, the costs go down even more significantly. With a virtual service, guests do not have to travel. They can attend from the convenience of their own home. Going the virtual route insures that a tombstone or plot will not deteriorate with time. Everything stays sparkling clean! You can avoid fees for the funeral director services, casket, cemetery, and church/chapel. All around, a virtual burial is great alternative to consider with options as low as $12 at *EasyPlots.com*.

SAVINGS – $4,500; TIME INVOLVED – 15 MINUTES (purchase an online plot and tombstone); TIME SAVED – 3 HOURS (you can do everything quickly online)
FINAL SAVINGS – $4,569

11. **USE COUPONS, SNAG DEALS, AND EAT CHEAP.** My family enjoys our tradition we call "Burrito Night". Every Wednesday, I gather up our free coupons and deep discount coupons; and we head out to the shopping strip. We usually start with dinner at Taco Bell. (It's been my favorite restaurant since the age of 7 when I first discovered it.) They have a great dollar menu right now! My whole family can walk away with satisfied stomachs for just $4 and change (we do not overeat and we always order tap water). Never underestimate the power of ordering from the dollar menu and consuming free tap water.

After that, we head next door to the proclaimed, largest thrift store in America. At 74,000 square feet, it is not hard to believe that it is the biggest (Krize). There are bins and bins of toys, rack after rack of clothing, shoes, and shelves full of household goods. Oh, you might be wondering why we choose Wednesday to be "Burrito Night". Wednesday is 50% off family day at the thrift store. That is pretty exciting because you get 50% off of already low prices. Last night I spent $11.61 at the thrift store and walked away with a pair of dress pants for my husband, 6 pairs of shorts plus 1 shirt for my daughter, a shirt for myself, and a large grab-bag of toys. All of the clothing that we purchased was stylish and in great condition. Oh, I also got a vintage, local branded mug for my dad's private collection.

Next, we use up any free or deep discount retail store coupons that I received in the mail or through email. If I have multiple of the same coupon and it is one per customer, I have each family member stand in line with one. This might annoy the staff. So whenever I can, I have us break up and go to two different registers. They should be glad we only have two children. Just think if we were that TV family with 19 kids and counting.

We wrap up our shopping extravaganza by heading to the grocery store. My husband and I each get a cart and use our separate club cards to double up on all of the week's deals. What is really nice is that while we shop, we are also saving on gas for our vehicles by using our store rewards cards. After completing checkout, the bottom of the receipt shows our savings. Last night I saved 54%. My husband saved 65% and we barely put forth an effort. We don't clip coupons for hours like some people. We spend a minute just clipping the front page coupons from our local flyer and pick up any deals we like that are flaunted in the flyer. We don't like the headaches of clipping. Though we like to get the biggest discount possible, we only want to purchase items we really need. Our goal isn't to beat some record boasting that our bill only came to 50 cents. Using a lot of coupons almost always causes holdups at the register. I enjoy purchasing items with instant savings attached (no hassles). Spending a lot of time rooting through coupon flyers isn't worth the trouble in my opinion. We are simply overjoyed when we snag a 50% savings on 2 carts full of goods that we *wanted*, *needed*, and *enjoy* (not items we purchased just because they were a deal); all the while investing only a few minutes of effort.

SAVINGS – $400/PERSON (snag deals, use coupons, eat cheap)

12. **REWARDS CARDS** and credit cards are great. Make sure you are not the only one in your family signed up for store rewards. Have every adult and kids (if applicable) sign up for a rewards card so that you can get the amount your family deserves. Everybody should get a birthday reward (if it is offered). You can visit the actual location to sign up or many times you can complete the process easily online.

One thing I never have to buy for myself is underwear. I get free underwear at a particular store just for having their store card. I even had my husband sign up for a card so that I would get double underwear (he gives them to me). I have so many pairs of new underwear that I am saving some of them for my daughter when she grows big enough. I hope the elastic holds up in the test of time! I suppose it will if I store them in a regulated environment (not in the attic).

SAVINGS – $500; TIME INVOLVED – 1 HOUR (sign up and take advantage of rewards cards)

13. **SAVE AT THE REGISTER.** Whenever you are standing in line getting ready to make a purchase at a store register, check out the signage on the counter. Look for deals that you can get right now.

I was recently in a brand name clothing outlet looking for the counter deal. I thought the clothing was over-priced, but my daughter really likes the brand and we don't buy secondhand socks or underwear. In my opinion, that would be creepy to wear pre-used intimates. But believe it or not, many secondhand stores sell personal items such as that. We decided to shop at a clothing outlet on vacation because she was ready for the next size up. Anyway, there happened to be a deal where you could get 10% off your order by texting the store. Well luckily, I just got pushed into an unlimited texting plan (before that, I was text free). So I went to get my phone out, but when I opened my purse, my phone was not there. My son had snatched it out of my purse for some gaming action and he was waiting in the car with my husband. So, I asked if I could run to my car real quick. I ran back in with my phone quickly since I was parked just outside the front door and I proceeded to complete the text. This automatically enrolled me in texting where I would receive about 6 texts a month from the store (that could get annoying). I received the discount and immediately texted "STOP" so that I would not continue to receive texts on a weekly basis. I figure I'll try enrolling again next time we have to shop at the store to see if I can get another 10% off since I already unenrolled.

I'm not a fan of gimmicks such as store club cards, reward cards, coupons, and the like. I think it is a waste of everyone's time and that all stores should offer everyone the true price at all times. With my business, I keep prices as low as I can for all customers. Like I said, I think the whole process of having to complete an offer or bring a club card to a store is a waste of everyone's time. It just causes more work and more expense.

SAVINGS – $75; TIME INVOLVED – 15 MINUTES (sign up for offers at the register)
FINAL SAVINGS – $69

14. **DO NOT BUY WARRANTIES.** I have never purchased a warranty and I feel great about it. Don't you just love it when you are buying a new gadget and they ask if you want the extended warranty plan? I always say, "I am my own warranty" or "I'll take the chance". I don't regret it. The chances of having to use a warranty are slim. If you purchased a warranty plan for every item that offers one, think of how much money you would be out! Plus, you don't need to organize paperwork or keep track of all of those plans if you avoid them altogether.

SAVINGS – $300 (don't sign up for warranties)
TIME SAVED – 3 HOURS (no need to sign up or organize paperwork)
FINAL SAVINGS – $375

15. **DITCH DIGITAL ITEMS.** It can be tough to find replacement parts for digital gadgets when they break. They are constantly being updated or discontinued. When possible, I opt to go with old-fashioned devices that get the job done without electricity or batteries. I own a cuckoo clock (got it for $5 at auction) and a grandfather clock (free from grandma) that both keep time just beautifully! I don't have to pay for electric or batteries. If something needs repair, I trust myself to solve the problem with a little glue, oiling, or tinkering. One time, our cuckoo clock fell off of the wall because I didn't use a large enough nail when hanging it. Even though the clock broke, I was able to repair it myself in about twenty minutes; and to this day, it still keeps accurate time.

Sometimes by going the old-fashioned route, you can save money. There is no need to upgrade to new products just because an item is outdated. These days outdated could mean a matter of one year. A friend of mine has one of those high tech cell phones that are on the market, but the battery won't keep a charge. The company that designed the phone made it that the batteries were not user-re-placeable. So my friend is forced to purchase a new phone, upgrade, or have the phone unavailable for days to weeks while an authorized person replaces the battery (which is costly). I told her that maybe she could downgrade to the model before her phone for only 99 cents (it's the model I have). I saw it on sale this weekend. She said she only moves forward and acted like this was a ghastly idea. I don't know what she is thinking because I'm happy with my phone and consider it to be awesome. But my friend won't take a step backward and because of that, it is almost certain that she will end up shelling out hundreds of dollars for the next best phone as she doesn't want to send her current phone away for a long stretch of time. She has no back up form of communication such as a landline.

My family went out last week to upgrade my husband's flip phone (battery was shot). The entire process took hours. One store had us run to another store because they were missing a part in the box and so on and so forth. The company representative said that our plan was ancient and that a new plan could actually save us money. In the end, the new plan that we signed up for was actually more expensive. We had already signed though. Before we signed the pa-per, I had asked if the price included hidden fees and taxes. The rep-resentative either pulled one over on us or doesn't know his stuff. It looks like we got stuck in another 2 year plan. I have to say I am peeved. When my contract is up, I may just revert to CB's. If you don't know what a CB is (Citizen Band Radio), I will tell you. When I was a kid, truckers and even my parents used the devices to talk to each other for free during road trips. They were cool. Everyone had a han-dle (a nickname) that they went by. Ah, the good old days.

SAVINGS – $300 (be old-fashioned)
TIME SAVED – 3 HOURS (skip dealing with upgrades and new purchases)
FINAL SAVINGS – $375

16. **BUY REFILLS!** If you purchase large refills for products such as soaps, detergents, and cleaners instead of purchasing another small bottle, you can save a buck here, a buck there – adding up to bigger savings each year.

SAVINGS – $25 (purchase refills for products)
TIME SAVED – 1 HOUR (no need to shop as often throughout the year)
FINAL SAVINGS – $50

17. **GET GENERIC.** I usually just go with the generic store brands when I shop for food and household supplies because they are cheaper and I don't notice much of a difference in taste or quality. In fact, I like store quality cheese better than the name brand cheeses! This savings can apply to many products including soaps, cereals, snacks, medicine, and more. Do you know what makes fancy shampoo expensive? Often times it is the fragrance in the product. The shampoo itself cleans about as well as a generic shampoo.

SAVINGS – $1,500 (purchase generic brands)

18. **THROW TRASH BACK WHERE IT CAME FROM.** Whenever possible, get rid of garbage at the source. Let's say you eat at a fast food restaurant. Be sure to throw out all of your trash using their garbage can and don't take any with you. That way you do not have to pay for the garbage removal. If you go through the drive through and eat on the road, then throw the trash out the next time you pay a visit. I wonder if this works the same way with grocery stores. If you buy a gallon of milk there, can you throw the jug away in their trash can later on? Hmmm . . . something about that seems very strange, but not illegal. Everyone is cool if you buy a drink or candy bar from the store and throw the wrapper or container in their trash, but a large amount of items would surely attract attention. If you buy a hunk of hamburger meat, do you think you should throw the bloody tray and wrapper in their gar-

bage can when you are through with it? Uh, it seems like more of a hassle than it is worth. When I buy clothing, I tear the tags off and throw them in the garbage when I get outside of the store. I always try on clothing before I buy it so there is no need for me to keep the tags. Junk mail is harder to deal with. However, you can return some items back to the sender using the enclosed return envelope. If you don't open the junk mail, you can write "Return to Sender" on the envelope and stick it in your mailbox. The postal carrier will return it at no cost to you. In return, the company who sent the junk mail to you will probably remove you from their mailing list. However, I like junk mail because I use the mail as paper for taking notes in my home and office. It is useful to me. All in all, the less garbage you have to deal with the better. It saves a few dollars throughout the year.

SAVINGS – $24 (throw garbage out at the source)

19. **MAKE GOOD USE OF YOUR OLD CELL PHONE.** My children enjoy playing on my cell phone so much that I plan to get a new phone this spring even though I don't need an upgrade. I have two kids and they are constantly fighting over who gets to play on the phone. If I get a new phone which is free or almost free with my plan, then I will have two phones and my kids will no longer fight. The cost of a phone upgrade is way cheaper in my situation than purchasing a handheld game system. Both of my kids want iPods like their friends, but I tell them that my iPhone is basically the same thing – seriously. Currently, I can get one for 99 cents plus a few dollars in fees when I am due for an upgrade. I'm not going to pay a couple hundred dollars for an iPod when I can just disable the calling features on my old phone and hand the device to my children.

There are many other uses for old cell phones. My husband uses his old flip phone as a camera and also as an alarm clock in the bedroom. I use mine as a calculator. It even has an advanced, scientific calculator function. So if one of my kids needs it for math class in high school, I won't need to purchase one of those fancy calculators at the store. You can even use your old phone as a flashlight. I can't tell you how many times I have made my way to bed using my phone as a flashlight and then set my alarm on it before dozing off for the night.

If you want to get a little more advanced, there is so much more that you can do with an old smartphone. Check out the latest apps that will allow you to use your phone as a baby monitor, GPS unit, or home surveillance system. **Presence** is an app that I use to monitor my home when I am away. I can do this because I have WiFi in my home. If motion is detected, I will receive a short video of the motion via email. It is so cool and I downloaded the app for free. If you want free GPS capability, you can use an app called **TeleNav**. Simply download your travel route at a free WiFi location and then be on your merry way. There is no need to have connection during your actual travel. I've done this when hunting for geocache treasures. I didn't want to add to any usage on my data plan. So I turned data roaming off on my phone and used a free app to lead the way.

SAVINGS – $850 (use your old phone as a game system, scientific calculator, flashlight, alarm clock, camera, GPS unit, and home surveillance system)

20. **DO NOT GET A CREDIT CARD PROTECTION PLAN.** When I first met my husband, I was surprised to find out that he was paying a monthly fee for credit card protection services. I told him that he would never need them. That it was a complete waste. I asked him why he had the service and he didn't even know why. The representative on the other end of the phone that signed him up for the card talked him into it. Month after month, money just went down the drain. These plans are there to help people if they are injured or laid off of work and are not able to make their credit card payments. Basically the service will protect your credit, but not under all circumstances. Read the fine print. What really

didn't make sense is that my husband was keeping a zero balance anyway, so he didn't even need the service. It only protected him if he carried a balance. He actually thought it was protecting him if someone would hack and use his credit card without him knowing. In my history of credit card use, I have always been protected against this sort of thing automatically. You should not have to pay extra.

SAVINGS – $120 (do not sign up for a protection plan)

21. **DO NOT PURCHASE LIFE INSURANCE.** I had my husband cancel his life insurance policy when I first met him. I just don't feel comfortable with it. It feels much safer to care for my own money. If you just set aside the money each year that you would have put into life insurance, you could invest it yourself in better ways. I feel very confident that I will have more in the end handling the money myself than if I had put it into a life insurance policy. Plus, I can access my money any time I want without a penalty. Life insurance is there so that debt can be paid off if you pass away. It's there to help your family get by if they no longer have your income to depend on. Life insurance can cover your mortgage so that other family members do not suffer if you would leave them with your debt. Dude, you shouldn't have debt to begin with and you should have some cash stowed away for backup! Instead of putting your money into life insurance policies, put the money towards paying off your debt and then never again should you buy something that you can't afford.

If you purchase a standard term life insurance policy and live until a ripe old age, then you will see no return whatsoever on your money. You could have made interest on that money by investing it elsewhere. Yikes! If you get one of those twenty year term plans and live another twenty years . . . guess what? The same thing applies! That's a real eye-opener. Like I stated before, put the money aside, let it collect interest, and save it for an emergency.

Now, there are other life insurance policies that you can buy that offer some sort of return. But you have to pay a bit more each month and I'm certain that the money could be invested in much better ways. I think these types of policies are designed to make people feel better like their money is not being wasted.

One more thing to factor in when considering life insurance is inflation. So the money you put into the policy will most likely be worth less when it comes out than when you put the money in. For all of these reasons stated, I am staying away from life insurance. I'll make my own policy called my bank account.

SAVINGS – $350; TIME SAVED – 1 HOUR (no need to sign up for a policy or pay the bill each month)
FINAL SAVINGS – $375

22. **USE RECHARGEABLE BATTERIES.** Always have a battery when you need one by keeping rechargeable batteries on hand. It is very convenient. You don't need to waste time running to the store when you run out. Plus, you don't have to worry about battery disposal.

Trent from The Simple Dollar did a study and found that rechargeable batteries really are more cost effective than regular batteries. Trent used a device called a ***Kill-A-Watt*** to measure how much electricity is used when charging batteries using a charger. When figuring the yearly savings, the initial cost of batteries was factored in (Trent). The annual savings is shown below.

SAVINGS – $77; TIME SAVED – 2 HOURS (no need to purchase batteries)
1ST YEAR'S FINAL SAVINGS – $0; **2ND YEAR** – $56; **FUTURE YEARS** – $127

23. **BECOME A MYSTERY SHOPPER.** Get paid to shop and go on adventures; and/or receive discounts on lots of things including vacations in return for your feedback. If being an undercover detective sounds exciting, then this is for you. I have to admit that being a

secret shopper takes guts. Sometimes I have to pretend interested in something when I'm really not. I only do this type of undercover work for monetary payment. As a bonus, I usually walk away having learned something new. If a job only reimburses for making a purchase and does not offer payment by check, then I make sure I like the item or adventure before agreeing to it. A lot of the assignments are not glamorous. But if you are going on a vacation, you can pick up jobs right along your travel route. The reviews that you complete can literally pay for your vacation. You can sign up to be a secret shopper at *secretshopper.com*. Keep in mind that if you make money being a mystery shopper, this is reported to the IRS for amounts over $600. You are considered an independent contractor and would receive a 1099 in the mail in January to be used for tax purposes. For this reason, they will ask for your social security number when you sign up.

There are certain dates that new shopping assignments are made available. You will want to be one of the first to snatch up the best jobs, so keep an eye on the *next release* section of the Secret Shopper website. Please note that you can make more money than listed in my calculation. My scenario does not bank on someone doing this for a living and takes into account that the person reading this book is probably completing most of the tips and will not have time to do just one tip full time. But if it is something that you enjoy, go for it! I base the calculations partly on my own lifestyle to see what is reasonable and can be expected.

SAVINGS – $200; TIME INVOLVED – 5 HOURS (investigate assignments along your travel routes); EARNINGS – $150 (payment by check)
FINAL SAVINGS – $225

24. **GET A TATTOO STAMP MADE.** Instead of getting a real tattoo that will fade and become smudgy over time, opt to go a less permanent route. Order a custom stamp from **StampsByDesign.com**. Then stamp it right onto your body using body ink. Complete a search online to find places that carry temporary tattoo ink pads. When I

shop for temporary ink, I find it available at **WalMart** and **Staples**, among other places. You'll never have to worry about paying for a removal procedure if you grow tired of your design and think of all the pain that will be avoided. You'll also save a bundle of cash. Stamps by Design can even make several stamps so that you can stamp multiple colors for a flashy tattoo. Oh no! Don't you like the color? That's okay, just switch ink pads and you're good to go. You can submit your own design to **Stamps by Design** or have a tattoo designed for you. Simply email your art or idea to **stampsbydesign@verizon.net**.

SAVINGS – $300 (order a stamp instead of getting a real tattoo)

25. **SHOP SMART WHEN PURCHASING TOWEL SETS.** Did you ever notice that towels are reasonably priced? But where the stores really get ya is on the hand towels and washcloths. I randomly checked out some pricing and found a collection where the towel was priced at $25, the hand towel was $19, and the washcloths were each $12. I do not even use washcloths, but I might have guests 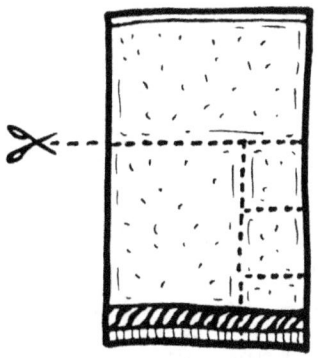 who do. So, here is what you can do. Purchase an extra towel and cut it into 2 hand towels and 3 washcloths in order to save $49. Or you can cut the extra towel into 1 hand towel and 9 washcloths saving yourself $102. If there is a special pattern on the towel take note of it when cutting your new accessories. Your hand towel can still have the matching border. So can one of your washcloths. Check out my diagram. Instead of making an extra hand towel, the top part of the towel which is plain with no pattern could be used as a matching bathroom floor mat. The edges of your new pieces can be finished off using a sewing machine set on the zigzag stitch using matching thread.

SAVINGS – $76; TIME INVOLVED – 30 MINUTES (cut towel, sew edges)
FINAL SAVINGS – $63

26. **RETURN UNWANTED ITEMS.** I know so many people who are either too lazy or too shy to return an item. If an item is defective, doesn't fit, or lacks quality, then return it. It's really not that hard to do. When you are running another errand, simply bring the item with you along with the receipt. Often times you do not even need a receipt and you can just get store credit for the item or do an even exchange.

One time I bought a pair of pants for my son. I splurged on a nice, new pair. I think I spent $15 to $20 using my percent off coupon. Ha, I know that is really not that much money, but I'm used to spending $1.50 on a pair of pants at the thrift store. Anyway, he fell on our smooth laminate, wood floor and the pants literally melted like burnt plastic. They looked hideous! He only got a half of a day's wear out of them. A regular pair of pants would have held up in this situation. Seriously, my kids are always crawling around on the floor, being goofy, and their pants hold up for quite some time. I thought it was a long shot to return them, but the store let me choose another brand for the exchange. I was told that I wasn't the first customer to bring this product back to the store. I checked the tag and made sure to never buy that material again. Darn you Polyester!

Get it? It's a pun . . . you can *darn* material. Darn – to sew, stitch, repair, or mend. Okay, you probably already knew the meaning. I'm wasting your time and that's not very nice. Onto the next tip we go! Hoorah!

SAVINGS – $100 (return items to store)

27. **TALK THE PRICE DOWN ON ITEMS.** If you go to a flea market, always offer less than the price on the item. They almost always will go lower. Believe me . . . they are desperate. I tried to run

a flea market booth one time and the cost of the booth was so high, it was almost impossible to get my money back. Ugh, poor booth tenders. They need to do something else with their time. I took notice that the flea market big wig drives a fancy car while the poor booth tenders suffer.

Don't stop there! You can get discounts at more places than just flea markets. I have a home business that does shipping with FedEx. I asked my advisor for cheaper shipping rates and he gave them to me and asked me to sign. I asked if he could go any lower and to my surprise – he did. It will save me hundreds per year and only took me a minute to ask. Now that is a minute well spent. You can try this tactic at yard sales, auctions, buying cars, houses, when getting labor estimates, and when signing business contracts. If you take just one minute to squeeze a couple of dollars out here and there, it adds up to something substantial over the course of a year.

I received a generous refund on our Disney vacation because I was displeased with many aspects of it. Our adventure started with me stepping on a piece of glass in the hotel room and cutting my foot. Then we got on a shuttle to go to one of the parks and got stuck on it for an hour or so. I don't remember the exact reason why, but their system was hard to understand. I think we almost missed breakfast because of it. Then one of the ride staff crinkled our family photograph that we just had taken while dining at the castle and we had to wait a considerable amount of time to get a new one. Several of the rides we wanted to go on were closed including the one we were most excited about. A bunch of rides at the water park were closed because of water conservation issues. We waited in line for several hours at one ride just to have it close down when we got to the front. There was a bunch of other stuff that went wrong, but it was an adventure of a lifetime. After a several calls and a very long letter, I received a nice, partial refund for our troubles.

SAVINGS – $1,090; TIME INVOLVED – 5 MINUTES (ask if companies or individuals can do any better on the price of products or services)
FINAL SAVINGS – $1,088

28. **RESEARCH BEFORE YOU BUY.** If you see something in a store, don't buy it right away. Use your phone to look up the price online to see if it is fair. If you don't have the capability to research in the store, look things up when you get home. You can always purchase the item the next time you run errands. Many times, store prices are higher than online prices. I usually end up ordering online, especially if my son wants a video game. I usually use *eBay* to buy the game for him. He might not like to wait for it to come in the mail, but patience is a good quality and it pays off. If you have a large purchase to make, you have the opportunity to save even more money.

I've noticed that some stores offer items cheaper online. You don't even have to wait to get the item either. For example, there was a tool I needed at *Sears*. It was more expensive in the store than it was online. I had the option to order the tool online and pick it up at the store on the same day since they had it in stock. If I had purchased the item in the store rather than ordering it online, I would have paid several dollars more. Shopping online had benefits in this situation. Just take five minutes to weigh your options before you commit to a purchase. It is worth it.

SAVINGS – $180; TIME INVOLVED – 2 HOURS (research prices before you buy)
FINAL SAVINGS – $130

29. **GET ART FOR CHEAP.** Buy art at second-hand stores or auctions. If you can get hand-painted art for $5, you are getting an awesome, super, spectacular deal – unless the painting is really ugly. It takes an artist a minimum of about twelve hours to paint a fine painting whether big or small. Twelve hour paintings deserve at least $300 for time and materials! Heck, if you are an artist and see an ugly

painting, paint over it. The canvas is worth a couple of bucks and the frame could be worth a hundred easy if it is good quality. Oh, don't buy stupid prints. They are mass printed by a machine. There is nothing special about that. Handmade is always best. Uh, unless you are looking to save a couple of extra dollars of course.

SAVINGS – $295

30. **DON'T SHOP AT CONVENIENCE STORES.** Never, ever shop inside a convenience store unless you have an awesome coupon, are picking up a copy of the newspaper, or buying milk. Milk prices are regulated by the government so it's all cool. Dude, it is mostly dumb to shop inside of a convenience store. Yes, I would like to pay double for an item please. That would be lovely. I am too lazy to go somewhere else – so please take more money. I would like a small bottle of soda for the same price as a huge two liter bottle. Ugh. Stock up at the grocery store once a week and make sure that you don't run out of anything. Carry extra food in your purse or bag while traveling if you tend to need a bite to eat every time you stop to fill up your gas tank or need to use a restroom.

SAVINGS – $104

31. **SAVE SHOPPING BAGS.** I never buy garbage bags because I just reuse bags from the store. I keep the larger bags separate from the smaller bags so I can easily grab the right size for a specific trash can. You can also use shopping bags to organize things in the attic, as a shower cap, shoe covers when painting, or to protect your shoes from getting wet when going out in the rain. Just tie the bag around your foot using the handles and you'll be protected from water and mud. I have even used a large shopping bag as a raincoat. They roll up real small. For instance, I kept one in my pocket at an amusement park. When we got ready to go down the steep hill on a water ride, I put the bag over my head so that I would not get drenched. I'm so uncomfortable when I'm soaked and have to walk

around a park, so sticking a bag over me solved the problem. I could have just skipped the ride, but I wanted to experience it with my family. I actually enjoyed it more than if I would have gotten wet.

SAVINGS – $20; TIME SAVED – 1 HOUR (no need to shop for bags during the year)
FINAL SAVINGS – $45

32. **BUY A BIG COMPUTER.** You can get a large desktop computer for less money than a compact laptop. Desktop computers take up more space, but they are cheaper and usually come with loads more memory for about half the price of a laptop. I think it is well worth it. A desktop computer is also easier to repair and you usually get a bigger viewing screen/monitor which is a nice bonus.

On the other hand, the positive benefit of a laptop computer is that it is easily portable – if you would have to work on road trips it would be very handy to have. I do have a laptop, but the battery usually only lasts me half an hour while on the road, after that, I have to find a power source. Over the years, I have rarely used the battery on my laptop. I keep it plugged in and only occasionally take it on trips to hook up in hotel rooms.

SAVINGS – $500

1. **RECYCLE GREETING CARDS.** Never buy a greeting card again. I save cards when they are given to me. I can't believe some people spend $5 or more on greeting cards that will probably just get thrown away. I have cardstock on hand that I can print a new saying onto and then glue right over the previous saying. This process hides hand-written messages and the signature as well. The cards looks fresh and new when I am done with them. I also have a bulk box of envelopes so that I can just grab one when I need it. A box of envelopes is only a few dollars and will last years.

My mom is so sweet. When she gives out a greeting card, she writes her message on a sticky note so that the person can easily re-use the card. This makes the card a gift within a gift because the receiver saves money in that they don't have to purchase a card for the next person.

SAVINGS – $50; TIME INVOLVED – 30 MINUTES (save and revamp greeting cards in one session); TIME SAVED – 4 HOURS (no need to shop for cards throughout the year)
FINAL SAVINGS – $138

2. **MAKE YOUR OWN GREETING CARDS.** If you already have the materials on hand, it makes sense to create your own greeting cards rather than purchasing them in order to save a few dollars. You

can print cards from your computer or fold a piece of cardstock and decorate the card using stamps, stickers, glitters, glue, and more. I get a lot of my craft supplies in clearance bins at stores, from auctions, and at yard sales. People really seem to enjoy receiving a handmade card with lots of love put into it.

SAVINGS – $40; TIME INVOLVED – 3 HOURS (make greeting cards)
TIME SAVED – 4 HOURS (no need to shop for cards throughout the year)
FINAL SAVINGS – $65

3. **MAKE YOUR OWN WRAPPING PAPER.** I use plain newsprint paper to make wrapping paper. I happen to have a good supply of newsprint paper on hand since I ship a lot of items through the mail for my business. At just four cents per sheet, this is a good deal on wrapping paper. I can simply purchase a few sheets from my business each year for personal use. Sometimes I have my kids stamp shapes onto the paper to create designs. I like to jazz the paper up to make it special. If I get an old can of spray paint at auction in a dollar box, I can also add large blocks of color to the paper very easily (metallic varieties really add class). Not everyone has access to large sheets of newsprint, but keep your eyes peeled. For instance, my mom works at a job where they throw out large sheets of paper. She brings it home for me because she knows I will use it as wrapping paper or to protect the surface of my table when working on art projects.

My father doesn't care so much about impressing people. He simply gets away with using newspaper to wrap gifts every now and then. Everyone just laughs. Hey, I can't blame him. Wrapping paper is a waste of money the way I see it.

SAVINGS – $25; TIME INVOLVED – 1 ½ HOURS (make your own wrapping paper); TIME SAVED – 1 HOUR (no need to shop for wrapping paper)
FINAL SAVINGS – $13

4. **RE-GIFT.** I'm all for re-gifting as long as you don't give the

gift back to the person who gave it to you, as long as you think the person will like it, and as long as it is not an obvious re-gift.

Now I'll tell you about the *non-classy* way of re-gifting. This way of giving is a complete turn-off and will make the receiver think that you don't care about them at all. I share this story from personal experience on the receiving end of things. It is better to give no gift at all than to give a gift that means nothing and is obviously regifted. One Christmas, a couple (one of them worked for a hotel chain) gave my family the following gifts:

8 year old Nicole was given a stick of **lip balm** and a single serve **pack of hot chocolate** and marshmallows (the kind you would find in a hotel room). She threw up after drinking it (maybe it was outdated). My daughter is rarely sick (and I do mean rarely), so I'm judging that it was food poisoning.

9 year old Travis received a **hotel-branded baseball** (he's not into sports at all, he's my little computer genius) and a **pack of paper**. The paper was a small size and was to be used to print gift cards. You have to purchase a gift card online and then you can use this paper to print your gift cards out. What 9 year old boy would want to purchase a gift card for himself using his own money and then have to print it out?

I got a tiny **flip book** of a belly dancer shaking her boobies in my face. Why? Maybe the gifts got switched and I was supposed to get the pack of gift card paper instead of my son (it sounds more appropriate). I also got a **hotel-branded domino set** which I'm assuming was a re-gift from the gift-giver's company.

Nathan (my husband) got a **sample rap CD** (Nate does not like rap) and a **hotel keychain** from the gift-givers' honeymoon trip.

It seemed obvious that everything was re-gifted junk. It left a sour taste in our mouths (especially my daughter's). Gifts are supposed to make people happy. So keep this story in mind when you plan on re-gifting an item. Now, I'm not saying I'm the perfect re-gifter, but I try my darndest to do an awesome job. I really care about the people that I give gifts to and I want to put a smile on each and every face.

SAVINGS – $125 (save gifts you don't need, re-gift appropriately)
TIME SAVED – 3 HOURS (no need to shop for gifts)
FINAL SAVINGS – $200

5. **GIVE HANDMADE GIFTS.** Sometimes handmade gifts are the most meaningful gifts. Here is a list of some things that you can make yourself and give to the special people in your life:

- Wreaths, baskets, flower arrangements

- Paintings, scrapbooks, framed photographs

- Blankets, scarves, hats, decorative pillows

- Stuffed animals, hair clips, slime

- Cookies, cakes, candy, other baked goods

- A coupon book of things you will do – carwash, clean, cook, massage

- Jewelry, candles, soap

- Christmas tree ornaments, paper flowers

- Write and record a song for someone

- Breakfast in bed, cook a meal

- Can food and create a gift basket

- Wallets and purses

SAVINGS – $225; TIME INVOLVED – 7 ½ HOURS (Make in bulk if possible, give throughout year); TIME SAVED – 22 ½ HOURS (no need to shop for gifts during the year)
FINAL SAVINGS – $600

6.   **DRAW NAMES.** At Christmas time my family draws names to see who gets who for gift-giving purposes. This way we don't have to spend a fortune each year on gifts. However, the adults still buy for all of the children as it is a very magical time for them. We draw names a year in advance since everyone is already together (it saves time) and allows a whole year to pick out the perfect gift for that special someone! Besides that, when people have to buy for so many different people, they tend to spend less on a gift. We would rather receive a nicer quality gift with lots of thought put into it than a bunch of cheaper items.

SAVINGS – $200; TIME INVOLVED – 4 MINUTES (write down names, then draw names); TIME SAVED – 4 HOURS (no need to shop for as many people)
FINAL SAVINGS – $298

7.   **SHOP FOR GIFTS AT LOCAL AUCTIONS.** I find great gift items at local auctions (both new and used). Anyway, one year I pulled my Dad's name in our gift exchange. We are supposed to spend $50. So I spent $50 at auction and got him so much cool stuff that everyone thought I went well over the budget (but I didn't). I spoiled him big time. This is really a great idea because the receiver is getting more than anticipated. I made sure to let everyone know that I did not go over budget. I just got really good deals at auction!

By the way, if you don't know how to find auctions near you, visit *auctionzip.com* and you'll be on your way to saving some cash.

SAVINGS – $250 (find an auction, bid on stuff instead of shopping)

8.   **GIVE PAPER ROSES.** When I was dating my husband, he bought me a bouquet of real roses. I taught him early on that it was a waste of money. In order to erase his mistake and make use of the roses, I dried them and they are still hanging on my dining room wall twelve years later. I just can't see paying all of that money for some-

thing that lasts such a short amount of time that I don't get much enjoyment out of. I would much rather eat a chocolate bar. But if you feel the urge to give roses, why not make some out of paper? I have made roses out of coffee filters and even out of dollar bills. Now wouldn't you just love to receive some *money roses*? You can stare at them for a while and when you are done you can spend them. There are many paper flower projects on the internet if you care to try this out for yourself.

My husband and I do not exchange gifts. We share a bank account, so it just seems strange to spend each other's money to buy a gift that the other might not even like. I have told my husband that if he were to ever surprise me with a gift, make it a bouquet of Taco Bell burritos. I would be the happiest woman on earth. I love edible gifts because food brings me great enjoyment.

SAVINGS – $100 (make flowers, don't shop for them)

9. **SAVE BOWS AND GIFT WRAP.** I never purchase bows or gift bags. When a gift is given to me, I save everything for reuse. At Christmas time I watch to be sure that nobody throws a gift bow in the garbage bag that is being passed around. What a waste if one is thrown out. If I receive a gift, I open it carefully, roll the wrapping paper up, and reuse it later on. If somebody puts this technique down, maybe they are just jealous that they don't have the character to do it themselves. Why would anyone frown upon saving resources? Maybe they have too much pride. Well, I don't. My mother always said that I was uninhibited.

Here is another tip. I don't do this because I am too cheap to buy Mylar balloons, but I knew a lady who saved balloons, flattened them out, and would take them to the store to be re-filled with helium because it was cheaper than buying a new one. I might buy a pack of rubber balloons, but I would rather tape them to the ceiling than buy helium ones. Air is free and a piece of tape is cheap enough to warrant using.

SAVINGS – $30; TIME SAVED – 1 ½ HOURS (no need to shop for gift wrap, bows, or bags)
FINAL SAVINGS – $68

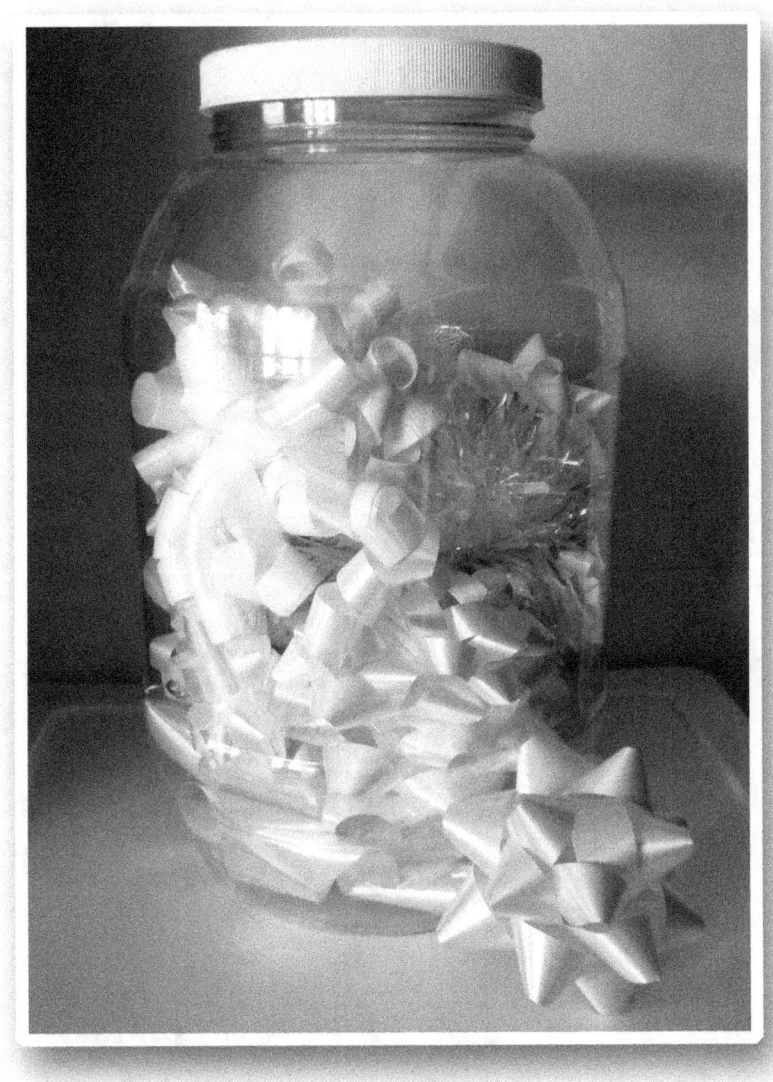

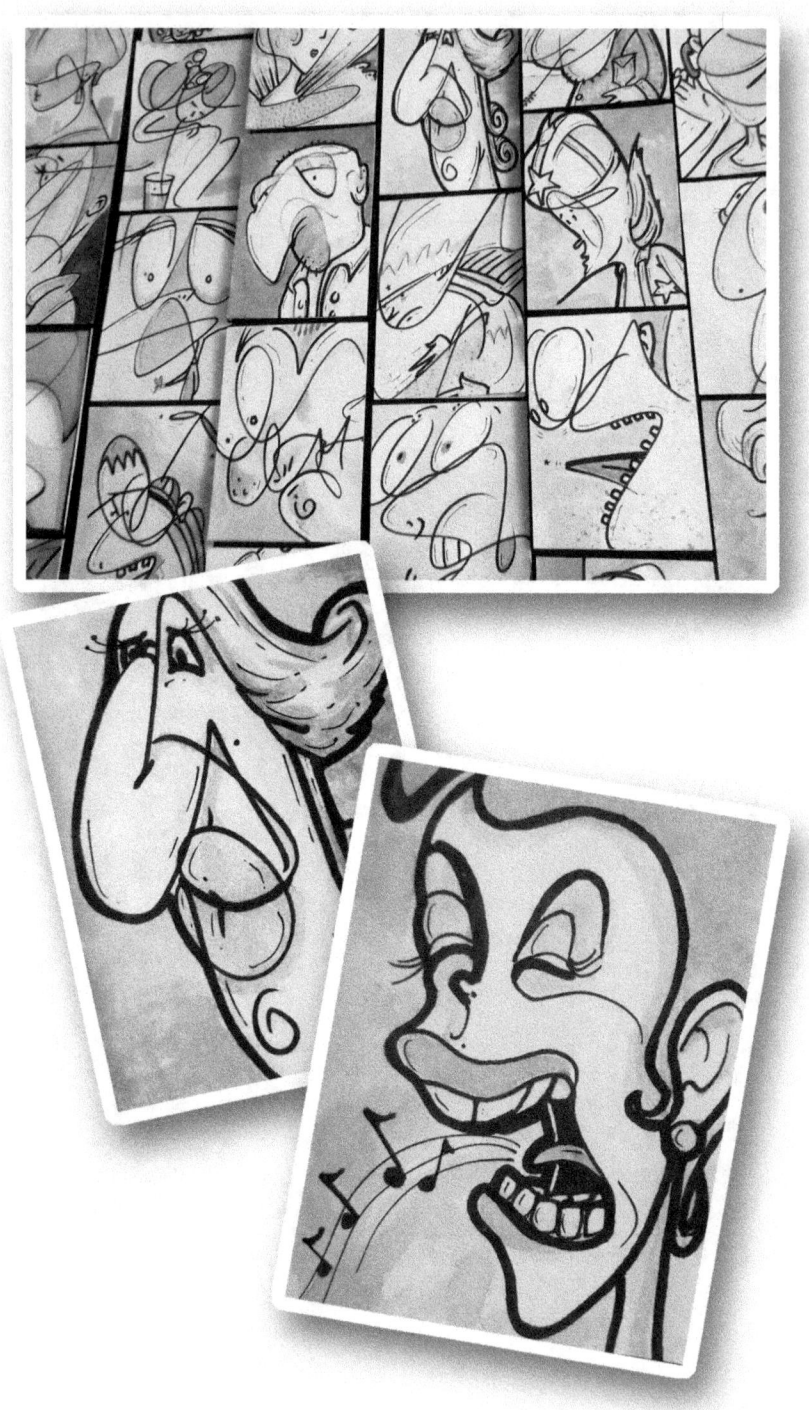

Living Big on a Small Income

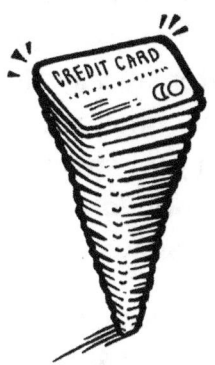

$

1. **ENTER CONTESTS.** Take it from the *Queen of Contests* (me), avoid sweepstakes because your chances of winning are usually low. There are many types of other contests out there and your chances of winning can be pretty good – especially if the contest requires a skill. For example, I entered an Oprah contest called "The Creative Mind Challenge". The theme was "What Inspires You". My entry was a video of me scribbling on used mail envelopes. I titled my piece "Inspiration is Everywhere". I showed how a scribble on paper inspires me to turn it into a work of art. Check out some of my scribble drawings on the left. I am an artist and when I don't know what to draw, I scribble, turning that scribble into something cool. It only took me about five minutes to create the video and enter it online. I spent nothing as I used materials that were lying on my desk. I won the grand prize and enjoyed a trip to New York City with a friend to take film classes. We got a free round trip flight and a hotel stay as well. It was a great experience. I paid the taxes and in return, my friend paid for meals. Bartering is great!

Please keep in mind that some of the ideas in this chapter may need to be reported on your yearly taxes. For example, if you win an Oprah contest like I did, you'll need to plan on reporting the value of your winnings and paying a portion of that to the government.

Other ways to win things fairly easily include online magazine contests. Visit magazine websites and check out their current contests. They often have random drawings and usually no skills are required to enter. If you are entering many online contests, you may wish to have your information automatically fill in for you so that you do not have to type it in every time you enter something. You may already have a program on your computer that will do this for you. If not, you could try using **RoboForm** available at **roboform.com**. It is a program that acts as a password manager and form filler.

If you have more than one person living under your roof, by all means, enter everyone in a contest (if the rules allow). You may have to clear your internet browser's history before entering another family member in the same contest. Some contests check to see if an entry is coming from the same location. Other contests require emails to differ, so be sure to have an email address for each family member.

One time I entered a live dance contest (I am not a professional dancer). I won because I was entertaining (smacked my butt, shook some booty, and did a few cartwheels). However, the prize was an extra-large shirt (I found that out only after I won). I happen to wear the opposite size, an extra-small. When I got home I tailored the shirt so that it would fit me. I simply turned it inside out and sewed it smaller all around.

Another time I entered a pie-eating contest just for the free pie. I made sure to stick my entire face and some hair in the pie to please the audience. I didn't win and I didn't intend to win. I was just hungry for some free Lemon Meringue pie. My picture made it into the newspaper. I am petite, weighing just about ninety pounds, and measuring 4' 10" tall. Not exactly the type that would be in a pie-eating contest. I find this hilarious.

Another thing that my family does is try to win games at a nearby roller skating rink. They have games such as the *Limbo* and Four *Corners*. We practice the limbo on skates when we can and usually win a prize such as a free drink, ice cream, or a hot pretzel. From what I remember, my husband and I are the only adults that ever take part in the Limbo on skates. There are some college guys who take part every now and then to show off their moves. My husband is 6' tall and has practically no chance of winning up against a short and slender 4 year old, but he does it for the exercise. Doing this sort of thing sure keeps both of us young and flexible. Hey, I've been asked if I was a professional skater which made me laugh. I've never had a lesson. I must bend my body in fancy ways to try to fit under that Limbo stick. It is usually my daughter who wins the game since she is young and petite – two great qualities for playing the Limbo. There is another game called four corners. Whoever is left standing wins the prize. Since we have four people in our family, we each take a different corner to increase our odds of winning. Most families stick together during the game, but we are in it to win it.

Try not to enter contests where the public votes to choose the winners. There are programs and systems where people can cheat to beat everyone else. It is not even worth trying to win in my opinion. I concentrate on contests where there are a select amount of judges that choose the winner.

So the moral of this story is – enter contests – even if they take guts. What have you got to lose – your dignity? I don't know how you look at it, but I place entertaining others higher up in importance than dignity. So if I have to embarrass myself to win a contest, at least I added some excitement to the lives of those around me. Excitement is a good thing. Plus, maybe you can walk away with dignity if you are awesome!

When I was just a young child (maybe the age of seven), I submitted a cartoon/comic sketch to **Better Homes and Gardens** magazine. I wanted to make $300. I don't even think my parents knew I did this. **Better Homes and Gardens** sent me a letter back pretty much saying that the comic was good, but that it was inappropriate for their magazine. For the comic, I had drawn a family enjoying dinner out at a restaurant in which the father was bending over with his butt crack sticking out. The woman said, "Honey, your buns are getting cold". Yep, I should have thought that one over. But I thought adults liked that kind of humor. Guess I was wrong. My point is, it never hurts to try. I learned something from the experience. I learned to consider the target audience when creating art for a project.

SAVINGS – $2,300; TIME INVOLVED – 6 HOURS (enter lots of contests throughout the year); TIME SAVED – 3 HOURS (no need to shop for various items because they'll be given or shipped to you)
FINAL SAVINGS – $2,375

2.   **TAKE PART IN CHINESE AUCTIONS.** I enjoy taking part in Chinese auctions when they come up (also known as chance auctions). I buy an arm's length or two of tickets (best deal) and throw my tickets into the containers with the least amount of entries. Try to wait until the last minute possible to enter your tickets. Then you'll have a good idea of what your chances are. Usually people go for the fancy prizes, but I don't even bother. The chances are too slim. After I got married, I won a free will (to be drawn up by a lawyer) and a free wedding frame at a Chinese auction. For some reason, not many people want the gift certificates. I tend to win a lot of free car washes because of that. I have never in my life paid for a fancy car wash thanks to Chinese auctions.

SAVINGS – $75; TIME INVOLVED – 1 HOUR (take part in Chinese auctions, enter wisely); TIME SAVED – 2 HOURS (no need to shop for items because you won them)
FINAL SAVINGS – $100

3.   **SPIN THE PRIZE WHEEL AT FAIRS AND EVENTS.** My husband was the last person in our family to win. Oh, for your information, we only enter if it is free to spin the wheel and if we are conveniently walking past one. You won't find us paying for a spin. You can pick up some useful (and not so useful) items by taking part in the fun. He won a country music CD this last time. We don't listen to much music, so we put the CD up for sale on eBay. It's very simple

really – snap a photo of the item, list it, and ship it. There you go.

4.   **ENTER TO WIN DOOR PRIZES.** Who knows, maybe you will be the only person who enters (especially if the prize seems dumb). Hey, you might be able to use that dumb prize someday or even sell it. Maybe you have a friend who can use it. Give and you shall receive. If you think of your friend, they will tend to think of you in return.

Last year I entered into a door prize for a $20 yard plant. I was the only person on the entry list so I was pretty sure I would win. Guess what? I won, Yay for me!

5.   **HAVE A HOUSE PARTY.** Simply visit **houseparty.com** and get started with your adventure. Here is how it works. You sign up to be a party host. If you get selected, you are required to invite a certain amount of people to your party. Each party has a theme which usually advertises a product. Parties vary from month to month boasting products that range from coffee to pizza to water guns. Soon after completing your tasks such as inviting people, a party pack will arrive at your door including cool party supplies such as coupons, products, and decorations for your party. The party pack is completely free. You receive it as a token of thanks for advertising products during your party. Hey, I think I'll sign up for one right now! They are so much fun!

6. **SIGN UP FOR CREDIT CARDS.** I sign up for a credit card only when there is an offer tied to it. Some credit cards offer $100-500 in credit or rewards. They may require you to spend so much money in so many months to earn a reward or simply complete a transaction. It is not that hard to earn the reward if you do all of your spending using the credit card. Even pay your bills with the card to get to your goal faster. Try not to use the card to purchase things you would not normally buy just to hit a goal. After I take advantage of a credit card offer and receive my incentive, I go as far as cancelling the credit card. By the way, my credit is exceptional.

I have a favorite card that I keep open at all times. I've had it for many years. It gives me great rewards every time I use the card. Another benefit to keeping it open is that it helps to boost my credit score. I keep a zero balance – paying my card off every month. So the positive history and age of the account help to further increase my credit score.

Be certain to read the fine print associated with credit card offers. Some cards do not let you receive the reward again if you cancel the card and then sign up for the same card again. By the way, also be sure to pay your bill off each month (in full and on time) and never spend what you don't have. Also, if you don't receive credit card offers through the mail like I do, you can search online for one.

For the record, my husband and I have signed up for over 200 credit card offers (that we have counted). If we received just $50 for each offer, that amounts to over $10,000 in incentives. Check this out – we don't even have to pay tax on the money.

Here is how it works – the Internal Revenue Service considers the money to be a *rebate* if you had to complete a financial transaction to earn the money. Rebates are considered to be discounts and are not taxable. So if you had to make a purchase or purchases to earn the reward, then you are good to go because it is considered to be a discount. But, if all you did was sign up for the credit card to earn a reward, then it is considered an *award* and is taxable. It is considered to be a financial gain (Herron). I choose to avoid this type of offer altogether because it sounds like a headache waiting to happen. Don't forget, laws can change. So try to keep yourself in the know each year.

SAVINGS – $1,000; TIME INVOLVED – 4 HOURS (sign up for credit card offers)
FINAL SAVINGS – $900

7. **PICK UP PENNIES.** Some people consider it stealing if you pick up a penny, coins, or other objects that you find on the ground. If you find a penny on the street, the common consensus is that the person who dropped it was irresponsible, and you may now keep the penny. You have probably dropped your fair share as well. If you find a twenty dollar bill in a store, it seems right that you should notify the courtesy desk that you found money. You should give them your contact information. I would not want to just hand the money over to the worker as they will probably just pocket it. If someone contacts you and can tell you the amount they lost, then you hand it over. If nobody contacts you in a good amount of time, I think it would be reasonable to say that it is yours to use. You can always refund them the money if they call in the future.

By picking up spare change, you can accumulate a few extra dollars over the course of a year. This is especially true if you have a job that gets you out an about like a delivery person or mall security guard. Keep in mind that you are getting exercise every time you bend down. How great is that? You are getting paid to work out!

When my family is on vacation, we make a game out of it. Whoever finds the most change gets to keep everyone's coins at the end of the day. You can look for coins near meters, behind vending machines, in arcades, or simply on the sidewalk. Some people even use metal detectors to find lost change or jewelry. If you do this, you'll want to search a high traffic area which could make you look like a weirdo. People will stare at you, but maybe they are just jealous.

EARNINGS – $5 (bend down, pick up change during the year)

8. **GATHER UP FREE BOXES.** I love neighborhood yard sales (mostly when they are over with). After a sale, I travel around with my family and grab up all of the boxes that are marked "FREE." Pots and pans with no lids and other useless metal items that we collect go immediately into our scrap (recycling) pile. We obviously keep the things we need or want. Things such as backpacks, office supplies, and handy gadgets. Everything else gets sold at our consignment center booth. For more information on the free consignment booth visit chapter 2.

Oh, I need to share something with you. Sometimes when you see a "FREE" box along a highway, you might breeze right by it (like we usually do). By the time you realize it is a free box, you have already passed it. Then you think – is it worth turning around? Yes! Yes it is. Don't be lazy. Each box is usually worth $25 or more in objects that you can use. It is well worth the time to turn around. I don't think we have ever regretted it.

SAVINGS – $125; TIME INVOLVED – 15 MINUTES (grab some free boxes during your travels); TIME SAVED – 3 HOURS (no need to shop for these items throughout the year)
FINAL SAVINGS – $194

9. **GET FREE STUFF ON FACEBOOK.** When one of my friends lists an item for free on *Facebook*, giving it away to the first person who says they want it, I usually respond, "I'll take it!" If I can't use the item in one of my homes, I can sell it, or scrap it. It seems pretty harsh to take a free item and sell it. But that's the way I roll. They could have sold the item themselves, but must be too busy – preferring to get rid of the item quickly. I can use the money from selling an item to get something that I really need. Recently I acquired a shower door and a ceiling fan through Facebook. They are both great items for fixing up a foreclosure that my husband and I purchased.

SAVINGS – $225; TIME INVOLVED – 30 MINUTES (snag free stuff on Facebook)
TIME SAVED – 2 HOURS (no need to shop for the items)
FINAL SAVINGS – $263

10. **SIGN UP FOR FREE SAMPLES.** Have automatic free sample offers sent to your email every day with the help of *AllYou.com*. That is how I obtain my free samples. Some of the more recent samples I have received through the mail are feminine pads, bandages, soft cat food, dry cat food, coffee, tea, energy bars, and detergent, among other things. When I sign up for a free sample offer, I usually have additional samples sent to my parents and sister who live elsewhere. I give them samples that I don't use and they give me samples that they don't use. It's a win-win.

SAVINGS – $30; TIME INVOLVED – 1 HOUR (sign up for free samples all year long)
TIME SAVED – 2 HOURS (no need to purchase the items)
FINAL SAVINGS – $55

11. **DON'T BE EARLY.** When there is an event or item on your schedule, arrive at the specified time – no sooner. Time is a valuable resource in this world. When there is something we really want in our lives, one of the first things we consider is if there is enough *time* and enough *money. Time* is *money*, so scrimp and save every minute. Make every second count.

The benefit of being early to some activities is that you might get a good seat. In that case, bring something to do while you sit there for a half hour or more. I personally don't care about getting a good seat that much. I would much rather be doing other things, so I am on time for events or fashionably late. If I need a good photo, I just squat in the center isle down front with other photographers and then go back to my seat when needed.

I drive my children to school instead of having them ride the bus. If they rode the bus, then we would have to wake up a half hour earlier. The bus picks the kids up around 8:00, but school does not start until 8:30. In order to make sure we catch the bus, we would have to arrive five minutes early because the bus schedule varies. I only live one minute from the school, so I simply drive my children. The process takes two minutes as compared to ten minutes with the bus stop routine. The walk to the bus stop actually takes longer than my driving. So, every morning I save my children a half hour that they would have spent sitting in a cafeteria or gym waiting to enter their morning class, plus ten minutes walking to and standing at the bus stop.

You can do this for work, school, church, parties, and everything in your life. Waiting is no fun. Arrive for the good parts! We even did this when we visited Walt Disney World. We used the *Fastpass* service as often as we could that allowed us to go in a special line where there was very little waiting involved. If we had gone in the regular lines every time, we would have had typical hour or longer waits. We tried using the regular line for a ride and ended up standing in line for three hours only to have the ride shut down on us when we got to the front. That kind of thing blows. It's *Fastpass* for us baby!

TIME SAVED – 100 HOURS; **FINAL SAVINGS** – $2,500

12. **LEAVE LARGE EVENTS EARLY OR STAY LATER.** Plan your getaway! When you are at an event with lots of vehicles, leave early or at least plan to stay an extra fifteen minutes or more. Let me explain this type of situation. Every year my family goes to a fireworks display that brings in a big crowd. At the end of the event, there is a huge traffic jam where people sit in their cars anxiously waiting to leave. However, they just sit in their cars annoyed because they cannot move forward. If someone were to leave early, they would be driving easy avoiding the traffic jam. However, it is not desirable to leave early or the fireworks finale would be missed. So what is someone to do in this type of situation? Well, I have the answer. Don't leave when everyone else does. Bask in your smart way of

thinking. Purposely stay in your chairs and have a snack that you pre-packed just for this very moment. Opt to play a fun game like Hacky Sack which can easily fit in a purse or pocket. Everyone is happier when they feel in control of a situation. So if you are visiting a drive-in theater, community or public event, school function, stage show, sporting event, or similar; simply plan to stay a little later than usual. Bring something fun to do. Instead of sitting in a long line of traffic going nowhere and complaining, plan ahead and get creative!

Good things happen to those who are late. I was just late for orientation with the kids' new principal. I only caught the end of the principal's informal speech and then partook of some yummy cookies and out the door we went. It was short and sweet. Sometimes when we are late to events, the parking lots become filled and we end up getting a spot right at the front door because people are allowed to park anywhere at that point out of desperation. In conclusion, late is great!

SAVINGS – GOOD TIMES; TIME SAVED – 3 HOURS
FINAL SAVINGS – $75

13. **TAKE SURVEYS TO EARN REWARDS.** My favorite survey site is *e-Rewards*. You can sign up to take surveys at *e-rewards.com* earning rewards such as free magazine subscriptions (my personal favorite), music, gift cards, certificates, sky miles, and more. If you can make more than $15 per hour with your spare time or don't need these rewards, then this technique is probably not for you because taking surveys takes time.

EARNINGS – $260 (take surveys every now and then, redeem earnings for rewards)

14. **PAY BILLS ONLINE.** I don't know about you, but I have a lot of bills every month. I pay them online whenever possible to avoid spending money on a stamp. I also use my online checking account

which gives me ten cents credit for every bill paid online and every check that is written. I keep a password protected list of my passwords in a spreadsheet program on my computer. If I had to memorize every password and website, I would go insane. I can log in to pay my bill quickly by copying and pasting the password right from my spreadsheet document. It takes me the same amount of time to pay a bill online as it does for me to mail one the old fashioned way.

SAVINGS – $120 (pay bills online)

15. PAY ALL AT ONCE. If you pay for things in one lump sum for the year, you will save time by not having to write checks as often. For example, I pay for my kids lunches up front at the beginning of the school year. This saves a lot of time writing checks each week. It also saves a lot of checks. This is a big savings considering the amount of checks and time saved. Remember . . . time is money. You cannot buy time.

You can also pay for other things all at once. Check into this. For example, some insurance companies have different plans available. If you pay in one lump sum, they may even cut you a break on your bill (mine does). You may even save stamps if you usually mail your payments.

SAVINGS – $120; TIME SAVED – 3 ¾ HOURS (write less checks, receive discounts, save stamps)
FINAL SAVINGS – $214

16. GET ELDER CARE. A tip for the wise, more mature folks. Visit **eldercare.gov** to find local agencies that might be able to help with home care, meals, and transportation. It can be very helpful and save you lots of money adding peace of mind to your golden years. There is probably even free transportation in your area to a center where people of your age can meet and share similar hobbies. There might be things available such as quilt making, knitting, arts, crafts, entertainment, and more!

SAVINGS – $3,500

CONCLUSION

Hopefully by now, you have had a chance to read all of the completely awesome, classy tips that I shared with you in this valuable book. As I think of and come across new tips, I will share them on my website at *classycheapskate.wordpress.com*. Feel free to share your own ideas with everyone in the *comment* area on the website. Also, if you see any errors in this book, I'd love to know! I spent countless hours calculating and proofreading, but nobody is perfect.

So here is the exciting conclusion to this book – if you are able follow every tip in this book, you have the potential to save and/or earn an average of **$509,395** worth of cash and time in your first year. Wow! That's half a million dollars. Holy cow! You should be able to stash away a lot of extra savings each year and live the life of someone with a much higher income. I think it would be really fun if you kept track of your own savings each year. So I'm going to include some pages at the end of this book that you can use to track your progress. Each year you can try to beat the savings from the year before!

I want everyone to remember that money does not control you, you control it. Do not let greed get the best of you. Do work in your life that you enjoy no matter what it pays. You can always find ways to make your money stretch farther. Just look at all of the ways outlined in this book. Protect your health and guard it like you would a precious treasure. For example, I left a job at one of the top design firms in the country because I was getting carpel tunnel in my hand and an ulcer in my stomach from the stress and overtime that the job required. Once I left, my health returned to its normal state. I also quit because I wanted to be closer to my family which is very important to me – more important than money. I resigned from a job once that paid about $45 an hour because it made me vomit after every work session. I worked with chemicals and the gas mask didn't help either. I quit a comfortable job that paid approximately $17.50 an hour because I didn't think the work environment was fair. One time I took a job that paid around $7.50 just because I wanted to work with doughnuts. It's just silly. I don't usually work for the money (though it is an added bonus), most of the time I work purely for the experience. Nowadays I am only working for myself and it is the most enjoyable job I've ever had. I really like my boss. She understands me so well and even lets me keep all of the profits. I would just love to see you be able to take some of these values and apply them to your life. I hope you find great happiness and joy by implementing some of this knowledge.

Well, the time to say goodbye (for now) is drawing near. I'm happy that I had the chance to share my best money and time saving tips with you in such an organized manner. I had a lot of fun writing this book and I hope that you enjoyed reading it. I encourage you to reference it again and again, year after year, to continue to see huge savings! That's all for now folks! You have just graduated from the "School of Classy Cheapskates". **Congratulations**!

Before you go though, check this out! If everyone in America spent money like me, they would save this much per year on the following items mostly because I don't buy them! And this isn't even a complete list!

$96 billion on Beer (Reilly) Brewers Association
$550 million on Pretzels (Reilly) Reuters
$1.4 billion on St. Patrick's Day (Reilly) National Retail Federation
$310 million on Pet Halloween Costumes (Reilly) National Retail Federation/American Pet Product Association
$10 billion on Romance Novels (Reilly) Romance Writers of America
$1.7 billion on Valentine's Day Flowers (Reilly) National Retail Federation

$16 billion on Chocolate (Reilly) IBIS

$4.2 billion on Perfume (Reilly) Research and Markets

$5 billion on Household Fragrances (Forbes)

$11 billion on Coffee (Reilly) Franchise Direct/North American Organic Coffee Industry Report

$2.3 billion on Tattoos (Reilly) INC.

$66 million on Tattoo Removal (Reilly) IBIS

$500 million on Golf Balls (Reilly) Forbes

$800 million on Girl Scout Cookies (Reilly) Girl Scouts of America

$65 billion on Soft Drinks (Reilly) National Soft Drinks Association

$11 billion on Bottled Water (Reilly) Beverage Marketing Corp.

$25.4 billion on Professional Sports (Reilly) WR Hambrecht

$5 billion on Ringtones (Reilly) NY Times

$18 billion on Credit Card Late Fees (Reilly) RK Hammer

$49 billion on Credit Card Interest (Krasny, Lubin, Sprung)

$40 billion on Lawn Care (Reilly) Bloomberg

$47 billion on Child Care (Reilly) IBIS

$500 million on Twinkies (Reilly) WSJ

$100 billion on Illicit Drugs (Zobeck)

$165 billion on Wasted Food (Muniz) National Resources Defense Council

$7 billion on ATM Fees in 2010 (Muniz)

$66.5 billion on Lottery Tickets in 2011 (Muniz) CNN

$44 billion on Tobacco Products (Krasny, Lubin, Sprung) BLS

$6 billion on Unused Gift Cards (Krasny, Lubin, Sprung) TowerGroup

$12 billion on Speeding and Traffic Tickets (Krasny, Lubin, Sprung) The National Motorists Association

$29 billion on Candy (Krasny, Lubin, Sprung)

$69 billion at Casinos (Krasny, Lubin, Sprung)

$30 billion on supplements (Bellows, Moore, Gross)

Do you know how much money that amounts to? It is just shy of 1 trillion dollars! **$939,226,000,000** to be exact.

Though I make the income of a pauper (okay, not really), I live like that of a Queen (okay, not really – again). But seriously, check out my bed! It's shown over there on the right. Check out the detailing! It really is fit for royalty. In times of old, someone very special slept in this bed. It was hand carved by a master carver, gently layered with white gesso, and masterfully painted in exquisite detail. My husband and I have named it "The Chastity Bed". It depicts historical Christian figures/characters such as the virgin princess Saint Catherine of Alexandria with her martyr's palm in hand and breaking wheel below; various angels/cherubs; Adam, Eve, and the serpent in the Garden of Eden. The bed is covered in a fish scale pattern, the fish being a symbol in Christianity. An artisan or two surely spent a year of their lives or more crafting this ornate bed for a regal figure. This bed may have been commissioned by an elaborate person such as Pope Pius IX. Upon inspecting his Miter (hat), you would be able to notice similar qualities to that of the bed. Pope Pius IX passed away in 1878. Coincidentally, I was born in 1978. Now, in these more modern days, I have the privilege of sleeping in this work of art because I am able to save in many other aspects of my life. I have the ability to set so much money aside, that I can splurge on a masterpiece every now and then. If this bed were to be remade today, it would surely cost a fortune. The bed requires a custom mattress because times have changed drastically since the making of this bed. I could order a custom mattress online, but have made due by placing two cots within the frame. The cots were in my attic when I bought my house and I use them because I do not want to invest in a mattress. I plan to sell the bed to the right person in the near future. Anyway, it's not like sleeping on a cot is anything new to me!

Until next time, folks! Take care of yourself – *the classy cheapskate way.*

WORKS CITED

American Lung Association. "Cleaning Supplies and Household Chemicals." *lung.org*. American Lung Association, n.d. Web. 2 September 2014. <http://www.lung.org/healthy-air/home/resources/cleaning-supplies.html>.

apardue. "How much Ice Cream is Consumed in the U.S.?" *voice4nations.org*. Voice4Nations, 25 January 2013. Web. 27 August 2014. <http://www.voice4nations.org/content/how-much-ice-cream-consumed-us>.

BabyCenter. "How much you'll spend on childcare." *babycenter.com*. BabyCenter, L.L.C., n.d. Web. 28 August 2014. <http://www.babycenter.com/0_how-much-youll-spend-on-childcare_1199776.bc>.

Bankrate. "Amortization Schedule Calculator." *bankrate.com*. Bankrate, Inc., n.d. Web. 30 August 2014. <http://www.bankrate.com/calculators/mortgages/amortization-calculator.aspx>.

Barlow, Tom. "How much does an hour of fun cost you?" *dailyfinance.com*. AOL Inc., 28 April 2008. Web. 24 August 2014. <http://www.dailyfinance.com/2008/04/28/how-much-does-an-hour-of-fun-cost-you/>.

Bellows, L., R. Moore, and A. Gross. "Dietary Supplements: Vitamins and Minerals." Rev. ed. *ext.colostate.edu*. Colorado State University Extension, September 2013. Web. 22 September 2014. <http://www.ext.colostate.edu/pubs/foodnut/09338.html>.

Bon Appétit. "15 Ways to Use Leftover Pickle Juice." *bonappetit.com*. Condé Nast, 30 August 2012. Web. 15 September 2014. <http://www.bonappetit.com/test-kitchen/cooking-tips/article/15-ways-to-use-leftover-pickle-juice>.

Bowman, Zach. "Report: Water as windshield wiper fluid causes 20% of Legionnaires' Disease cases in UK." *autoblog.com*. AOL Inc., 15 June 2010. Web. 22 September 2014. <http://www.autoblog.com/2010/06/15/report-water-as-windshield-wiper-fluid-causes-20-of-legionnair/>.

Brogan, Kelly. "A Shot Never Worth Taking: The Flu Vaccine." *vaccinationcouncil.org*. International Medical Council on Vaccination, 27 November 2013. Web. 23 September 2014. <http://www.vaccinationcouncil.org/2013/11/27/a-shot-never-worth-taking-the-flu-vaccine-by-kelly-brogan-md/>.

Brunot, Trudy. "How Much Do Lights Affect an Electric Bill?" *budgeting.thenest.com*. Demand Media, n.d. Web. 12 August 2014. <http://budgeting.thenest.com/much-lights-affect-electric-bill-27123.html>.

Bureau of Labor Statistics. "Average annual expenditures on sweets, flowers, stationery, jewelry, and other items in 2012." bls.gov, 14 February 2014. Web. 15 September 2014. <http://www.bls.gov/opub/ted/2014/ted_20140214.htm>.

Caldwell, Marleen. "Dreaming of a Good Night's Sleep?" *my.clevelandclinic.org*. Cleveland Clinic, n.d. Web. 2 September 2014. <http://my.clevelandclinic.org/be_well/sleeping__healthy_spine_bewell1008.aspx>.

Cancio, Colleen. "How much money can I save with a water filter?" *home.howstuffworks.com*. InfoSpace LLC, 8 July 2010. Web. 31 August 2014. <http://home.howstuffworks.com/appliances/energy-efficient/save-money-with-water-filter1.htm>.

Carvertise LLC. "To Qualify, Our Drivers Need to Meet a Few Criteria." *carvertise.com*. Carvertise LLC., n.d. Web. 10 September 2014. <http://www.carvertise.com/>.

Cetawayo, Ameerah. "How Much Money Does an Average Family Spend on Cleaning Products in a Year?" *budgeting.thenest.com*. The Nest, n.d. Web. 1 September 2014. <http://budgeting.thenest.com/much-money-average-family-spend-cleaning-products-year-23539.html>.

Chao, Julie. "White, Green or Black Roofs? Berkeley Lab Report Compares Economic Payoffs." *newscenter.lbl.gov*. Berkeley Lab, 21 January 2014. Web. 12 August 2014. <http://newscenter.lbl.gov/2014/01/21/white-green-or-black-roofs-berkeley-lab-report-compares-economic-payoffs/>.

Cheung, Nadine. "Use Rags to Keep Your Riches." *dailyfinance.com*. AOL Inc., 6 November 2012. Web. 12 August 2014. <http://www.dailyfinance.com/2012/11/06/use-rags-to-keep-your-riches-savings-experiment/>.

---. "Wash and Save on Laundry." *dailyfinance.com*. AOL Inc., 28 August 2012. Web. 3 September 2014. <http://www.dailyfinance.com/2012/08/28/wash-and-save-on-laundry-savings-experiment/>.

Clark, Josh. "What is gray water, and can it solve the global water crisis? *howstuffworks.com*. HowStuffWorks, n.d. Web. 17 September 2014. <http://home.howstuffworks.com/green-living/gray-water1.htm>.

COLLEGEdata. "What's the Price Tag for a College Education?" *collegedata.com*. COLLEGEdata, n.d. Web. 14 August 2014. <http://www.collegedata.com/cs/content/content_payarticle_tmpl.jhtml?articleId=10064>.

Collignon, Peter. "Does vinegar really kill household germs?" *abc.net.au*. ABC, 2 February 2012. Web. 1 September 2014. <http://www.abc.net.au/health/talkinghealth/factbuster/stories/2012/02/02/3407024.htm>.

Dempsey, Bobbi. "Make money by simply driving your car." *bankrate.com*. Bankrate, Inc., 3 August 2009. Web. 10 September 2014. <http://www.bankrate.com/finance/auto/make-money-by-simply-driving-your-car-2.aspx>.

Energy Impact Illinois. "Close your blinds during summer days." *energyimpactillinois.org*. Energy Impact Illinois, n.d. Web. 12 August 2014. <http://energyimpactillinois.org/waystosave/close-your-blinds-during-the-summer-days/>.

Fishman, Stephen. "Tax Issues When Renting Your Home on Airbnb or VRBO." *nolo.com*. Nolo, n.d. Web. 24 September 2014. <http://www.nolo.com/legal-encyclopedia/tax-issues-when-renting-your-home-airbnb-vrbo.html>.

Focused Care Dental, Valley Dental Group. "Dental Hygiend Statistics." *statisticbrain.com*. Statistics Brain, 19 July 2013. Web. 2 September 2014. <http://www.statisticbrain.com/dental-hygiene-statistics/>.

Forbes. "Household Items You're Paying Too Much For." *forbes.com*. Forbes.com LLC, 2014. Web. 11 August 2014. <http://www.forbes.com/pictures/ehhh45glf/room-fragrances-and-candles/>.

Fox, Emily Jane. "Number of U.S. millionaires hits new high." *money.cnn.com*. Cable News Network, A Time Warner Company, 14 March 2014. Web. 30 August 2014. <http://money.cnn.com/2014/03/14/news/economy/us-millionaires-households/>.

Geonarcissa. "Thumbs down to soliciting and advertising with geocaches." *geonarcissa.wordpress.com*. Geonarcissa, 21 July 2009. Web. 24 August 2014. <http://geonarcissa.wordpress.com/2009/07/16/thumbs-down-to-soliciting-and-advertising-with-geocaches/>.

Gillam, Carey. "Americans waste, throw away nearly half their food: study." Ed. Dan Grebler. *reuters.com*. Thomson Reuters, 21 August 2012. Web. 31 August 2014. <http://www.reuters.com/article/2012/08/21/us-food-waste-idUSBRE87K0WR20120821>.

Gordon, Lisa Kaplan. "Why Fake Grass is Gaining Popularity." *houselogic.com*. National Association of Realtors, n.d. Web. 19 September 2014. <http://www.houselogic.com/home-advice/lawns/fake-grass/#.>.

Groundspeak. "GEOCACHING." *geocaching.com*. Groundspeak, Inc., n.d. Web. 30 August 2014. <http://www.geocaching.com/>.

Group Communications Inc. "Starting Your Own Bulletin-Billboard Advertising Business." *bizkits4u.com*. Group Communications Inc., n.d. Web. 9 September 2014. <http://www.bizkits4u.com/billboard-biz.htm>.

Heiting, Gary. "Why Do Contact Lenses Expire?" allaboutvision.com. All About Vision, n.d. Web. 15 September 2014. <http://www.allaboutvision.com/contacts/faq/why-cls-expire.htm>.

Herron, Janna. "Do credit card rewards count as taxable income?" *bankrate.com*. Bankrate, Inc., 6 November 2013. Web. 5 September 2014. <http://www.bankrate.com/finance/credit-cards/credit-card-rewards-count-taxable-income.aspx>.

IRS. "Topic 420 – Bartering Income." *irs.gov*. IRS, 19 August 2014. Web. 3 September 2014. <http://www.irs.gov/taxtopics/tc420.html>.

Johnson, Caitlyn. "Sweet Dreams? Not With That Old Pillow." *cbsnews.com*. CBS Interactive Inc., 6 August 2007. Web. 2 September 2014. <http://www.cbsnews.com/news/sweet-dreams-not-with-that-old-pillow/>.

Josef, Natalie. "What Are the Odds?" *divinecaroline.com*. Meredith Corporation, n.d. Web. 30 August 2014. <http://www.divinecaroline.com/entertainment/what-are-odds-0/>.

Judson, Olivia. "Stand Up While You Read This!" *opinionator.blogs.nytimes.com*. The New York Times Company, 23 February 2010. Web. 1 September 2014. <http://opinionator.blogs.nytimes.com/2010/02/23/stand-up-while-you-read-this/>.

KidsHealth. "Fluoride and Water." Reviewed by Steven Dowshen. *kidshealth.org*. Nemours, October 2012. Web. 2 September 2014. <http://kidshealth.org/parent/general/teeth/fluoride_water.html#>.

Krasny, Jill, Gus Lubin, and Shlomo Sprung. "13 Ways Americans Throw Away Money." *businessinsider.com*. Business Insider Inc., 30 September 2012. Web. 5 September 2014. <http://www.businessinsider.com/biggest-money-wasters-2012-9?op=1>.

Krize, Nikki. "New Thrift Store Opens in Snyder County." *wnep.com*. WNEP, 12 March 2014. Web. 4 September 2014. <http://wnep.com/2014/03/12/new-thrift-store-opens-in-snyder-county/>.

Segre, Liz. "Disposable Contacts: A Healthy Choice." *allaboutvision.com*. All About Vision, n.d. Web. 15 September 2014. <http://www.allaboutvision.com/contacts/disposable.htm>.

Lisaviolet. "Advantage flea control." *lisaviolet.com*. lisaviolet, n.d. Web. 29 September 2014. <http://www.lisaviolet.com/cathouse/advantage.html>.

Lowrey, Annie. "National Health Costs vs. Your Health Costs." *economix.blogs.nytimes.com*. The New York Times Company, 24 September 2013. Web. 1 September 2014. <http://economix.blogs.nytimes.com/2013/09/24/national-health-costs-vs-your-health-costs/?_php=true&_type=blogs&_r=0>.

Maranjian, Selena. "Holy Smokes! Some People Spend 25% of Their Income on What?!" *dailyfinance.com*. DailyFinance, 22 September 2012. Web. 2 September 2014. <http://www.dailyfinance.com/2012/09/22/cigarettes-cost-poor-quarter-income-spending/>.

Mathisen, Tyler. "Cremation is the hottest trend in the funeral industry." *nbcnews.com*. NBC News, 22 January 2013. Web. 4 September 2014. <http://www.nbcnews.com/business/business-news/cremation-hottest-trend-funeral-industry-f1B8068228>.

Miracle II Angels. "Miracle II Laundry Ball / Therapeutic Ball." *miracle2angels.com*. Miracle II Angels, n.d. Web. 3 September 2014. <http://miracle2angels.com/>.

Muniz, Katherine. "20 ways Americans are blowing their money." *Usatoday.com*. The Motley Fool, 24 March 2014. Web. 13 August 2014. <http://www.usatoday.com/story/money/personalfinance/2014/03/24/20-ways-we-blow-our-money/6826633/>.

Northam, Wanda. "Saving Comparison: LASIK Vs. Glasses & Contact Lenses." *texarkanalasik.com*. Collom and Carney Eye Institute, n.d. Web 15 September 2014. <http://texarkanalasik.com/704-2/>.

Outsidepride.com. "Ground Cover Seeds, Flower Seeds, Grass Seed ,Herb Seeds, & More." *outsidepride.com*. Outsidepride.com, Inc., n.d. Web. 20 September 2014. <http://www.outsidepride.com/>.

PCE Fitness. "Bringing Physical Activity Back into the Workplace, Treadmill Desks." *lifespanfitness.com*. PCE Fitness, n.d. Web. 11 September 2014. <http://www.lifespanfitness.com/workplacesolutions-treadmill-desk-and-bike-desk.html>.

Powerball. "Powerball – Prizes and Odds." *powerball.com*. Multi-State Lottery Association, n.d. Web. 30 August 2014. <http://www.powerball.com/powerball/pb_prizes.asp>.

Rampenthal, Chas. "Is Your Home-Based Business Illegal?" *inc.com*. Inc., 31 May 2012. Web. 29 August 2014. <http://www.inc.com/chas-rampenthal/legal-checklist-home-based-business.html>.

Reader's Digest. "11 Home and Beauty Uses for Mayonnaise." *rd.com*. The Reader's Digest Association, Inc., n.d. Web. 29 September 2014. <http://www.rd.com/health/beauty/11-home-and-beauty-uses-for-mayonnaise/>.

Reilly, Lucas. "By the Numbers: How Americans Spend Their Money." *mentalfloss.com*. mental_floss, 17 July 2012. Web. 11 August 2014. <http://mentalfloss.com/article/31222/numbers-how-americans-spend-their-money>.

Roach, John. "Source of Half Earth's Oxygen Gets Little Credit." *news.nationalgeographic.com*. National Geographic Society, 7 June 2004. Web. 29 September 2014. <http://news.nationalgeographic.com/news/2004/06/0607_040607_phytoplankton.html>.

Robb, John. "Use Air Conditioning? Then Read This." *resilientcommunities.com*. Resilient Communities, 14 March 2012. Web. 12 August 2014. <http://www.resilientcommunities.com/if-you-use-air-conditioning-read-this/>.

St. John, Allen. "How Much Is That Doggie In The Window? The Surprising Economics Of Purchasing A Purebred Puppy." *forbes.com*. Forbes.com LLC, 17 February 2012. Web. 30 August 2014. <http://www.forbes.com/sites/allenstjohn/2012/02/17/how-much-is-that-doggie-in-the-window-the-surprising-economics-of-purchasing-a-purebred-puppy/>.

SFGate. "Wide range of costs for having your taxes done." *sfgate.com*. SFGate, 24 February 2011. Web. 29 August 2014. <http://www.sfgate.com/business/networth/article/Wide-range-of-costs-for-having-your-taxes-done-2473420.php>.

Shapley, Dan. "5 Ways to Save Money on Air Conditioning." *goodhousekeeping.com*. Hearst Communications, Inc., n.d. Web. 12 August 2014. <http://www.goodhousekeeping.com/family/budget/save-money-air-conditioning>.

Shapouri, Beth. "Poll: Do You Use a Shower Pouf, Washcloth Or Just the Bar of Soap?" *glamour.com*. Condé Nast, 21 October 2008. Web. 3 September 2014. <http://www.glamour.com/lipstick/blogs/girls-in-the-beauty-department/2008/10/poll-do-you-use-a-shower-pouf>.

Shin, Laura. "Retirement Savings by Age: How Do You Compare?" *dailyfinance.com*. LearnVest, 26 November 2012. Web. 11 August 2014. <http://www.dailyfinance.com/2012/11/14/retirement-savings-by-age-how-do-you-compare/>.

Shutterfly. "Shutterfly" *shutterfly.com*. Shutterfly, Inc., n.d. Web. 28 August 2014. <http://www.shutterfly.com/prints/prints?esch=1>.

Simplee. "Simplee Q1 2012 Medical Spending Statistics Show Continued Consumer Burden." *finance.yahoo.com*. Yahoo! Finance, 10 April 2012. Web. 2 September 2014. <http://finance.yahoo.com/news/simplee-q1-2012-medical-spending-120600917.html>.

SlumberWise. "Real Men Sleep on Rocks." *slumberwise.com*. SlumberWise, 24 September 2013. Web. 2 September 2014. <http://slumberwise.com/trivia/real-men-sleep-on-rocks/>.

snapfish. "snapfish by hp." *snapfish.com*. snapfish worldwide, n.d. Web. 28 August 2014. <http://www.snapfish.com/snapfish/photo-gifts/photo-prints>.

Statista. "Average amount spent per child on toys by country in 2013 (in U.S. dollars)." *statista.com*. Statista, n.d. Web. 14 August 2014. <http://www.statista.com/statistics/194424/amount-spent-on-toys-per-child-by-country-since-2009/>.

---. "Average amount of money spent on recorded music in the U.S. from 2002 to 2012 (in U.S. dollars per person per year)." *statista.com*. Statista, n.d. Web. 30 September 2014. < http://www.statista.com/statistics/191044/us-consumer-spending-on-recorded-music-since-2002/>.

Stock Logos. "Famous logo designs and how much did they cost?" *stocklogos.com*. Media Bistro, 7 August 2012. Web. 29 August 2014. <http://stocklogos.com/topic/famous-logo-designs-and-how-much-did-they-cost>.

The Holy Bible, King James Version. *Kingjamesbibleonline.org*. Cambridge Edition, 1769. Web. 30 August 2014. <http://www.kingjamesbibleonline.org/>.

The Huffington Post. "How Much Americans Spend On Gas Every Year [GRAPHIC]." *huffingtonpost. com*. The Huffington Post. 3 April 2012. Web. 13 August 2014. <http://www.huffingtonpost. com/2012/03/04/gas-prices-infographic_n_1316919.html>.

The Wedding Report, Inc. "Average Wedding Cost in United States." *costofwedding.com*. The Wedding Report, Inc., n.d. Web. 13 September 2014. <http://www.costofwedding.com/index.cfm/action/search.weddingcost/zipcode/00000.>

TLC. "Do You Have What It Takes To Be a Cheapskate?" *tlc.com*. Discovery Communications, LLC, n.d. Web. 11 August 2014. <http://www.tlc.com/tv-shows/extreme-cheapskates/cheapskate-quiz.htm>.

Trent. "Freezer and Fridge Hacks: Seven Ways to Maximize the Value of Your Refrigerator and Freezer." *thesimpledollar.com*. The Simple Dollar, 29 July 2014. Web. 12 August 2014. <http://www.thesimpledollar.com/freezer-and-fridge-hacks-seven-ways-to-maximize-the-value-of-your-refrigerator-and-freezer/>.

---. "Saving Pennies or Dollars? Dishwasher or Hand Washing." *thesimpledollar.com*. The Simple Dollar, 10 December 2013. Web. 9 September 2014. <http://www.thesimpledollar.com/saving-pennies-or-dollars-dishwasher-or-hand-washing/>.

---. "Are Rechargeable Batteries Really Cost Effective?" The Simple Dollar, 15 September 2014. Web. 23 September 2014. <http://www.thesimpledollar.com/are-rechargeable-batteries-really-cost-effective/>.

TurboTax. "Guide to Short-term vs Long-term Capital Gains Taxes (Brokerage Accounts, etc.)" *turbotax.intuit.com*. Intuit Inc., n.d. Web. 30 August 2014. <https://turbotax.intuit.com/tax-tools/tax-tips/Investments-and-Taxes/Guide-to-Short-term-vs-Long-term-Capital-Gains-Taxes--Brokerage-Accounts--etc--/INF22384.html>.

United States Census Bureau. "USA, People QuickFacts." *quickfacts.census.gov*. U.S. Department of Commerce, 8 July 2014. Web. 30 August 2014. <http://quickfacts.census.gov/qfd/states/00000.html>.

University of Manchester. "Pillows: A Hot Bed Of Fungal Spores." *sciencedaily.com*. ScienceDaily, 15 October 2005. Web. 2 September 2014. <http://www.sciencedaily.com/releases/2005/10/051015093046.htm>.

University of Michigan-Flint. "Surviving College." *umflint.edu*. University of Michigan-Flint, n.d. Web. 3 September 2014. <http://www.umflint.edu/advising/surviving_college>.

Wade, Leslie. "Sugary drinks linked to 180,000 deaths worldwide." *cnn.com*. Turner Broadcasting System, Inc., 19 March 2013. Web. 30 August 2014. <http://www.cnn.com/2013/03/19/health/sugary-drinks-deaths/>.

Walmart. "Prints." *Photos.walmart.com*. Wal-Mart Stores, Inc., n.d. Web. 13 August 2014. <http://photos.walmart.com/walmart/storepage/storePageId=Prints/>.

Waters, Shari. "What will it cost to lease a store front?" *retail.about.com*. About.com, n.d. Web. 29 August 2014. <http://retail.about.com/od/startupcosts/f/startupcosts2.htm>.

Weliver, David. "The Annual Cost of Pet Ownership: Can You Afford a Furry Friend?" *moneyunder30. com*. Moneyblogs, LLC, n.d. Web. 2 October 2014. <http://www.moneyunder30.com/the-true-cost-of-pet-ownership>.

wikiHow. "How to Toilet Train Your Cat." *wikihow.com*. Wikimedia Foundation, Inc., n.d. Web. 24 August 2014. <http://www.wikihow.com/Toilet-Train-Your-Cat>.

YCharts. "US Average Hourly Earnings." *ycharts.com*. YCharts, August 2014. Web. 5 September 2014. <https://ycharts.com/indicators/average_hourly_earnings>.

Zisko, Dan. "How Much Does It Cost to Cater a Wedding?" *ehow.com*. Demand Media, n.d. Web. 28 August 2014. <http://www.ehow.com/facts_5061446_much-cost-cater-wedding_.html>.

Zobeck, Terry. "How Much Do Americans Really Spend on Drugs Each Year?" *whitehouse.gov*. www.whitehouse.gov, 7 March 2014. Web. 5 September 2014. <http://www.whitehouse.gov/blog/2014/03/07/how-much-do-americans-really-spend-drugs-each-year>.

NOTES

SAVINGS CHART

Please use the charts which appear on the following pages to track your savings each year. You will see that there are columns for the 1st year, 2nd year, 3rd year, 6th year, and 7th year. Each column shows the average savings/earnings as it pertains to each tip. Just browse through to find the associated tip. The tips are arranged in order. If you are completing a tip for the first time, you would look at the 1st year's savings column. The savings could differ each year due to several factors including cost or time associated with the initial investment. If it is your fourth or fifth year completing the same tip, just refer to the 3rd year column. The figures are the same.

There are plenty of note pages throughout this book. Use one of them to begin recording your savings right now. At the end of each year, you can compare to see if you have outdone yourself. Make it a game and have some fun!

CHAPTER 1 - Home	1ST YEAR	2ND YEAR	3RD YEAR	6TH YEAR	7TH YEAR
1. SHOP AT AUCTIONS	$925	$925	$925	$925	$925
2. PLANT ARTIFICIAL FLOWERS	$440	$440	$440	$440	$440
3. LAY ARTIFICIAL GRASS	$0	$344	$590	$590	$590
4. PLANT GROUND COVER	$105	$375	$375	$375	$375
5. USE A REEL LAWN MOWER	$185	$35	$35	$35	$35
6. ACCEPT A HAND-ME-DOWN	$775	$775	$775	$775	$775
7. ASSIGN COLORS	$400	$425	$425	$425	$425
8. FILL FRIDGE	$48	$48	$48	$48	$48
9. SAVE NAPKINS	$20	$20	$20	$20	$20
10. DON'T BUY PAPER TOWELS	$182	$182	$182	$182	$182
11. SKIP USING TISSUES	$24	$24	$24	$24	$24
12. SAVE MAIL ENVELOPES	$60	$60	$60	$60	$60
13. AVOID PURCHASING SCENTS	$375	$375	$375	$375	$375
14. REMOLD JUNK CANDLES	$17	$17	$17	$17	$17
15. DON'T LAUNDER TOWELS OFTEN	$725	$725	$725	$725	$725
16. DON'T WASH BEDDING OFTEN	$213	$213	$213	$213	$213
17. LET NATURAL LIGHT IN	$112	$112	$112	$112	$112
18. CLOSE BLINDS TO KEEP HEAT OUT	$25	$25	$25	$25	$25
19. OPEN WINDOWS FOR COOL AIR	$125	$125	$125	$125	$125

CHAPTER 1 - Home	1ST YEAR	2ND YEAR	3RD YEAR	6TH YEAR	7TH YEAR
20. REPAIR BLINDS	$19	$19	$19	$19	$19
21. USE GLOW IN THE DARK PAINT	$200	$250	$250	$250	$250
22. LIVE CLOSE TO LOVED ONES	$1,000	$1,500	$1,500	$1,500	$1,500
23. PAINT ROOF WHITE	$0	$0	$0	$40	$40
24. HAVE BILLBOARD ON PROPERTY	$41,400	$45,400	$45,400	$45,400	$45,400
25. PAY BILLS ON TIME	$788	$788	$788	$788	$788
26. PUT BRICK IN TOILET TANK	$18	$22.50	$22.50	$22.50	$22.50
27. FLUSH LESS OFTEN	$35	$35	$35	$35	$35
28. HOOK HOSE TO DEHUMIDIFIER	$440	$465	$465	$465	$465
29. HOOK BARREL TO DOWNSPOUT	$0	$30	$30	$30	$30
30. USE BATHWATER ON LAWN	$15	$15	$15	$15	$15
31. USE DRYER LINT TO START FIRES	$20	$20	$20	$20	$20
32. USE EVERY DROP OF PRODUCT	$8	$8	$8	$8	$8
33. ORDER PHOTO PRINTS ONLINE	$60	$60	$60	$60	$60
34. USE DIGITAL PHOTO FRAME	$30	$30	$30	$30	$30
35. GET FREE INTERNET PROTECTION	$35	$35	$35	$35	$35
36. WORK WITH WHAT YOU'VE GOT	$520	$520	$520	$520	$520
37. HEAT OR COOL JUST 1 ROOM	$1,700	$1,713	$1,713	$1,713	$1,713
38. ACCEPT ELECTRIC COMPANY OFFERS	$208	$208	$208	$208	$208

CHAPTER 2 - Storage

	1ST YEAR	2ND YEAR	3RD YEAR	6TH YEAR	7TH YEAR
1. GET CONSIGNMENT BOOTHS	$1,200	$1,250	$1,250	$1,250	$1,250
2. GET A SECOND HOME	$1,075	$1,200	$1,200	$1,200	$1,200
3. KEEP A DIGITAL FILING CABINET	$125	$125	$125	$125	$125
4. UTILIZE YOUR LOCAL LIBRARY	$250	$250	$250	$250	$250
5. SMASH YOUR TRASH	$33	$33	$33	$33	$33

CHAPTER 3 - Transportation

	1ST YEAR	2ND YEAR	3RD YEAR	6TH YEAR	7TH YEAR
1. USE LEFTOVER METER TIME	$1	$1	$1	$1	$1
2. PURCHASE A USED VEHICLE	$2,475	$2,500	$2,500	$2,500	$2,500
3. SCRAP VEHICLE / SELL PARTS	$375	$375	$375	$375	$375
4. LIVE NEAR WORK	$4,550	$4,950	$4,950	$4,950	$4,950
5. OBEY TRAFFIC LAWS	$150	$150	$150	$150	$150
6. CARPOOL	$725	$725	$725	$725	$725
7. ADVERTISE ON YOUR VEHICLE	$9,600	$9,600	$9,600	$9,600	$9,600
8. MAKE YOUR VEHICLE YOUR HOME	$0	$13,500	$13,500	$13,500	$13,500
9. SKIP WINDSHIELD WASHER FLUID	$30	$30	$30	$30	$30
10. USE YOUR TURN SIGNAL LESS	$20	$20	$20	$20	$20
11. STICK WITH MANUAL OPTIONS	$145	$145	$145	$145	$145
12. DON'T PAY FOR AIR	$10	$10	$10	$10	$10
13. GET GAS FOR LESS	$208	$208	$208	$208	$208
14. WASH YOUR CAR IN THE RAIN	$80	$80	$80	$80	$80

CHAPTER 4 - Marriage

	1ST YEAR	2ND YEAR	3RD YEAR	6TH YEAR	7TH YEAR
1. GET MARRIED	$9,400	$10,000	$10,000	$10,000	$10,000
2. PROPOSE WITH A PLASTIC RING	$3,344	$0	$0	$0	$0
3. FREE ESCORT	$483	$0	$0	$0	$0
4. BAKE YOUR WEDDING CAKE	$340	$0	$0	$0	$0
5. CATER YOUR OWN WEDDING	$11,200	$0	$0	$0	$0
6. BE YOUR OWN DJ	$970	$0	$0	$0	$0
7. MAKE YOUR OWN BOUQUETS	$475	$0	$0	$0	$0
8. DECORATE YOUR OWN WEDDING	$1,225	$0	$0	$0	$0
9. BORROW YOUR WEDDING ATTIRE	$1,464	$0	$0	$0	$0
10. STYLE YOUR OWN HAIR	$174	$0	$0	$0	$0
11. KEEP WEDDING PARTY SMALL	$1,200	$0	$0	$0	$0
12. WED AT A FREE LOCATION	$3,615	$0	$0	$0	$0
13. SKIP THE PHOTOGRAPHER	$2,610	$0	$0	$0	$0
14. MAKE INVITES AND MORE	$915	$0	$0	$0	$0

CHAPTER 5 - Children	1ST YEAR	2ND YEAR	3RD YEAR	6TH YEAR	7TH YEAR
1. ENROLL KIDS IN FREE PROGRAMS	$1,388	$1,388	$1,388	$1,388	$1,388
2. ATTEND FREE WORKSHOPS FOR KIDS	$90	$90	$90	$90	$90
3. SAVE SCHOOL PROJECT MATERIALS	$9	$9	$9	$9	$9
4. WATCH YOUR OWN KIDS	$12,000	$12,000	$12,000	$12,000	$12,000
5. SHARE A BIRTHDAY	$498	$500	$500	$500	$500
6. USE A FREE PARTY VENUE AND MORE	$190	$190	$190	$190	$190
7. GET FREE CANDY	$97	$97	$97	$97	$97
8. BUY TREATS AT THE LOCAL GROCER	$14	$14	$14	$14	$14
9. NEVER USE A VENDING MACHINE	$250	$250	$250	$250	$250
10. TURN STAIRS INTO SLIDING BOARD	$148	$0	$0	$0	$0
11. SAVE YOUR CHILDHOOD TOYS	$446	$446	$446	$446	$446
12. SELL UNWANTED TOYS	$100	$100	$100	$100	$100
13. MAKE DOLL CLOTHING	$75	$75	$75	$75	$75
14. MAKE SLIME	$20	$20	$20	$20	$20
15. DRESSING ROOM PHOTO SESSION	$213	$213	$213	$213	$213
16. LIFT CHILDREN FOR EXERCISE	$350	$350	$350	$350	$350
17. TURN TORN PANTS INTO SHORTS	$125	$125	$125	$125	$125

CHAPTER 5 - Children

	1ST YEAR	2ND YEAR	3RD YEAR	6TH YEAR	7TH YEAR
18. BUY GENDER NEUTRAL ITEMS	**$250**	$250	$250	$250	$250
19. SWAP CAR SEATS FOR GIFT CARDS	**$10**	$10	$10	$10	$10
20. CRAFT YOUR OWN COSTUMES	**$35**	$35	$35	$35	$35
21. BUY DISCOUNTED CLOTHING, RESELL IT	**$2,200**	$2,200	$2,200	$2,200	$2,200
22. DON'T PURCHASE KIDS' MEALS	**$150**	$150	$150	$150	$150
23. SAVE YOUR CHILDREN'S TEETH	**$4**	$4	$4	$4	$4
24. MAKE YOUR OWN VALENTINES	**$3**	$3	$3	$3	$3

CHAPTER 6 - Education

	1ST YEAR	2ND YEAR	3RD YEAR	6TH YEAR	7TH YEAR
1. LEARN ON THE JOB, SKIP COLLEGE	**$164,913**	**$165,038**	$165,038	$165,038	$165,038
2. LEARN BY WATCHING	**$4,325**	**$4,325**	$4,325	$4,325	$4,325
3. LEARN BY READING	**$4,275**	**$4,275**	$4,275	$4,275	$4,275
4. DON'T TAKE PART IN FUNDRAISERS	**$225**	**$225**	$225	$225	$225

CHAPTER 7 - Business	1ST YEAR	2ND YEAR	3RD YEAR	6TH YEAR	7TH YEAR
1. START A HOME BUSINESS	$21,500	$35,000	$35,000	$35,000	$35,000
2. DESIGN YOUR OWN LOGO	$675	$675	$675	$675	$675
3. DESIGN YOUR OWN WEBSITE	$1,450	$1,450	$1,450	$1,450	$1,450
4. DO NOT KEEP AN INVENTORY	$21,571	$21,571	$21,571	$21,571	$21,571
5. MAKE YOUR OWN MACHINE	$895	$0	$0	$0	$0
6. COMPARE SHIPPING RATES	$9,850	$9,850	$9,850	$9,850	$9,850
7. SAVE BOXES	$8,500	$8,500	$8,500	$8,500	$8,500
8. USE NEWSPRINT FOR CUSHIONING	$9,140	$9,140	$9,140	$9,140	$9,140
9. FIND OTHER USES FOR THINGS	$450	$450	$450	$450	$450
10. CREATE MULTI-PURPOSE SPACES	$7,175	$7,200	$7,200	$7,200	$7,200
11. CREATIVE FREE ADVERTISING	$5,000	$5,000	$5,000	$5,000	$5,000
12. COMBINE TONER FROM PRINTER	$246	$246	$246	$246	$246
13. REUSE PRINTER PAPER	$70	$70	$70	$70	$70
14. BE YOUR OWN STAFF	$3,200	$3,200	$3,200	$3,200	$3,200
15. DO NOT HAVE CALLER ID	$548	$560	$560	$560	$560
16. DO YOUR OWN TAXES	$275	$275	$275	$275	$275
17. DO NOT GET A ROLLING CHAIR	$103	$103	$103	$103	$103
18. LET PEOPLE RENT YOUR SPACE	$190	$190	$190	$190	$190
19. PAY CASH IF THERE IS A DISCOUNT	$125	$125	$125	$125	$125
20. COPY AND PASTE	$188	$188	$188	$188	$188

CHAPTER 8 - Saving and Investing

	1ST YEAR	2ND YEAR	3RD YEAR	6TH YEAR	7TH YEAR
1. START EARNING INTEREST	$85	$85	$85	$85	$85
2. INVEST IN TANGIBLE ITEMS	$2,500	$2,500	$2,500	$2,500	$2,500
3. GET FREE CHECKS	$3	$3	$3	$3	$3
4. AVOID LOANS	$5,000	$5,000	$5,000	$5,000	$5,000
5. BE YOUR OWN FINANCIAL ADVISER	$700	$700	$700	$700	$700
6. SAVE TIME BY MULTI-TASKING	$6,850	$6,850	$6,850	$6,850	$6,850
7. PUT THINGS IN THEIR PLACE	$350	$350	$350	$350	$350
8. HANG UP THE PHONE, SAVE TIME	$450	$450	$450	$450	$450

CHAPTER 9 - Giving Back

	1ST YEAR	2ND YEAR	3RD YEAR	6TH YEAR	7TH YEAR
1. GIVE 10%	ETERNAL RICHES	ETERNAL RICHES	ETERNAL RICHES	ETERNAL RICHES	ETERNAL RICHES
2. SPLIT THE BILL	FRIENDSHIP	FRIENDSHIP	FRIENDSHIP	FRIENDSHIP	FRIENDSHIP
3. CLEAN UP THE WORLD	$125	$125	$125	$125	$125
4. CREATE A BLOG	$15	$15	$15	$15	$15
5. MAKE YOUTUBE VIDEOS	$15	$15	$15	$15	$15
6. HELP THOSE IN NEED	$50	$50	$50	$50	$50

CHAPTER 10 - Pets

	1ST YEAR	2ND YEAR	3RD YEAR	6TH YEAR	7TH YEAR
1. CREATE A PET CARRIER	$24	$0	$0	$0	$0
2. ADOPT A PET, DON'T PURCHASE ONE	$1,750	$0	$0	$0	$0
3. MAKE YOUR OWN PET TOYS	$59	$59	$59	$59	$59
4. TOILET TRAIN YOUR CAT	$850	$925	$925	$925	$925
5. TAKE ADVANTAGE	$168	$168	$168	$168	$168
6. GET A CHICKEN AS A PET	$91	$91	$91	$91	$91
7. SHOP AROUND FOR A VET	$79	$79	$79	$79	$79

CHAPTER 11 - Entertainment

	1ST YEAR	2ND YEAR	3RD YEAR	6TH YEAR	7TH YEAR
1. CANCEL CABLE, GET NETFLIX	$1,092	$1,100	$1,100	$1,100	$1,100
2. GO GEOCACHING FOR FUN	$225	$225	$225	$225	$225
3. UTILIZE PLAYGROUNDS	$195	$195	$195	$195	$195
4. GET YOUR OWN GEAR	$505	$530	$530	$530	$530
5. SWIM AT OFF HOURS	$20	$20	$20	$20	$20
6. PURCHASE GROUPONS	$30	$30	$30	$30	$30
7. GAMBLE FOR FREE	$59	$59	$59	$59	$59
8. DON'T PLAY THE LOTTERY	$775	$775	$775	$775	$775
9. BRING DRINKS TO EVENTS	$3	$3	$3	$3	$3
10. DO NOT PAY FOR MOVIES	$60	$60	$60	$60	$60
11. SKIP IN-APP PURCHASES	$15	$15	$15	$15	$15
12. VISIT FAIRS, COLLECT FREEBIES	$50	$50	$50	$50	$50
13. TAKE PRACTICE SHOTS IN MINI GOLF	$9	$9	$9	$9	$9
14. DO NOT PAY FOR MUSIC	$93	$93	$93	$93	$93

CHAPTER 12 - Vacations	1ST YEAR	2ND YEAR	3RD YEAR	6TH YEAR	7TH YEAR
1. WORK WHILE TRAVELING	**$880**	$880	$880	$880	$880
2. UTILIZE BARGAIN HOURS	**$45**	$45	$45	$45	$45
3. GET FREE HOTEL STAYS	**$140**	$140	$140	$140	$140
4. DON'T INCUR HOTEL FEES	**$112**	$112	$112	$112	$112
5. STAY FOR LESS OR STAY FOR FREE	**$900**	$900	$900	$900	$900
6. USE SLED AS BOOGIE BOARD	**$50**	$50	$50	$50	$50
7. USE AN AWESOME CHEAP CAMERA	**$913**	**$13**	$13	$13	$13
8. SAVE BY BOOKING IN ADVANCE	**$130**	$130	$130	$130	$130
9. VACATION WITHIN YOUR OWN CITY	**$1,425**	$1,425	$1,425	$1,425	$1,425
10. USE CHEAPEST METHOD OF TRAVEL	**$228**	$228	$228	$228	$228
11. PACK LIGHT, AVOID BAGGAGE FEES	**$56**	$56	$56	$56	$56
12. CARRY YOUR OWN BAGS	**$4**	$4	$4	$4	$4
13. STAY CHEAPER ON A CRUISE SHIP	**$1,247**	$1,247	$1,247	$1,247	$1,247
14. AVOID THE TOLL ROUTES	**$13**	$13	$13	$13	$13
15. BRING YOUR OWN FOOD	**$369**	$369	$369	$369	$369
16. GET FREE RIDE TICKETS	**$8**	$8	$8	$8	$8

CHAPTER 13 - Food and Beverages	1ST YEAR	2ND YEAR	3RD YEAR	6TH YEAR	7TH YEAR
1. BUY ICE CREAM AT HALF PRICE	$72	$72	$72	$72	$72
2. DO NOT DRINK SUGARY DRINKS	$850	$850	$850	$850	$850
3. BREW YOUR OWN COFFEE	$675	$675	$675	$675	$675
4. REUSE TEA BAGS	$18	$18	$18	$18	$18
5. DRINK TAP WATER	$775	$775	$775	$775	$775
6. PLANT A GARDEN	$138	$138	$138	$138	$138
7. DON'T WASTE FOOD	$3,070	$3,070	$3,070	$3,070	$3,070
8. SKIP USING THE OVEN	$40	$40	$40	$40	$40
9. USE CRUMB REMAINS	$15	$15	$15	$15	$15
10. NO ALCOHOL WHILE DINING	$100	$100	$100	$100	$100
11. PACK LUNCHES	$2,425	$2,425	$2,425	$2,425	$2,425
12. EAT WELL, SKIP VITAMINS	$740	$740	$740	$740	$740
13. SAVE FOOD CONTAINERS	$6	$6	$6	$6	$6
14. DO NOT BUY PLASTIC WRAP	$20	$20	$20	$20	$20
15. ATTEND SEMINARS, EAT FREE	$50	$50	$50	$50	$50
16. AVOID LEAVING TIPS	$100	$100	$100	$100	$100
17. GET DISCOUNTS AT RESTAURANTS	$215	$215	$215	$215	$215
18. SAVE FOOD PACKAGING	$250	$250	$250	$250	$250
19. TAKE TURNS COOKING	$2,275	$2,275	$2,275	$2,275	$2,275
20. USE LEFTOVER BOILED WATER	$30	$30	$30	$30	$30
21. CLEAN WITH FOOD SCRAPS	$50	$50	$50	$50	$50

CHAPTER 14 - Exercise

	1ST YEAR	2ND YEAR	3RD YEAR	6TH YEAR	7TH YEAR
1. STAY FIT	$843	$843	$843	$843	$843
2. EXERCISE FOR FREE	$11,050	$11,050	$11,050	$11,050	$11,050
3. STAND INSTEAD OF SIT	$350	$350	$350	$350	$350
4. USE A TREADMILL AT YOUR DESK	$8,549	$6,500	$6,500	$6,500	$6,500

CHAPTER 15 - Health

	1ST YEAR	2ND YEAR	3RD YEAR	6TH YEAR	7TH YEAR
1. USE LESS CLEANING SUPPLIES	$750	$750	$750	$750	$750
2. REUSE VACUUM SWEEPER BAGS	$37	$37	$37	$37	$37
3. USE A DISHWASHER	$1,690	$1,690	$1,690	$1,690	$1,690
4. USE DISPOSABLE DINNERWARE	$1,425	$1,425	$1,425	$1,425	$1,425
5. DON'T USE A PILLOW	$37.50	$37.50	$37.50	$37.50	$37.50
6. ONLY BRUSH TEETH ONCE PER DAY	$180	$180	$180	$180	$180
7. DRINK FLUORIDATED TAP WATER	$50	$50	$50	$50	$50
8. QUIT SMOKING	$5,600	$5,600	$5,600	$5,600	$5,600
9. TREAT YOUR OWN AILMENTS	$1,100	$1,100	$1,100	$1,100	$1,100
10. DON'T USE FEVER MEDICATION	$10	$10	$10	$10	$10
11. SOOTHE WITH A HOT TODDY	$8	$8	$8	$8	$8
12. TREAT PINK EYE AT HOME	$53	$53	$53	$53	$53
13. WEAR GLASSES	$420	$420	$420	$420	$420
14. MAKE CONTACTS LAST LONG	$823	$823	$823	$823	$823
15. SKIP THE FLU SHOT	$68	$68	$68	$68	$68

CHAPTER 16 - Grooming	1ST YEAR	2ND YEAR	3RD YEAR	6TH YEAR	7TH YEAR
1. USE ROCK SALT DEODORANT	$73	$73	$73	$73	$73
2. TURN CRAYONS INTO MAKEUP	$100	$100	$100	$100	$100
3. USE MEDIUM-THICK TOILET PAPER	$30	$30	$30	$30	$30
4. USE A BIDET	$0	$0	$0	$0	$25
5. WATER DOWN PRODUCTS	$75	$75	$75	$75	$75
6. BUY BULK SHAMPOO/CONDITIONER	$80	$80	$80	$80	$80
7. SHOWER EVERY OTHER DAY	$650	$650	$650	$650	$650
8. WASH WITH YOUR HANDS	$35	$35	$35	$35	$35
9. WASH HAIR EVERY OTHER DAY	$350	$350	$350	$350	$350
10. LET HAIR AIR DRY	$555	$555	$555	$555	$555
11. CUT YOUR OWN HAIR	$465	$465	$465	$465	$465
12. DYE OR LIGHTEN YOUR OWN HAIR	$1,300	$1,300	$1,300	$1,300	$1,300
13. FIND OTHER USES FOR MAYO	$45	$45	$45	$45	$45
14. DON'T BUY TOOTHBRUSHES	$33	$33	$33	$33	$33
15. SKIP WEARING JEWELRY	$594	$594	$594	$594	$594
16. CLEAN GLASSES WITH BREATH	$12	$12	$12	$12	$12
17. PAMPER YOURSELF	$900	$900	$900	$900	$900
18. SHARPEN YOUR DULL RAZORS	$40	$40	$40	$40	$40
19. DON'T SHAVE IN THE WINTER	$410	$410	$410	$410	$410
20. USE YOUR FACE OILS	$50	$50	$50	$50	$50

CHAPTER 17 - Clothing

	1ST YEAR	2ND YEAR	3RD YEAR	6TH YEAR	7TH YEAR
1. WEAR A UNIFORM	$2,750	$2,750	$2,750	$2,750	$2,750
2. RE-WEAR CLOTHING	$770	$770	$770	$770	$770
3. DON'T WEAR SOCKS OFTEN	$63	$63	$63	$63	$63
4. SAVE OLD SOCKS TO USE AS RAGS	$16	$16	$16	$16	$16
5. WEAR SHOES UNTIL THEY FALL APART	$130	$130	$130	$130	$130
6. DO NOT BUY FAT PANTS, EXPAND	$750	$750	$750	$750	$750
7. DON'T BUY LAUNDRY DETERGENT	$57	$57	$57	$57	$57
8. USE HOTEL BAR SOAP ON STAINS	$10	$10	$10	$10	$10
9. USE THE COLD CYCLE	$50	$50	$50	$50	$50
10. DON'T USE DRYER SHEETS	$30	$30	$30	$30	$30
11. DON'T IRON	$1,300	$1,300	$1,300	$1,300	$1,300

CHAPTER 18 - Shopping

	1ST YEAR	2ND YEAR	3RD YEAR	6TH YEAR	7TH YEAR
1. SHOP SECONDHAND	$1,700	$1,700	$1,700	$1,700	$1,700
2. BARTER	$100	$100	$100	$100	$100
3. SHOP AT WALMART	$400	$400	$400	$400	$400
4. SHOP CLEARANCE SECTIONS	$500	$500	$500	$500	$500
5. SHOP AT THE END OF SEASON	$750	$750	$750	$750	$750
6. STOCK UP WHEN THE PRICE IS RIGHT	$179	$179	$179	$179	$179

CHAPTER 18 - Shopping	1ST YEAR	2ND YEAR	3RD YEAR	6TH YEAR	7TH YEAR
7. FIX DAMAGED ITEMS	$1,525	$1,525	$1,525	$1,525	$1,525
8. DEAL WITH IT, GET CREATIVE	$168	$168	$168	$168	$168
9. MAKE A TOMBSTONE	$850	$0	$0	$0	$0
10. GO WITH A VIRTUAL BURIAL	$4,569	$0	$0	$0	$0
11. USE COUPONS, DINE CHEAP	$400	$400	$400	$400	$400
12. USE REWARD CARDS	$500	$500	$500	$500	$500
13. SAVE AT THE REGISTER	$69	$69	$69	$69	$69
14. DON'T PURCHASE WARRANTIES	$375	$375	$375	$375	$375
15. DITCH DIGITAL ITEMS	$375	$375	$375	$375	$375
16. PURCHASE REFILLS	$50	$50	$50	$50	$50
17. PURCHASE GENERIC PRODUCTS	$1,500	$1,500	$1,500	$1,500	$1,500
18. THROW TRASH OUT AT THE SOURCE	$24	$24	$24	$24	$24
19. MAKE USE OF YOUR OLD PHONE	$850	$850	$850	$850	$850
20. SKIP THE CREDIT CARD PROTECTION PLAN	$120	$120	$120	$120	$120
21. DO NOT BUY LIFE INSURANCE	$375	$375	$375	$375	$375
22. USE RECHARGEABLE BATTERIES	$0	$56	$127	$127	$127
23. BECOME A SECRET SHOPPER	$225	$225	$225	$225	$225
24. GET A TATTOO STAMP MADE	$300	$0	$0	$0	$0
25. SAVE MONEY ON TOWEL SETS	$63	$63	$63	$63	$63

CHAPTER 18 - Shopping

	1ST YEAR	2ND YEAR	3RD YEAR	6TH YEAR	7TH YEAR
26. RETURN OR EXCHANGE ITEMS	**$100**	$100	$100	$100	$100
27. TALK THEM DOWN IN PRICE	**$1,088**	$1,088	$1,088	$1,088	$1,088
28. RESEARCH BEFORE YOU BUY	**$130**	$130	$130	$130	$130
29. GET ART FOR CHEAP	**$295**	$295	$295	$295	$295
30. DON'T SHOP AT CONVENIENCE STORES	**$104**	$104	$104	$104	$104
31. SAVE SHOPPING BAGS	**$45**	$45	$45	$45	$45
32. BUY A BIG COMPUTER	**$500**	**$0**	$0	$0	$0

CHAPTER 19 - Gifts

	1ST YEAR	2ND YEAR	3RD YEAR	6TH YEAR	7TH YEAR
1. RECYCLE GREETING CARDS	**$138**	$138	$138	$138	$138
2. MAKE GREETING CARDS	**$65**	$65	$65	$65	$65
3. MAKE WRAPPING PAPER	**$13**	$13	$13	$13	$13
4. RE-GIFT ITEMS	**$200**	$200	$200	$200	$200
5. GIVE HANDMADE GIFTS	**$600**	$600	$600	$600	$600
6. DRAW NAMES FOR GIFT GIVING	**$298**	$298	$298	$298	$298
7. SHOP FOR GIFTS AT AUCTIONS	**$250**	$250	$250	$250	$250
8. GIVE PAPER ROSES	**$100**	$100	$100	$100	$100
9. SAVE BOWS AND GIFT WRAP	**$68**	$68	$68	$68	$68

CHAPTER 20 - Easy Money and More	1ST YEAR	2ND YEAR	3RD YEAR	6TH YEAR	7TH YEAR
1. ENTER CONTESTS	$2,375	$2,375	$2,375	$2,375	$2,375
2. TAKE PART IN CHINESE AUCTIONS	$100	$100	$100	$100	$100
3. SPIN PRIZE WHEELS	$34	$34	$34	$34	$34
4. ENTER TO WIN DOOR PRIZES	$45	$45	$45	$45	$45
5. HOST A HOUSE PARTY	$25	$25	$25	$25	$25
6. SIGN UP FOR CREDIT CARD OFFERS	$900	$900	$900	$900	$900
7. PICK UP COINS	$5	$5	$5	$5	$5
8. GATHER UP FREE BOXES	$194	$194	$194	$194	$194
9. ACCEPT FREE STUFF ON FACEBOOK	$263	$263	$263	$263	$263
10. GET FREE SAMPLES	$55	$55	$55	$55	$55
11. DON'T BE EARLY	$2,500	$2,500	$2,500	$2,500	$2,500
12. LEAVE EVENTS EARLY OR LATE	$75	$75	$75	$75	$75
13. TAKE SURVEYS FOR REWARDS	$260	$260	$260	$260	$260
14. PAY BILLS ONLINE	$120	$120	$120	$120	$120
15. PAY IN ONE LUMP SUM	$214	$214	$214	$214	$214
16. GET ELDER CARE	$3,500	$3,500	$3,500	$3,500	$3,500

JAMIE JAY – also known as "The Classy Cheapskate" and "The Junk Artist" – is a woman of many talents. She is an artist, designer, entrepreneur, author, and more! Through all of her endeavors, she manages to use resources to the best of her ability in order to save a lot of dough while still enjoying the best things in life. As an artist, she uses junk and even garbage to create her whimsical masterpieces. In her

personal and business life, she is a role model on saving and conserving. Jamie uses her creativity and frugalness in all aspects of her life. She shares her artistic and money saving skills through many outlets including the writing and illustrating of books, she is a presenter for eHow, artist for several stock art companies including iStockphoto and Shutterstock; volunteers her time in the church, school, and community; and has been featured in many media outlets including TLC's Extreme Cheapskates where she starred in season 3, episode 9 demonstrating her creative money saving tips including how to repurpose used kitty litter to create clay art sculptures.

In 2011, Jamie won the GRAND PRIZE in the OPRAH WINFREY NETWORK "Creative Mind Challenge" with her video entry titled, "Inspiration is Everywhere!" The video featured Jamie scribbling on used junk mail envelopes. She quickly turned the scribbles into works of art using an ordinary black marker. She showed that even junk can become useful and beautiful.

Jamie currently lives in central, Pennsylvania with her family of four where she has spent the majority of her life. She graduated top of her class from Bradley Academy for the Visual Arts majoring in Graphic

Design (schooling paid for, courtesy of Jamie's parents). She also graduated from Dov Simons two Day Film School (gift from Oprah); and Pennsylvania Governor's School for the Arts; her focus being video, animation, and creative writing (scholarship with only forty visual artists being accepted into the program each year).

At the start of her career, Jamie was a package designer, concept artist, and more; creating art mainly for The Hershey Company. She then moved on to working on a larger scale creating wall murals and foreground art – her largest mural being located in the Oakes Museum in Grantham, PA; in which she worked closely with her twin sister, Jennifer Haupt. They collaborated together creating foreground displays for the museum as well.

In 2004, at the age of 25, Jamie started a family and became her own boss; teaching herself web design by reading books. From there she started her first website with sales taking off quickly. For over a decade, she has been working out of her home running several businesses at once, all while raising a family. With zero debt and a flexible schedule, she has found freedom to pursue her dreams in life. Jamie biggest pursuits are to glorify God, live an adventurous life with her husband and children, try new things, and share her knowledge with mass audiences. Jamie always had a love for entertaining people, however, lacked the skill to memorize lines. So she found a way to enjoy her love for entertaining by demonstrating her skills online and on television (no memorizing needed when you do what comes naturally).

Jamie says, "If you have read this far, I want you to know that I just pretended I was someone else in order to write these last two pages. Dude, I'm not paying someone else to write my bio for me! You all take care now and become great successes! Keep in touch! Visit anytime at *classycheapskate.wordpress.com*.